More than Merkle

More than Merkle

A History of the Best and

Most Exciting Baseball Season

in Human History

DAVID W. ANDERSON

with a foreword by Keith Olbermann

University of Nebraska Press

Lincoln and London

© 2000 by the
University of Nebraska Press
All rights reserved
Manufactured in the
United States of America
⊗
Library of Congress
Cataloging-in-Publication Data
Anderson, David W. (David Wallace),
1948–
More than Merkle : a history of the best
and most exciting baseball season in
human history / David W. Anderson.
   p.   cm.
Includes bibliographical references
(p.   ) and index.
ISBN 0-8032-1056-6 (cl.: alk. paper)
1. Baseball — United States — History —
20th century.   I. Title.
GV863.A1A52   2000
796.357′0973 — dc21   99-35024
                            CIP

To my father

Thanks for teaching me to

enjoy books and the Go Go Sox

Contents

Illustrations

Tables

Foreword

Fred Merkle's great-grandson was quietly scuttling across the floor of my Los Angeles apartment in 1991, unexpectedly sturdy for a fourteen-month old, honing in on a piece of ornamental wood on a mirrored wall while his mother regaled me with *her* mother's stories of the years "after" in the Merkle household. Suddenly the baby grunted, pulled the wood slat off the mirror, and began to wave it around his head.

"My God," I said. "He's *swinging* it."

His father smiled, and his mother moved towards her young clean-up hitter. "Heredity," she said, matter-of-factly.

I have done a report of some kind on the Fred Merkle story, whether in print, on radio, or on TV, on or about its anniversary, September 23rd, virtually every year since I was in college. The saga has always seemed to me a microcosm not just of baseball or of celebrity, but of life. The rules sometimes change while you're playing the game. Those you trust to tell you the changes often don't bother to. That for which history still mocks you would have gone unnoticed if you had done it a year or a month or a day before.

That's who Fred Merkle is.

I have often proposed September 23rd as a national day of amnesty, in Fred Merkle's memory. Not forgiveness; forgiveness requires guilt. But amnesty means merely an acknowledgment that something that could deserve blame, might in fact be far more complicated, and meriting not of reproach but of understanding and dismissal from retribution.

If anybody deserves dismissal from retribution, it's Fred Merkle. Dave Anderson will tell you in the coming pages of all that led up to his extraordinary collision with history, a day that went from being a moment in the sun to a moment in infamy. "Merkle's Boner" will be explained for what it is, and what it isn't; why the never-enforced arcane baseball rule requiring men on base to advance while a two-out game-ending, winning run scored, suddenly began to *be* enforced just as Fred veered off the baseline toward the safety of his team's clubhouse in the outfield, and, ultimately, toward eternal, misplaced blame.

To appreciate the story you are about to read, you must remember that while now, nearly a century later, the "Merkle game" is remembered only on its anniversary, for the first forty years after the play itself, it was as constant a part of American culture as the Johnstown Flood had been, or as Neil Armstrong's moon landing would be.

Merkle's youngest daughter told me that in the '30s, a quarter century after that 23rd of September, 1908, a visiting minister had come to her family's church in Florida. "I want to begin," he chuckled from the pulpit, "by admitting to you an ugly secret. I am from Toledo, Ohio; birthplace of the infamous Fred 'Bonehead' Merkle." Fred Merkle silently stood up and led his family out the door.

"At home, we didn't talk much about the game," she added. "Needless to say."

Merkle's life was like that from the year this book recounts through the rest of his major league baseball career. Daily somebody would shout from the stands "Hey Fred, don't forget to touch second." His last name was a synonym for stupidity, for blundering. That he survived to play seventeen seasons and manage in the minors should have earned him, in my opinion, immediate and unanimous election to the Baseball Hall of Fame the day it opened.

Fortunately it will spoil no retelling of easily the greatest season in baseball's history that late, rather than early, Merkle's odyssey ended at an old-timers' game with a surprisingly happy twist.

Now he lives again here in these pages. Dave Anderson will introduce him to you, along with dozens of other unforgettable, sometimes equally tragic, characters: Addie Joss, Harry Pulliam, Warren Gill, Bonesetter Reese, Hank O'Day, Dr. Joseph Creamer. Read on: remember that, remarkably, this is not fiction but fact, and remind yourself always that tomorrow, events that would require a book to fully explain could conspire to make you into a new Fred Merkle.

Keith Olbermann

Acknowledgments

This book is a study of the 1908 major league baseball season, using contemporary accounts as primary sources with other descriptions of the season as secondary references. My intent is to develop a comprehensive history of this controversial and important year and to augment another study of this season, *The Unforgettable Season* by G. H. Fleming (New York: Holt, Rinehart and Winston, 1981). Anyone studying 1908 or the Dead Ball Era will find Fleming's book must reading. It is also an outstanding reference work for the study of sports journalism of the day.

But Fleming's work was not a comprehensive study of the entire year. He tells the New York Giants' story and barely mentions the equally exciting American League pennant race. In *More than Merkle* I address what Fleming did not intend to address: the American League race and other events during this most significant year in baseball history.

For pitchers and pitching there was no better year than 1908. The only other season that has come close was 1968. Pennant races in both leagues were decided on the last day of play, with visiting teams emerging victorious. For the owners, the game's popularity reached a historic high in 1908. Their confidence in the future stimulated the construction of steel and concrete ballparks, two of which opened in 1909. The year was nearly stained by scandal. An attempted bribe of umpires had no impact on the field, but the resulting investigation raised more questions than it answered. The gambling issue was not raised seriously again until 1920, in the wake of the Black Sox scandal.

This study details play during each month of the season, featuring the contending teams in each league. Each chapter about the season concludes with an afterword examining an issue or subject of interest that impacted the game during this season of all seasons. Individual chapters are devoted to the players and umpires who took part in the regular-season action, the 1908 World Series, as well as the post-season scandals involving ticket scalping and an attempted bribe of umpires by the New York Giants' team physician.

I would be remiss not to thank the staff at the University of Notre Dame's Hesburgh Library and the curator of the Joyce Sports Research Collection, George Rugg, a member of the Society for American Baseball Research. His insights and ability to find arcane facts deserve several assists in the scorebook. His staff's discovery of the obituary of Dr. Creamer is an outstanding example of the value of libraries as repositories of information and librarians as retrievers of fact. Mr. Rugg also oversees one of the finest collections of sports literature in the United States.

I recognize that this work would not have been possible without the help of my fellow members of the Society for American Baseball Research (SABR). They are the keepers of the flame and able stewards of the lore and history of our national game. Larry Gerlach, 1998–99 SABR president, deserves special recognition for his help and encouragement in reviewing the chapter on umpires. Fellow umpire and Rules Committee member Doug Pappas rates a high five for his sharing ejection data from the season. Baseball historian Marc Okkonen earns a nod of thanks for recommending several helpful changes to the manuscript, giving it accuracy and an improved perspective. SABR member Steve Krah of the *Elkhart Truth* rates a thank-you for his encouragement and kind words when this project was just a dream. Other fellow SABR members John Kovach and Cappy Gagnon were generous with their expertise about railroads and college players respectively. Any errors in the final draft are mine alone.

This book is dedicated to my father, who imparted to me a love of reading, a respect for knowledge and learning, and the often frustrating appreciation of the Go Go Chicago White Sox and the real Comiskey Park. He took me to my first major league game. The last game we attended together was my treat. We saw the Sox clinch the 1983 American League West Championship. We were mighty pleased, and the drive home from Chicago was an unforgettable moment in my life.

A special word to my wife Judy, who is indifferent to baseball and its intricate strategies, except for the movie *Bull Durham*. She supported me in my dream to publish this work—one can ask no more from a life partner and friend. She tolerates and understands my work as a high school and Babe Ruth umpire. I share my umpire fees with her. I am sure the time I spend wearing a mask and chest protector will not be subtracted from the time I have on this Good Earth.

Finally, a word of thanks to my teachers. This work would not have happened if they hadn't pushed me to read and express myself. Our teachers are underappreciated. They, after all, give us our start in the world of research and writing. It would be arrogant of me not to express gratitude for their work.

I conclude with this passage from the Bible, which provides a divine reference to the optimism and hope that emerges on the opening day of every baseball season. It was first revealed to me when I read of the work of Tiger broadcaster Ernie Harwell:

> For see, the winter is past!
> The rains are over and gone;
> the flowers appear in the countryside;
> the season of birdsong is come,
> and the turtle-dove's cooing is heard in our land.
> Song of Songs 2:11–12, Revised English Bible

Introduction

If you didn't honestly and furiously hate the Giants, you weren't a real Cub. —Joe Tinker, Second Base, Chicago Cubs

For better or worse, it's called the Dead Ball Era—that's what some baseball historians generally call the two decades between 1900 and 1919. The 1919 or 1920 season has been used as a convenient divide between the Dead and Lively Ball eras, primarily due to the emergence of Babe Ruth and the home run as a significant offensive weapon and the resolution of the 1919 World Series scandal.

However, a technical argument can be made that the Dead Ball Era ended when the major leagues adopted the cork-centered baseball in 1910 and 1911. Run production increased as a result of the new tighter, livelier ball, but the strategy of the game did not change significantly until Ruth became an everyday player. Thus the extension of the Dead Ball Era to 1919 can be defended, despite being technically incorrect. If some historians dispute the duration of the Dead Ball Era, there is no argument that early-twentieth-century baseball was as exciting and competitive as any other brand of ball played during the past hundred years.

Meant to describe dominant pitching and low scoring using a mush ball, the term *Dead Ball Era* does a huge injustice to those pioneering players, managers, umpires, and owners who lived during the era and participated in fierce competition both on and off the field. The Tinker epigraph stands as an example of how players approached competition with other teams and viewed the concept of team loyalty.

This competition was essentially among cities and their teams, but there was a personal element to it too. Players generally stayed with the same teams for a longer period than they do now, which allowed for a stronger sense of team and regional loyalty on the part of fan and player alike. This loyalty concept has been dampened by free agency and other modern influences.

The highly partisan local sports press contributed to building team loyalty and civic pride. Baseball executives eventually, and in some cases grudgingly, recognized the vital role newspaper coverage played in generating interest in teams, individual players, and in the game itself. During an age when most major cities were served by at least three or more daily newspapers, competition among them was fierce. The writing of the era was at once quaint, colorful, and an art form in and of itself.

The owners, slow to recognize the importance of newspapers, had to be forced into providing facilities for the news media. Late during the 1908 season, reporters established the Base Ball Writers Association of America (BBWAA), and poor conditions for newspapermen were a driving force behind its inception. The BBWAA eventually became known by fans for its annual selection of Most Valuable Player for each league and for Baseball Hall of Fame elections. The founding of the BBWAA received little notice in 1908; BBWAA's glory days were still years away. As the game and the sportswriting profession developed, the BBWAA became part of the institution of baseball, evolving into an organization that became almost as significant to the game as are the players themselves.

There can be absolutely no argument that the rubber-centered, yarn-entwined ball was dead, especially when compared to the so-called rabbit ball of the 1990s. But action on and off the field was anything but dull, as the era's name unfairly implies. Before those brought up on the clink and plink of the aluminum bat think of high-button shoes, handlebar mustaches, and pillbox-style baseball caps (back in 1908 they were called cheesebox hats) and allow their eyes to glaze over, an explanation is owed.

The Dead Ball Era witnessed some of the most thrilling and competitive pennant races in baseball history. Those early races helped establish the foundation upon which baseball, as the national pastime and as a business, was built. The Dead Ball Era also encompassed the careers of players named Young, Cobb, Joss, Mathewson, Wagner, Lajoie, and others you will read about later.

There has never been a baseball season like that of 1908, and it is very unlikely that we will ever witness one like it again. Recent changes in the structure of baseball — divisional play-offs and interleague play — have ensured that. The 1908 season was hard and fast in the middle of the Dead Ball Era and stands as its exemplar. It was a season of great pitching, few home runs, numerous feats of skill and endurance, and stellar performances by the stars of the era. The English language quickly runs out of superlatives to describe the 1908 pennant chase.

The 1909 *Spalding's Official Base Ball Guide* said the year afforded fans "all the pleasure of a Mardi Gras Base Ball carnival."[1] The 1909 *Reach Official American League Guide* noted that the 1908 season was a success because it "resisted successfully the blighting effects of a national election year with its unsettled conditions and political unrest."[2]

While subsequent seasons witnessed close pennant races, 1908 stands alone. In 1967 four American League teams battled until the last week of the season. The Indians and Red Sox ended the 1948 season tied for first, and thirty years later the Red Sox and Yankees settled a divisional crown with a one-game play-off. Over in the National League, play-offs determined pennant winners in 1946, 1951, 1959, and 1962, and the Dodgers were involved in each of them. In 1908, there were no play-offs. Three teams in both the American and National leagues finished within one game of one another, and pennants were decided on the last day of play.

The National League pennant was decided by the replay of an earlier game of a 154-game season, after the New York Giants received a tie for a game the team and their fans thought they had won. The game the Giants thought they had won was the infamous Merkle game. Giants rookie Fred Merkle followed tradition and had not touched second base but instead headed for the clubhouse after witnessing what he thought was a game-winning hit against the Cubs. Chicago won the 154th game at New York's Polo Grounds and went on to win the World Series to become repeat World Champions.

The American League pennant was also won on the last day of the season, when the Detroit Tigers defeated the Chicago White Sox at Chicago. The second-place Cleveland Naps finished a half game behind Detroit, while the Sox fell a full game short. A key late-season contest was a 1 to 0 perfect game hurled by Cleveland ace Addie Joss over White Sox stalwart "Big Ed" Walsh just a week earlier.

Cleveland finished a half game behind the Tigers because of a quirk of the weather and in the rules. League officials ruled that the Naps had finished their season and Detroit was not obligated to play a game that had been rained out. As a result of this outcome, in later years teams in contention were required to play any game that had a bearing on the pennant race.

It was a landmark season from a purely historical perspective as well. The year 1908 was a watershed in that it was the last year that all major league teams played in the small, wooden ballparks of the nineteenth century. The rickety bandbox grandstands that had served the game through the turn of the century were soon to be replaced in response to increased attendance and the growing popularity of baseball.

In short, the building boom made good business sense from the standpoints of timing and marketing. Land inside America's major cities was still relatively cheap, and even the weakest franchises experienced good if not spectacular attendance figures. Fireproof steel and concrete facilities were soon under construction in Pittsburgh (Forbes Field) and Philadelphia (Shibe Park). Both of these parks opened in 1909 and each remained in service for more than fifty years.

The St. Louis Browns chose not to build an entirely new ballpark. Instead, Browns President Robert Lee Hedges ended a three-year feud and bought land from a neighboring landowner in June 1908. Plans called for building a concrete and steel outfield grandstand. Upon completion of the structure, Sportman's Park was reoriented around the new pavilion and its seating capacity was almost doubled to twenty-five thousand.

The deal stirred some controversy in midseason when John E. Brown, secretary of the National Commission and a Browns stockholder, complained about the price of land. The so-called Solari Strip cost the club sixty-five thousand dollars, or more than twice what had originally been offered. Brown issued an awkwardly worded warning to his fellow baseball executives, using his team's experience as the lesson: "It goes to show that ball clubs are going to be confronted with a serious problem with the next few years so far as well locating grounds [sic] in the big cities are concerned. It is policy right now for the clubs in the major leagues to purchase their grounds, for in a few years, it will be impossible to get grounds in large cities which can be easily reached by the cars."[3]

The experience of the Pirates, Athletics, or St. Louis Browns, or John E. Brown's words themselves, may have set off a land rush. A month later the Giants signed a long-term lease for the Polo Grounds, a property the team would occupy until moving to San Francisco in 1958. In December 1908 Charles Comiskey bought the land upon which Comiskey Park would sit until it was demolished in 1990. The Old Roman purchased the parcel for $150,000 from Moses Wentworth and his sister Amelia Boehm. Also late in 1908, the crosstown Cubs moved to secure their future by purchasing the land occupied by the West Side Grounds. That move merely bought them time. The Cubs moved to the present-day Wrigley Field, previously named Weeghman Park, in 1916 after the Federal League folded.

Although "the cars" Brown referred to were street cars and other forms of public transportation, his words foreshadowed the impact the automobile would have on ballpark locations. Parking problems and access to land led some teams to move to other cities during the 1950s, while others sought new property with better automobile access and parking. Brown's concern about public access to playing fields also coincided with an unnoticed but important milestone: the rollout of the first Model T from Henry Ford's factory in Detroit was in 1908.

The ballparks that would occupy a special place in the hearts of fans during the post–World War II era were all built within a decade. The stadia — or, in the language of the day, baseball palaces — would soon be constructed in Chicago, New York, Boston, Detroit, Washington, Philadelphia, and St. Louis. Like Forbes and Shibe, these ballparks would last at least five decades. Three of them built during the early teens — Wrigley Field in Chicago, Boston's Fenway Park, and Tiger Stadium in Detroit — were still standing and in use late in the twentieth century. Tiger Stadium is slated for demolition at the turn of the century. In Boston, plans call for Fenway to be replaced in 2003. Of all the ballparks built during the early twentieth century, only Wrigley seems to have a secure future.

Significantly, the new permanent structures were financed by the owners, not by taxpayers. This entrepreneurialism and financial independence explains to a large degree why baseball owners treated the game as a purely private business during this era. It was this attitude that helped keep the lid on a potentially damaging gambling/bribery scandal late during the 1908 season. The worldview of baseball's leadership was no different from the prevailing business philosophies of other magnates during the Progressive Era. Government was breaking the bonds of laissez-faire policies during this time, using regulation and trust-busting lawsuits. Most businesses resisted notions of accountability to anyone other than themselves and their stockholders. While not thinking of asking for public financial help seems a quaint ideal today, in the politics of the time, such aid was deemed beyond the scope of what government should do.

The record-breaking attendance of 1908 was spurred by the hot pennant races in both leagues. The subsequent skyrocketing revenues provided the driving force that compelled owners to build new parks.

The "build it and they will come" mentality was best expressed by Pittsburgh player-manager Fred Clarke: "When I first came into baseball we used to consider 10,000 a big crowd. Now we have 20,000 crowds, and I expect to see 50,000 crowds some day when the stands are big enough to hold them."[4]

Big league paid attendance broke the seven million mark for the first time in history in 1908, after eclipsing the six million mark in 1907. Interest in the white-hot pennant races was so high in September and October that many people outside baseball expressed concern at the pennant races overshadowing the Taft-Bryan presidential race. On the flip side, many baseball people, other than *Guide* editors, expressed relief that the quadrennial presidential race did not hurt attendance or revenues. Both positions speak volumes about attitudes of the day regarding partisan politics and leisure time entertainment. Interest in the pennant races also drew crowds to view games with the help of electronic boards, an early version of the broadcast transmissions that today allow millions to witness games. These events were held in many large cities and some served as charitable fund-raisers.

Chicago and New York competed both on the diamond and at the turnstile for the title of greatest baseball city. The Giants easily drew the most fans; 880,700. The White Sox were the second most popular club, attracting 694,728 fans through the gates, while the World Champion west side Cubs ranked third with 619,807 paid. Over one third of all fans to witness games in 1908 saw them in either New York or Chicago. The Cubs and Sox combined drew 1.3 million fans, while the Giants and Highlanders attracted just under 1.2 million. New Yorkers could claim the title of baseball capital by including the gate in Brooklyn, but true Chicago fans would claim that three teams against two would not be fair. And Brooklynites would probably resent being lumped in with New York.

The 1909 *Spalding's Guide* notes that the attendance figures given were conservative and it would be impossible to obtain exact figures. Figures provided by the leagues and the sum of home attendance submitted by each club differed slightly from the official league numbers. Official figures increased American League attendance by four hundred and the National League gate by five hundred. No matter which numbers you believe, it is enough to say that baseball had been enjoying unprecedented and increasing popularity since the American League had established itself in 1901 (see appendix A).[5]

Oddly, attendance figures for 1908 did not reflect the final standings as much as reveal the strength of baseball in specific cities, despite the outcome of pennant races. Relatively poor attendance in Cleveland, Detroit, and Pittsburgh in comparison to the teams' final rankings in the standings was blamed upon poor local economic conditions rather than lack of fan interest. Mediocre teams in Philadelphia did little to dampen fan interest. For the Athletics, construction of Shibe Park was more of a recognition of the popularity of the team than an act of faith. The Athletics were only a couple of years away from dominating the American League. The Red Sox drew well despite — with the exception of Cy Young — a lackluster ball club (see appendix B).

The 1908 season witnessed innovations that impacted the game in later years. The Pittsburgh Pirates introduced an infield tarpaulin in order to cut down on postponements due to wet field conditions. This was a case of necessity being the mother of invention: Exposition Park, located near the Ohio River, was often soggy in the spring and early summer due to seasonal rains and flooding. Ironically, Exposition Park occupies the site of today's Three Rivers Stadium.[6]

The idea eventually caught on with other clubs because covering the diamond when it wasn't in use provided a measure of protection from the elements, which meant fewer postponements, which decreased the necessity of doubleheaders, allowing for improved opportunities to collect revenue. Weather-related postponements were a big issue in 1907 and 1908; during each season sixty-nine games were postponed due to inclement weather. In June 1908, *Sporting Life* noted the figures and opined that the weather gave "ground for the question whether the unnatural climatic conditions of the last two years are mere freakish coincidences or whether they are to become established conditions. Another year may shed some light on a question that will become of grave importance to the base ball schedule makers."[7]

Another trend, night baseball, would take longer to become commonplace. While other years would stake claims to its origination, the idea of night baseball received significant attention during the 1908 season. Late in the season, during the height of the pennant races, Cincinnati owner and National Commission member Garry Herrmann startled the baseball world by announcing that he would undertake an experiment with lights and night baseball. While the experiment was successful as undertaken in 1909 using semipro teams at the Cincinnati ballpark, night baseball didn't catch on in the big leagues until the mid-1930s, long after use of lights had been successfully pioneered by the barnstorming Negro League teams. Some Negro League teams used portable lights to give them the opportunity to play day and night, the idea being more games and more revenue. The major league owners were slow to embrace night baseball, despite its proven track record, due to cost considerations, little pressure to make a change, and concerns among officials that night games represented baseball played under unnatural conditions.[8]

The owners' contention that night baseball was unnatural has an odd ring to it. There was no other rationale presented for not adopting night contests. It seems owners were unwilling to spend the money on something they did not need. Dead Ball Era revenues were ample and there was no need for the boost in attendance that night baseball would bring. Night games were not embraced by owners until attendance had decreased to Dead Ball Era levels as a result of the Great Depression.

The season of 1908 was one of heartache, heartbreak, foreboding, and furious all-out controversy. It was a season of great achievement and abject failure. It was a season of personalities, competition, and courage. The Merkle incident, one of the most frequently written about moments in baseball history, has all the elements of conflict, passion, and tragedy one sees in classical theater. This single play overshadows many of the other exciting and momentous facets of this most remarkable season. And that is unfortunate. It forever stained Merkle's overall fine career and contributed to the breakdown and eventual suicide in the summer of 1909 of National League President Harry C. Pulliam.

Each league witnessed remarkable pitching performances. Within five days of one another in late September, Ed Summers of Detroit, Ed Reulbach of the Cubs, and Ed Walsh of the White Sox started and won both games of a doubleheader. Earlier in the month Walter Johnson threw three shutouts against the Highlanders in five days. In June Cy Young, a nineteen-year veteran, pitched a no-hitter. Young's performance should remind contemporary fans of Nolan Ryan, whose remarkable labors with underachieving teams are the stuff of modern legend. Cleveland's Addie Joss made his own legend with a perfect game against the White Sox during a crucial October encounter.

There was spirited debate over the spitball. While many associate the Dead Ball Era with the moist delivery, the assumption that the pitch was universally accepted and admired is quite untrue. The spitter was blamed for poor offensive production and poor fielding. It was also the meal ticket for a number of star pitchers. There was an outcry for banning the delivery, but those calls were ignored. As any fan knows, baseball is inherently conservative and slow to change. The spitter was not banned until 1920, and even then some pitchers were grandfathered and allowed to use it until their careers ended.

The game itself was maturing. The days of one umpire covering a regular season game were slowly ending. Most games were still covered by one umpire in 1908, but owners, players, sportswriters, and fans were realizing that the game needed more than one official on the field. Over half the games of 1908 were covered by only one official. In 1909, it would be the other way around, as enough umpires were hired to ensure that the majority of games were overseen by two officials. A commitment to two umpires helped keep order on the field and eventually improved overall officiating.

Additionally, 1908 was a year when the storm clouds of scandal formed, thundered, then disappeared for another eleven years. Two umpires were the targets of a bribery attempt, but the subsequent investigation and punishment of the perpetrator were hardly earth shattering. Contemporary newspapers constantly editorialized about the evils of gambling on baseball. American League President Ban Johnson declared war on gamblers. There were documented incidents of attempted bribes of National League players and umpires in New York. But in the end, little was done and the problem of gambling in big league baseball would not be fully addressed until a World Series was fixed in 1919.

In a less ominous vein, the year witnessed the writing of a song that has become indelibly etched into the fabric of baseball history and culture. Baseball's unofficial anthem, "Take Me Out to the Ball Game," made its debut onstage in October 1908, just after the fury of the pennant races had subsided and the World Series had concluded. Interestingly, neither composer Albert Von Tilzer nor lyricist Jack Norworth had ever been to a baseball game prior to writing this song, performance of which has become a seventh-inning ritual nearly everywhere the game is played. While the chorus has obviously survived, its verse about a baseball-crazy young woman has been largely forgotten. The song in its entirety is worth repeating:

Katie O'Casey was baseball mad,
Had the fever and had it bad;
Just to root for her hometown crew,
Ev'ry sou, Katie blew.
On a Saturday,
Her young beau called to see if she'd like to go see a show,
But Miss Kate said,
"No, I'll tell you what you can do.
Take me out to the ballgame,
Take me out to the crowd,
Buy me some peanuts and Cracker Jack,
I don't care if I never get back,
Let me root, root, root for the home team,
If they don't win its a shame,
For it's one, two, three strikes
"You're out"
At the old ball game."[9]

It would have been icing on the cake to a great story line, but Franklin P. Adams's poem "Tinker to Evers to Chance" was not published in 1908, as some sources indicate. Adams wrote it solely to fill space in his column in the *New York Globe* on July 10, 1910, during the last year of the great Cubs dynasty of the early twentieth century.

Sportswriters of the era were true artisans of the craft of writing. Poetry often accompanied stories and accounts of games or of events affecting the game. Adams was a rabid Giants fan, and ironically, his poem probably contributed more to the Hall of Fame status of three of the four Cubs infielders in 1908 than did their own field performance. Had third baseman Harry Steinfeldt's name been more melodic, the entire Cubs infield might have been immortalized.

These are the saddest of possible words —
    Tinker to Evers to Chance.
Trio of Bear Cubs and fleeter than birds —
    Tinker to Evers to Chance.
Thoughtlessly pricking our gonfalon bubble,
Making a Giant hit into a double,
Words that are weighty with nothing but trouble,
    Tinker to Evers to Chance.[10]

One follow-up note to this famous verse: the word *gonfalon* was not and is not widely used. It is defined as a banner with streamers hung from a crossbar. Thus, a gonfalon was more of a banner than a bubble. Adams's use of the word meant the Cub trio put an end to the Giants' pennant dreams.

Another historic note: the year 1908 was also when the world learned of the weighty decision by officialdom as to who invented baseball. In a decision released in late 1907 and becoming public in early 1908, the Mills Commission decided that baseball had been devised by Abner Doubleday at Cooperstown, New York, in 1839. The myth was embellished by the fact that Doubleday was a Civil War general. That, coupled with the dubious conclusion that baseball had no connection to any foreign game, gave the owners the ammunition they needed to promote baseball as the national pastime. Performance on the field led some to forget the commission's decision, but its conclusion helped lead to establishing Cooperstown as the site of the National Baseball Hall of Fame a couple of decades later. The Mills findings have been refuted by historians but remain firmly fixed in the game's mythology.

Finally, 1908 marks the last time the White Sox and Cubs were locked in simultaneous, hotly contested pennant races at the end of the season. The Cubs dynasty and the popular White Sox provided evidence that Chicago was the baseball capital of the world, besides being the headquarters of the American League. For long-suffering Cubs fans, 1908 marks the last World Championship (as of this writing) for the storied franchise. For equally long-suffering Sox fans, 1908 was just another heartbreaker and the precursor to a last (as of this writing) World Championship in 1917 and the humiliation of the Black Sox in 1919.

We begin the journey through 1908 two years earlier, when the Cubs and Sox met in the first intracity and, so far, the only Chicago-only World Series. In 1906, the Cubs won 116 games during the regular season and were heavy favorites over the White Sox, dubbed the "Hitless Wonders" due to an anemic .230 team batting average. In one of the biggest upsets in baseball history, the underdog Sox won the series 4–2. The 1906 World Series put Chicago on the baseball map. The 1906 season also cemented the bitter rivalries that carried over into the 1908 season.

More than Merkle

1 Baseball Turned Upside Down
The 1906 World Series

No club that wins a pennant once is an outstanding club. One which bunches two pennants is a good club. But a team which can win three in a row really achieves greatness. —John McGraw

New York Giants manager John McGraw never forgave the Cubs for what happened in 1906. His 1905 World Champion Giants were one of the strongest teams in baseball history. The '05 club was among McGraw's favorites because it was the first National League team to defeat the despised upstart American League in a World Series. The Giants had refused to play Boston in the 1904 World Series out of contempt, scorn, and outright hatred of the American League and its president, Ban Johnson.

McGraw's animus toward Johnson was due to their relationship when the Giants manager had been skipper of the American League Baltimore Orioles. The two clashed frequently over McGraw's abuse of umpires and other on-field behavior. While McGraw believed that Johnson arranged to throw him out of the league in 1902, in reality McGraw left for the National League before Johnson could have him removed. In truth, McGraw was happy to leave to manage the Giants. Johnson was equally glad to be rid of a major problem. Both men were capable of holding long-time grudges. They succeeded in maintaining their mutual loathing for the rest of their lives.

John McGraw wanted nothing more than to win a third straight National League pennant in 1906. In McGraw's mind, only then would the Giants achieve true greatness and assume their place among the immortals. The Giants chalked up ninety-six wins in 1906, enough to do the job in more than a mere handful of seasons. McGraw had cajoled, fought, ordered, and willed the team, overcoming the illness of Christy Mathewson, Mike Donlin's battle with booze and injury, and other assorted injuries and ravages of age to other key performers. But the third straight pennant was not to be.

It was not to be for a variety of reasons. An important one could have been pride. McGraw was always one to gloat. The Giants' uniforms had "World Champions" emblazoned across the chest and the team rode to the ballpark with "World Champions" embroidered on horse blankets.[1] Neither of these gestures endeared the Giants to their opposition, who could be counted on to give extra effort when New York was in town.

Also standing in the way of Giants greatness was an emerging dynasty. Frequently ungracious to his opposition, McGraw regarded these up-and-comers as upstarts, barely worthy of respect and quite deserving of scorn. The upstart bushers were the Chicago Cubs, managed by first baseman Frank Chance.

The 1906 Cubs had a year like no other big league team had ever had, winning 116 games and easily icing the pennant by twenty games over the also-ran Giants. The 1998 Yankees' regular season 114–48 (.703) mark came close to approaching the Cubs record, reminding modern fans of the Cubs' achievement. The Yankees' march through the 1998 play-offs and World Series set a major league record of 125 games won for the year, compared to the 1906 Cubs' regular and post-season mark of 116.

The enormity of Chicago's achievement has dimmed with the passage of time, but the numbers do not lie. At the end of July, the Cubs were in first with a 61–26 record. They won fifty-five and lost only ten more games the rest of the year, for a final 116–36 (.763) slate for the regular season. This first team of the great Cub dynasty of 1906–10 dominated the National League in nearly every significant statistical category; batting average (.262), slugging percentage (.339), fielding average (.969), shutouts (28), and earned run average (1.76).

Like all other sports successes, this Cubs dynasty was built over several years and was the result of a combination of luck, determination, money, and patience. It did not hurt to have a front office committed and smart enough to spot talent and to go out and get it. Each of the Cubs' key players was obtained by a trade and/or purchase. Each transaction was calculated to add personnel to fill weaknesses and buttress the assets of the club. Most of the credit for building the team ought to go to one of the most overlooked managers in baseball history, Frank Selee. Credit for execution of Selee's plan went to his successor, player-manager Frank Chance.

Selee managed the Cubs for three and half years, from 1902 until stepping down in midseason 1905 due to illness. Prior to coming to Chicago, Selee had managed the National League's Boston Beaneaters to five pennants from 1890 to 1901. Selee's overall record as a manager was 1,284–862 (.598). That winning percentage is fourth highest among managers in baseball history. Selee's trademark teams had outstanding offensive and defensive speed with excellent baseball intelligence. It is sad that Selee's achievements have been ignored for almost an entire century. His contribution to baseball was finally recognized in early 1999 when the Old Timers Committee voted him into the Hall of Fame.

While Selee didn't win any pennants for the Cubs, the core of this dominant team had been acquired by the time he resigned and handed over the reins to Frank Chance. The players Selee acquired or retained who played a key role for the Cubs from 1906 to 1910 were Chance, a converted catcher, at first; second baseman Johnny Evers; Joe Tinker at shortstop; outfielders Jimmy Slagle and Frank "Wildfire" Schulte; catcher Johnny Kling; and pitchers Carl Lundgren, Mordecai "Three Finger" Brown, and "Big Ed" Reulbach.

Chance wound up with all of the managerial glory and with membership in the Hall of Fame. After 1905 Chance reportedly said the club needed a pitcher, an outfielder, and a third baseman. In 1906, the team that terrorized the National League for five years added pitchers Jack Taylor, Jack Pfiester, and Orval Overall; outfielder Jimmy Sheckard; and, to round out the infield, third baseman Harry Steinfeldt, acquired in a trade with Cincinnati. Steinfeldt, overlooked because of his more famous infield mates, was a key part of these fine Cubs teams and anchored an already strong defensive unit. Sheckard added another bat and strong defensive skills to a solid outfield. Taylor, Pfiester, and

Overall, each in his own way, contributed significantly to Chicago's success during their five-year run.

From 1906 through 1910, the Chicago Cubs played 765 regular season games, winning 530 and losing only 235 for a staggering .693 won-lost percentage. That translated into four pennants and a second-place finish during those five seasons. The Cubs' World Series record during the dynasty was a more down-to-earth eleven and nine, winning two World Championships. The so-so World Series record aside, this Cubs dynasty was the best in the game's history in terms of total wins and winning percentage, beating out the great Cardinals teams of the early 1940s and Yankees teams of the thirties, fifties, and sixties (see appendix C).

Over in the American League, the crosstown White Sox scratched their way to their third American League crown since 1900. The 1906 American League race was close as the New York Highlanders and Cleveland Naps finished off the pace by three and five games respectively. The Sox were paced by a nineteen-game winning streak in August but still needed to fight off a late charge by New York in September to win the pennant.

The 1906 Sox were affectionately known as the "Hitless Wonders." As with most baseball nicknames, it fit. It could be said that if the Sox fell out of a boat into the ocean, they couldn't hit water, or if they did, they wouldn't hit it hard. The Sox .230 team batting average was last in the league. They ranked dead last in most other offensive categories, reflecting owner Charles Comiskey's philosophy of building a team around pitching and conditioning while utilizing a strategy of squeezing advantage out of every hit, walk, error, stolen base, or lapse by the opposition. Comiskey's philosophy about offensive baseball also applied to his finances. He squeezed every penny out of each dollar as much as his teams treasured each base runner.

Cubs second baseman Johnny Evers boiled the Hitless Wonders down to this simple declaration: "The team excelled any team ever organized in concentrating every move toward making runs, one at a time, and while nearly weakest in batting, scored the greatest average number of runs per hit of any club in the history of the game."[2]

Analysis of runs per hit in 1906 does not entirely bear out Evers's statement. The Sox were among the leaders, but not the leader in this obscure category. They scored .50 runs per hit, or a run for every two hits. The Cubs scored .53 runs per hit, the best in the game. The Giants were the only other 1906 team to exceed half a run per hit at .51 runs per hit. Significantly, both the Cubs and Giants clearly had more offense to work with, outhitting the Sox by a wide margin.

Further analysis of opponents reveals just how good the two Chicago teams were in 1906. Cubs opponents scored .374 runs per hit, while the Sox opposition was just off that pace at .379 runs per hit. This stinginess resulted in an interesting statistic, which gives truth to Evers's declaration about White Sox offensive efficiency. The Hitless Wonders scored 3.77 runs per game and surrendered 3.05, for an average margin of victory of just over half a run. The Cubs scored 4.62 and allowed 2.51 per contest, defeating opponents by over two runs a game.

Like the Cubs, the White Sox were led by a player-manager. Fielder Jones directed his team's fortunes from center field. Jones was a hard-nosed leader, able to get every bit of effort and ability out of his players. He enjoys the distinction of being one of only two White Sox managers ever to win a World Series, and his 426–293 record with the South Siders is among the best won-lost records in the checkered history of the franchise. Jones's .592 managerial winning percentage is best among White Sox skippers, but his achievement has been largely forgotten.

The White Sox featured a veteran lineup with ex–National League slugger George Davis at shortstop and Frank Isbell at second; they and first baseman John "Jiggs" Donahue were the only starters to hit above .250 in 1906. Defense and pitching were the Sox forte. It was a staff handled by one of the best defensive catchers in the Dead Ball Era, Billy Sullivan. The pitching staff was anchored by twenty-game winners Frank "Yip" Owen and Nick Altrock. Big Ed Walsh and Doc White bolstered the staff. Sox pitchers registered a team-earned run average of 2.13, just over a third of a run higher than that of the Cubs.

On paper, the White Sox seemed to have little hope of defeating the mighty Cubs. But, as the adage goes, games are played on the field. From October 9 through 14, the city of Chicago stood still as the Cubs and Sox waged a six-day war. Like all contests between nearby rivals, the Sox-Cubs series resembled civil war in some respects.

It was civil war with an ethnic flavor in a city where ethnicity was, and still is, an important matter. By accident or coincidence, the Cubs lineup was dominated by German surnames — Kling, Sheckard, Steinfeldt, Reulbach, Pfiester, Hofman. As for the South Side White Sox, the lineup looked like a list of voters from the nearby predominantly Irish-American Bridgeport neighborhood — Walsh, Sullivan, Dougherty,

Jones. This ethnic division was the source of amusement during a time when much was made of such things without arousing outrage.

Johnny Evers in *Touching Second* relates the following anecdote:

> When the West Side and the South Side were engaged almost in civil war, there was an Irishman named Faugh, a Ballagh Finnegan, better known as "Fog," who made a small fortune in trade on the West Side, and who, although he never had seen a game, was one of the most loyal supporters of the West Side team. On the day of the first game "Fog," gloriously arrayed, and with much money to wager, was the center of a group of ardent West Siders assembled in one section of the South Side stands. Standing on his seat he defied the White Sox supporters and flaunted his money in their faces.
>
> "Wan hundred to sixty on the Wist Side," he shouted.
>
> "Wan hundred to fifty. Wan hundred to forty."
>
> The South Siders, who were not betting on their team, ignored him. He shouted, challenged, and yelled the praises of the West Side. Presently the umpire brushed off the plate and announced:
>
> "Ladies and Gentlemen — the batteries for today's game will be Reulbach and Kling for the West Side. Walsh and Sullivan for the South Side."
>
> For an instant "Fog" blinked hard, wavering between loyalty to the West Side and love of Ireland. Then, leaping up again, he shouted,
>
> "Walsh and Sullivan — thim's they byes I meant. Wan hundred to sixty on the South Side."[3]

While a believable instance of ethnic division coupled with the depiction of the common Dead Ball Era occurrence of gambling in the stands, Evers's story is partly apocryphal. The existence of open gambling in the stands was accurate. But the series opener was played at the Cubs' West Side Grounds and Brown and Altrock started. Walsh and Reulbach locked horns in game five at West Side Grounds, not South Side Park. Evers can be forgiven for embellishing a credible story.

Chicago in October 1906 was not a place for a Sox fan in Cubs territory or vice versa. Some cooler heads managed to produce two-way buttons showing a dual allegiance, a bear cub wearing white socks![4] The series was a highly partisan affair, but fortunately, the spirit of sportsmanship prevailed during baseball's first intracity World Series and the last one to feature Chicago's teams. But no matter the outcome, it was a proud moment for Chicagoans.

Contemporary fans have witnessed some truly terrible Cubs and White Sox teams during the twentieth century. They can be forgiven for believing hell would freeze over before the Sox and Cubs would ever lock horns in a World Series. White Sox and Cubs loyalists would also understand the possibly divine message from the playing conditions of this Windy City World Series. Game one of the 1906 series was played in below-freezing weather with light snow falling. Nick Altrock and Three Finger Brown each allowed four hits. The Sox won 2–1 with a triple by reserve third baseman George Rohe and a single by Isbell providing the winning runs.

Game two moved to the South Side where Big Ed Reulbach threw a one-hitter, knotting the series at a game each in another game played in nasty cold weather. Cubs hitters rang out ten safeties. A three-run second inning, aided by a Sox throwing error, settled the issue early. Reulbach had a no-hitter going until the seventh inning, when Jiggs Donahue singled. Reulbach's effort, as was sometimes the case, was marred by wildness to the tune of six walks and a hit batsman. The 7–1 score seemed to indicate that the Cubs were back on track and the Sox were in trouble, if only the Cubs would play like they had during the regular season.

The third game of the series featured a stellar pitching duel between Big Ed Walsh and lefty Jack Pfiester. Walsh struck out twelve hitters and George Rohe, hero of game one, hit a two-out, bases-loaded triple in the sixth inning to give the Sox the 3–0 win. Rohe had appeared in only seventy-five games during the regular season, hitting .258. His 1906 World Series heroics were soon forgotten. He was out of the major leagues by 1908, becoming an early member of the "what have you done for me lately" wing of baseball's archives.

Game four saw the trend of the home team losing continue. Three Finger Brown threw a two-hit shutout at South Side Park to even the series at two games apiece. Johnny Evers's seventh-inning two-out single drove home Frank Chance for the sole run of the game. Chance had reached base when his fly ball was lost in the sun.

The Cubs returned home to the West Side Grounds for the pivotal game five. Chance, superstitiously noting that the visitors had won all games, dressed the Cubs in their road uniforms and started game two hero Ed Reulbach. Taking advantage of poor fielding, the Cubs jumped out to a 3–1 lead, but the White Sox roared back behind an uncharacteristic twelve-hit attack that chased both Reulbach and Pfiester for an

8–6 win. The Sox had miraculously overcome six errors, while the Cubs were flawless in the field.

Game six was no contest. The Sox chased Brown, scoring seven times in the first two innings on the way to an easy 8–3 win. Doc White went the distance to win the World Championship for the White Sox in one of the greatest sports upsets ever. For Cubs fans, the 1906 series represented a huge disappointment. For Sox fans it has provided bragging rights for several generations. Delirious Sox fans crowded the offices of Cubs owner Charles Murphy after the victory, and Murphy delivered a gracious concession speech on behalf of Chicago Cubs baseball.

Was it a case of complacency, or was it fate? Frank Chance would not let his charges forget the 1906 series. The Cubs were gracious in their public statements, to a point. Chance summed up: "The Sox played grand, game baseball and outclassed us in this Series. But there is one thing that I will never believe, and that is that the White Sox are better than the Cubs."[5]

The enemy named complacency would be put to ground in 1907. This edition of the Cubs won 107 contests and the pennant by seventeen games over the Pirates. McGraw's Giants were a distant third and would have to rebuild to return to serious pennant competition. The 1907 Cubs team had no .300 hitters, but five pitchers; Orval Overall, Three Finger Brown, Carl Lundgren, Jack Pfiester, and Big Ed Reulbach turned in earned run averages under 1.70. The entire staff threw thirty shutouts, or nearly one for every five games.

This time the series opponent for the Cubs was Hughie Jennings's Detroit Tigers, who had squeaked by Philadelphia by a game and a half. The Tigers were at the start of a three-consecutive-pennants run. In the series Cubs pitchers smothered the Tigers four games to none after game one resulted in a tie. Cubs pitchers held the Tigers' lineup, which included Ty Cobb and Sam Crawford, to a .209 average, posted a 0.75 earned run average, and erased the shame of 1906.

Going into 1908, the Cubs had won 223 games and lost only eighty-one during the previous two seasons. All key players were returning and it again looked as if the Cubs would be the team to beat in 1908. John McGraw had other plans, and the Pirates were hungry for revenge.

For the White Sox, 1907 yielded a disappointing third place, five and a half games off the pace. Following the season's end, manager Fielder Jones threatened to retire and join his brother in the lumber business in the Pacific Northwest. It was no secret that acting as an intermediary between disgruntled players and owner Charles Comiskey was wearing Jones down. In late 1907 Comiskey persuaded him to give it another try. Going into 1908, Jones was convinced that the Sox would be the team to beat. The Tigers would have something to say about that. So would Napoleon "Larry" Lajoie's Cleveland club and, surprisingly, the St. Louis Browns. The Browns had loaded up for the campaign by acquiring ace left-hander Rube Waddell from Philadelphia. Waddell's antics and drinking had worn out his welcome and would provide distraction for his new team. The stage was set for one of the most tumultuous, fascinating, controversial, and exciting baseball seasons ever.

2 The Game in 1908 Dead Ball Era Baseball

Baseball is a simple yet complex game. Its charm and appeal lie in its combination of simplicity and complexity, allowing fans to appreciate the game on many levels. This relationship between the elementary and complicated has led some to say baseball is like church. Many attend but few understand.

The game and its measurements of success and failure have remained essentially the same through the years; only the participants, environment, and equipment have changed. A late-twentieth-century fan would easily recognize the 1908 game and its overall strategy, but there were still differences separating the Dead Ball Era game from that of modern times.

BALLPARKS AND FANS

Examination of the 1908 season starts with the trip to the ballpark. Chances are you arrived for the afternoon game via horse-drawn carriage, streetcar, or urban railroad, or even on foot, because the ballparks of the day were within urban neighborhoods. A major difference between attending a modern game and one of the Dead Ball Era was how you got there. Today's fans usually drive and park near the stadium. In 1908 you drove if you were among the elite, or the daring. Mass production and availability of the automobile were still some years off. As already noted, 1908 was the year Henry Ford introduced the Model T. The vast parking lots and interstate highways that are the primary habitat of the modern day were nonexistent and undreamed of during the Dead Ball Era.

Because of the automobile and parking requirements, most modern ballparks are isolated from neighborhoods. Only two of today's standing early-century parks give this kind of neighborhood flavor: Boston's Fenway Park and Wrigley Field in Chicago. Among the newer ballparks, Oriole Park at Camden Yards and Jacobs Field in Cleveland are splendid examples of how the early concrete and steel ballparks looked and felt and how they blended into an urban neighborhood.

The 1908 game was played under the afternoon sun. Games started any time between 2:00 and 4:00 P.M. In some cities games would start earlier than in others. There were no league rules setting game times. Earlier starts may have been necessary because of travel requirements or a doubleheader. There was also the phenomenon of the morning-afternoon doubleheader, which gave owners revenues from two separate games, as opposed to two afternoon contests for the price of one.

Almost nonexistent today, twin bills were common during the 1908 season. Usually scheduled for the summer holidays, doubleheaders were also required because of postponements due to weather, or tie games due to weather or darkness, and because owners wanted to recover revenue. Tie games were more frequent during the Dead Ball Era because of low-score games, no lights, and teams pressed to leave town to make travel connections. The burden of doubleheaders to make up postponed or suspended games was a huge headache for managers, who had to juggle pitching staffs down the stretch, thus the rare necessity of forcing pitchers to start both games of a doubleheader. This happened on three separate occasions among the contenders during the 1908 stretch drive.

Sunday baseball was legal in the western cities of Chicago, St. Louis, Detroit, and Cincinnati. This posed a minor problem for schedulers. Sundays were game days for the at-home western teams and either a travel or a rest day when the eastern teams were at home. Sunday games were popular with the blue-collar class. That day represented the one day of leisure their work schedules would allow them. Afternoon games during the work week meant crowds were composed mainly of white-collar, middle-class workers.

On arrival at the ballpark, seating was classified mainly in three ways — bleacher, grandstand, and box or reserved — a classification that has generally remained the same today. There were no sky- or luxury boxes during the Dead Ball Era. Admission ranged from 25 to 50 cents for the bleacher or standing room, 75 cents for grandstand, and a dollar for reserved seats. During a World Series, these prices doubled.[1] In 1908, the Cubs' prices were 25 cents for bleachers, 75 cents for grandstand, and a dollar and a half for box seats.[2] While these prices seem ridiculously low by modern standards, the cost represented a significant portion of income to the average working person, as the bleacher seat accounted for as much as three hours of labor in 1908 dollars for the average worker.

If it was a big game, your bleacher admission could entitle you to stand behind ropes in the outfield or in foul territory along the infield and outfield. Among the utilitarian charms of the old wooden ballparks were huge outfield areas, which were often used to accommodate overflow crowds. In some cases these overflow crowds could affect the outcome of games by changing the dimensions of the outfield and foul territory.

Permanent seating was primarily located around the infield, where the action was. The old wooden ballparks all had one thing in common — little or no permanent seating behind the outfield fences. As a result, the vast majority of box or grandstand seats were close to the field, adding to the atmosphere of the Dead Ball Era game.

If you were fortunate enough to watch the game from a reserved seat or anywhere else, men would be dressed quite formally, with a bowler hat or straw boater during the summer. This was a reflection of the times, since no self-respecting person would go out in public dressed informally. A look at photos of the day leaves you with a striking impression of the formality of dress, especially compared to today's standards. There were none of the T-shirts, baseball hats, or halter tops common in today's crowds. Team-licensed sportswear was years away. About the only people wearing ties to today's games are the owners, some broadcasters, and those who rent expensive skyboxes.

As mentioned earlier, a feature of games during the Dead Ball Era was gambling in the grandstands. Fans would bet on just about anything. In *Touching Base*, Stephen A. Reiss notes: "Fans gambled on the outcome of a game, the total number of hits and runs, the call of a pitch, and even the possibility of a batted ball being caught. Bets were made on ball games in cities throughout the country, especially in cities like Boston and Pittsburgh where there was no horse racing to interest the gambling crowd."[3]

The matter of gambling was one in which the owners' antibetting rhetoric plainly did not match the action taken against it, despite fears that gambling would harm the appeal of the game. The question of baseball and gambling was a complex issue, involving internal and external politics, conflicts of interest, and desire to retain the status quo, which effectively blocked any conclusive action against betting. Throughout 1908, some baseball executives took turns either denouncing gambling or announcing that it was dying off, while others said or did nothing. In August American League President Ban Johnson announced a crusade against gambling in the league, ordering owners to enforce league rules against betting in the stands. National League President Harry Pulliam, calling on his ability to ignore problems, acknowledged Johnson's move as "commendable" while claiming the gambling problem had been "squelched" in his league.[4] As we shall see, Pulliam was sadly mistaken.

It would take scandal of earth-shaking proportions to change the status quo and forever remove the ambivalence shown during the Dead Ball Era over betting on games. Gambling in the stands is one practice rarely seen today; now betting on games is largely dependent on the use of radio and television coverage.

Gambling aside, owners were also concerned about a related problem, "rowdyism," both in the stands and on the field. In 1908 this issue received almost as much attention as gambling. While betting may have contributed to the problem, rowdyism was also fed by the flow of alcoholic beverages, ranging from beer to hard liquor and served in glasses and bottles. The atmosphere in the stands contributed to the notion that baseball was a sport for the uncouth underclasses. That was true in the 1890s.

By the middle of the first decade of the twentieth century moves were afoot to rid the game of its poor image. As one part of this effort, women were encouraged to attend games. This was both a bow to Victorian Age sensibilities — that women would or could be a civilizing influence — and a means of expanding the audience.

An outdated, discriminatory, and even perhaps chauvinistic practice by today's standards was Ladies' Day at the ballpark. It meant women with escorts were admitted to the ballpark free of charge, as the primary way of encouraging women to attend ball games. The Chicago

White Sox already had the policy in place on Fridays at South Side Park and Cubs President Charles W. Murphy initiated the practice at his West Side Grounds on Tuesdays. Interestingly, in Chicago, there was no limit on the number of women who could attend without charge in the company of one man — a curious twist to the moral sensibilities of the era.[5]

While the presence of ladies may or may not have had a civilizing impact on the largely male crowds, there was an amusing side to this story. While men were dressed in hats, suits, and ties, the well-dressed lady would not venture forth without the fashion statement of the age, the Merry Widow hat. With its oversized brim and feather adornments, the hat could obstruct the view of fans who had the misfortune of sitting behind a fashionably dressed woman. In *Unforgettable Season*, this occurrence was noted in several accounts of ball games, the best of which was this description of the situation by Jack Ryder of the *Cincinnati Enquirer:* "A number of thoughtful women removed their expensive millinery creations during the game, gaining the gratitude of many spectators. At a ball game you can tell whether a woman is a real lady or just a plain female by noting whether she has her hat on or not."[6]

Often sportswriters resorted to poetry to get their ideas across. It was only a matter of time before the Merry Widow hat would receive such attention. The hat crisis became so intense that early during the 1909 season none other than the immortal Grantland Rice was compelled to write this amusing poem in *Sporting Life,* titled "A Timely Warning":

Makers of bonnets the women wear —
   Moulders of fashion, whoe'er ye be —
Drear is the curse of my daily prayer,
   Deep is the hatred I have for thee;
This is the warning I fling afar:
   "Mould 'em more on a smaller plan —
Chop off a couple of yards of 'spar,'
   Or beware of the wrath of the angry fan!"

Yester year to the game I went,
   Daily the pilgrimage I made —
Oh, what a waste of coin I spent
   Wondering how the game was played.
Was it a hit or an error raw
   Was it a stolen base or score?

I peered in vain, but I only saw
   A hat that was nine feet WIDE or more.

Back to the park this spring I passed,
   Knowing the old styles out of date —
"Now," I thought, "I shall get, at last,
   A look once more at the old 'home plate.' "
Was it a hit or a fielding flaw?
   Why the deuce did the bleachers roar?
In vain I looked, but I only saw
   A hat that was nine feet HIGH or more.

Makers of bonnets the women wear —
   Moulders of fashion, whoe'er ye be —
Drear is the curse of my daily prayer,
   Deep is the hatred I have for thee;
This is the warning I hurl to-day:
   Cut on a narrower, shorter plan;
Chop off a couple of yards each way —
   Or beware the wrath of the maddened fan!"[7]

If the Merry Widow hat fashion presented a cultural and physical obstacle to some fans, another fashion of the age, the organized rooters' club, was beginning to run its course by running afoul of efforts to clean up fan behavior. Such fan clubs were organized in nearly every major league city as a means of promoting city pride and providing vocal support for the home team, but owners were not entirely pleased with the development. Increasingly, baseball officialdom was seeing these rooters' clubs as sources of rowdyism.

Rooting clubs made grand entrances to games waving banners and noisemakers. They were hard to miss or ignore in their support of the home team. Opposing players and fans, as well as umpires, were often targets of derisive cheers. One of the most visible of these clubs was Boston's Royal Rooters, who achieved fame of sorts during the first World Series in 1903 for their boisterous support of the Red Sox. Members of the Royal Rooters included community leaders and politicians. Among the members of this club was Boston Mayor John "Honey Fitz" Fitzgerald, grandfather of President John F. Kennedy.

In Chicago, fan clubs for the Cubs and White Sox had cut their teeth on the 1906 World Series and had become large and profitable enterprises. Fan clubs held fund-raisers to purchase noisemakers and other gear and to create interest during the off season.[8] Judging from contemporary accounts, the relationship between fan clubs and owners varied from year to year and city to city, but the scales were tilting against these organizations by 1908. During the preseason, Cubs President Charles W. Murphy expressed concern about the rooters' clubs. He charged that they coerced people to join, inhibited spontaneous and honest enthusiasm, and harmed the game by encouraging bad behavior. Murphy wanted Chicago's fans "to be sportsmanlike in defeat and courteous to visiting players because both Sox and Cubs must go on the road."[9]

A little more than a week after Murphy's remarks, American League President Ban Johnson, an opponent of rowdyism and other rude behavior by fan and player alike, weighed in from his league office in Chicago. He warned White Sox and other team boosters that they would be suppressed if they resorted to rooting tactics used during previous years. Specifically, Johnson was unhappy about what he called "artificial rooting" and the use of megaphones to insult opposing players and umpires. Johnson noted that such insults often led to vulgar retorts and summed up: "Any player should be punished for aiming insulting remarks at the spectators, but the players, too, deserve some measure of protection."[10]

A week before the season began, Sporting Life editor Francis Richter supported Johnson's stand, calling organized rooting "an insult to the intelligence of the baseball patrons, a disgrace to the game, a glaring disturbance of the peace, and a standing invitation to abuse, rowdyism and riot."[11] Richter's editorial concluded that Johnson's actions deserved support because they were an attempt to attract a better class of customer and were thus a means of combating rowdyism.

While these arguments seemed high-minded, owners were also focusing on matters that had always concerned them — attendance and revenue. They feared that organized rooters' clubs would scare fans away and hurt attendance. Also, because of the success of fund-raisers, the owners were concerned that the fan clubs were trading in on the sport and not helping the teams or the game of baseball.

During the 1908 season the White Sox Rooters' Association was involved in a serious field incident, which justified those opposed to organized rooting clubs. On Monday, September 28, at South Side Grounds, the White Sox and Red Sox played a ten-inning 2–2 tie that was called by darkness. As umpire John Kerin was leaving the field, he was sucker punched by prominent Chicago attorney Robert E. Cantwell, who was one of the organizers of the White Sox Booster Association. Kerin was knocked unconscious and suffered a broken nose. To Kerin's credit, he filed assault charges against Cantwell. Kerin was finished umpiring for 1908, but he remained an American League arbiter for two more seasons.

Cantwell admitted that he was involved in the association for business purposes and to become known to fans who could become jurors in cases he argued. Cantwell was not shy in expressing his hope of getting favorable verdicts from his fellow baseball fans. He had organized a successful fund-raiser in 1907 and, according to contemporary accounts, much of the money raised disappeared.[12]

The Kerin-Cantwell incident illustrated nearly all of the evils such groups were capable of perpetrating. Unruly fans, stirred by passions these rooting clubs could arouse, could pose security problems after games by storming onto the field. In some games, fans in overflow seating in the outfield were already on the field. Such overflow crowds were often kept behind temporary barriers with little or no security. Little more than rope, these barriers were easily breached by enthusiastic rooters, either elated or angry. One explanation for how the tradition of base runners leaving the base paths and heading for the clubhouse without touching base after a game-winning hit could be simple self-preservation. If you are looking for a reason why Fred Merkle ran to the clubhouse rather than touch second base on Al Bridwell's apparent game-winning hit, you need go no further than the security issue.

Once you fought your way through the rooter clubs, Merry Widow hats, gamblers, and other hazards you may have faced, you settled into your seat. Your five- to ten-cent score card may or may not have the lineups already printed in it. If you were lucky, you would hear the starters announced via megaphone; numbers wouldn't be used until about twenty years later. You could tell the home team from visitors because the traveling gray or dark-colored uniform convention had been adopted to contrast with the home whites.

Vendors sold peanuts, popcorn, and of course, Cracker Jack. Beverage sales were popular. Ominously, beer, wine, and soft drinks were sold in bottles and glasses; some fans would sneak in with flasks of spirits or would purchase liquor in the stands. These containers sometimes became projectiles when action on the field or the umpire's calls aroused displeasure. Disposable plastic or paper cups had yet to be invented.

During the February 1908 preseason meetings, the owners had considered banning bottles but eventually rejected the idea. The 1907 season had witnessed two incidents during which American League umpire Billy Evans and Cubs player-manager Frank Chance were seriously injured by thrown bottles. The rejection of the bottle ban prompted I. E. Sanborn of the *Chicago Tribune* to write: "Whenever the good of the game conflicts too seriously with the pockets of the club owners, no reform ever has been made until something happens to unite the public in demanding reform."[13]

The other side of the bottle issue was stated on the editorial pages of *Sporting Life* by Francis C. Richter. He called an outright ban unreasonable because fans needed to quench their thirst, but he felt it was reasonable that all parties involved in bottle throwing be held liable for civil damages and that the bottle thrower be subject to arrest.[14] Contemporary accounts do not report any major bottle-throwing incidents during the 1908 season.

Once the game started, it moved smartly compared to modern standards. Games usually ran no more than two hours, and games of between an hour and a half and an hour and forty-five minutes were common. Of course, comparisons to modern games are not fair. Dead Ball Era contests were played quickly because of infrequent pitching changes, low scoring, and few base runners to slow pitchers down, and because radio coverage was nonexistent; there were no two-minute-plus waits between innings for broadcast commercial breaks. Another reason for comparatively quick games was the size of rosters of eligible players, which would range from fifteen to twenty players, depending on injuries and other problems. Roster size made small allowance for substitution, platooning, or specialization.

HOW THE GAME WAS PLAYED

The truth is that about two or three hard hitting, big score games in a season is quite enough. These 15 to 6 games are too much like old-fashioned three-old-cat for the red blooded fans of today. The truth is too that the games that make new fans and bring the old ones out the next day are the 1 to 0, 2 to 1 and 3 to 2 contests in which from start to finish, a hit or a brilliant fielding play will turn the tide of victory or defeat.

—Umpire Frank "Silk" O'Loughlin, Sporting Life, June 27, 1908

American League umpire O'Loughlin's remark sets the groundwork for a debate as old as the game itself. That eternal argument involves the question: Which is better baseball, a high-scoring offensive show or a tightly played, low-scoring pitcher's duel?

During the Dead Ball Era, pitching was dominant. Baseball runs in cycles, and there is no argument that this Era belonged to the pitcher. The ball itself did not change from the 1890s to 1910. During the 1890s in the National League, the average of runs scored per game ranged from 10.2 to 14.9. In 1908, National League hitters managed 6.7 runs per game while American League batsmen tallied 7 runs per game.

What accounts for this drop in production? As Captain Louis Renaud said in the classic film *Casablanca*, round up the usual suspects. If the ball remained the same, what happened? The short answer involves rules changes that resulted in improved pitching. Defensive improvements are traced to the evolution of fielding gloves from mere hand covers to something used to catch a baseball more effectively.

Whenever you see an increase or a drop in run production in baseball during pre-expansion times, you can generally that assume a rule has changed. Baseball is a game of adjustments. Neither hitters nor pitchers can be dominant forever. The rise in run production in the 1890s can be attributed to lengthening the distance from the pitcher's mound to home plate to the current sixty feet and six inches, giving hitters a temporary edge. It took time for pitchers to adjust to throwing an extra ten and a half feet.

The first major rules change leading to pitching dominance during the Dead Ball Era was changing the shape of home plate from a twelve-inch square to the current seventeen-inch-across pentagon shape. While this turn-of-the-century change may seem trivial in passing, it added two hundred square inches to the strike zone. This change gave pitchers the chance to work corners more effectively than with the square plate, and it made good pitchers better and excellent pitchers almost unbeatable.

A second rules change was possibly more significant. In 1901, the National League adopted a new foul ball rule. Prior to the change, foul balls meant nothing. As of 1901 the first two foul balls were strikes and a foul bunt after the second strike was a strike out. The American League adopted the foul ball rule in 1903, the year of the first World

Series. This rule had significant impact on offensive production because hitters could no longer purposely foul off pitches, often bunting, to await something they could hit hard. As a result of the adoption of the foul ball rule, batting averages and run production plummeted.

Sometimes doing nothing about rules has an adverse impact on pitching or hitting. The condition of the ball itself was a major grievance filed on behalf of hitters. As a way to cut costs, owners were loathe to provide a new baseball until absolutely necessary. Dead Ball Era fans were not allowed to keep baseballs hit into the stands, although they sometimes eluded team authorities.

Fred Snodgrass played six games for the Giants in 1908. In the classic *Glory of Their Times* he described what would happen to a pearl, or new baseball: "We hardly ever saw a new baseball, a clean one. If the ball went into the stands and the ushers couldn't get it back from the spectators, only then would the umpire throw out a new one. He'd throw it to the pitcher, who would promptly side step it. It would go around the infield once or twice and come back to the pitcher as black as the ace of spades. All the infielders were chewing tobacco or licorice, and spitting into their gloves, and they'd give that ball a good going over before it got to the pitcher."[15]

During the 1908 winter meetings, big league executives decided to do something about the situation by adopting a rule prohibiting the pitcher from discoloring a ball. As you may have figured from the Snodgrass story, which was a description of events after the rule was enacted, ball players got around that rule in rapid fashion. It must be noted the rule was enacted in hopes of speeding up games, not to help the hitter.

Whenever there is change, there are always predictions. Chicago Cubs ace Orval Overall, the pitching star of the 1908 World Series, turned out to be a better pitcher than prognosticator when he predicted that the new rule would be a boon to hitters: "I believe the rule prohibiting a pitcher from soiling a glossy ball will greatly increase the hitting department of the game. You can't curve a glossy ball, and in my judgment there will be more pitchers knocked out of the box the coming season than ever before. Unless I am mistaken the hitting averages will go soaring."[16] As we shall see, Overall was mistaken.

Another reason for decreased offense was the quality and quantity of pitchers in the big leagues. During the Dead Ball Era pitchers tended to be much taller and heavier than everyday position players. By 1908 pitchers were on the average twelve pounds heavier than their colleagues. This physical edge was no small advantage and is not unlike the advantage a big-for-his-age twelve-year-old has over younger colleagues in Little League play.[17] Today pitchers at the professional level still tend to be taller, but this physical advantage has been countered by rules changes.

The pitcher's advantage also extended to increasing use of trick pitches. While most hurlers relied upon the traditional fast ball and curve, trick or altered ball pitches were gaining acceptance, and most teams employed at least one pitcher whose success depended upon a trick delivery. Pitchers wanting to alter the ball could use saliva, tobacco juice, licorice, slippery elm, paraffin, talcum, hair tonic, sandpaper, and sharp objects such as razors to cut or scuff the ball. Whether trick pitches, especially the spitball, gave an edge is subject to debate.

While trick pitches could be out pitches, hurlers specializing in altered ball deliveries were more often victims of stolen bases, passed balls, and unearned runs than were their more conventional colleagues. Sometimes faking a trick pitch would be just as effective as not faking it. The war between the hitter and pitcher is constant, and getting an absolute edge that works all the time is successful only in the short run. As soon as adjustments are made by hitters, the pitchers are developing something new.

If you want to associate the Dead Ball Era with speed, pitching, and defense, the weak link in the chain has to be defense. Simply attaching a leather strap between the thumb and forefinger of the glove early in the first decade of the twentieth century improved fielding percentages, which had been hovering in the high .930s and low .940s at the turn of the century. In 1908, National League defenders committed 2,022 errors for a .961 fielding percentage; over in the American League, 2,212 errors were chalked up for a fielding percentage of .958. This comes out to almost three and a half errors a game! By comparison, 1990s league fielding percentages are in the low .980s, and errors per game are just under one and a half per game, or less than half the rate of the Dead Ball Era. Observers of the day noted it when a game was error free, but those contests were few and far between in 1908.

Another factor affecting defense was how the ballparks were built and the relationship between the outfield and late-afternoon sun. Except on cloudy days, in the days before sunglasses, infielders and outfielders alike had to contend with the sun. Most ballparks today are situated so that only right field is the "sun" field. The parks of 1908 were laid out according to what the available land would allow, thus late afternoon sun could, in some cities, be in the eyes of hitters, and in other cities in right, left, or center field.[18] The impact of varying sun conditions is scarcely mentioned in the reporting of the day, but experience and circumstance indicate that the outcome of some games had to be influenced by these conditions.

If baseball history is viewed as a variation of themes, the controversies of the Dead Ball Era differed little from those of today. Pitchers will always complain about hitters, hitters will always complain about pitchers, and eventually someone will complain about fielding gloves. During the 1908 season, there was a brief controversy over fielding gloves, and the rhetoric strongly evokes the statements of those who rail against the huge gloves players haul around in the 1990s. In July 1908, Tim Murnane of the *Boston Globe* blamed the lack of hitting on "big gloves" and urged the rules committee to do something about it. Before we go further, it must be noted that gloves of the Dead Ball Era were little more than padding for the hand and were roughly half the size of modern equipment.

Not one to shy away from controversy, *Sporting Life*'s editor Francis Richter proposed that hitting could be improved by outright elimination of the foul strike rule—making three balls a walk or at least exempting foul flies to the outfield from the foul strike rule if that rule were retained. Richter noted that improved "big mitts, misnamed gloves" had caused the problem and that "while errors may be fewer the fielding is lacking in brilliance and has become exceedingly mechanical or machine like."[19]

None of Richter's ideas was taken seriously, however. As for Murnane, he was a former player turned sportswriter and was a founding member of the Base Ball Writers Association of America. He had played professional baseball from 1871 to 1885 as an outfielder–first baseman. As part of the game's old guard, he was conservative and fond of claiming that the game of the present day could not compare to that of his era, a sentiment that has been stated with conviction as long as the game has been played and that will continue to be stated.

It's all very well to blame the ball, the pitchers, and the gloves, but what carping hitters overlooked was themselves. The style of hitting in 1908 also inhibited offensive performance. Few hitters could be called free swingers; most batters used heavy, thick bats, which were useful for bunting and placing hits. Many hitters used an exaggerated split grip to facilitate bunting or place hitting. Few consistently took what we would term a full swing. The long ball was scorned. Inside Baseball was king in 1908 and for the balance of the Dead Ball Era.

Inside Baseball is a mental game. Yogi Berra raised eyebrows when he said, "Ninety percent of this game is half mental."[20] While he wasn't holding forth about the Dead Ball Era and Inside Baseball, the remark is apt. The game in 1908 was a form of unrestrained psychological warfare from the first pitch to the last out.

Inside Baseball involves what fans today would term manufactured runs, a game in which every ninety feet mattered and every edge was exploited to gain victory. Team play, rather than individual effort, was stressed. An example of the dominance of this team play philosophy was the debate in some quarters about the enactment of the sacrifice fly rule in 1908. This new rule gave the batter a run batted in and no at bat for a run-scoring fly ball to the outfield. The opposition to the new rule, simply put, arose from fear that it would be detrimental to team play and would encourage hitters to pad their personal statistics.[21] White Sox manager Fielder Jones expressed this viewpoint tersely: "That rule is the direct opposite of what is needed in base ball today. Team work is the goal of every club that wants to become a winner and individual records are a handicap."[22]

The Inside game featured frequent bunting for sacrifices and base hits, wearing down pitchers by fouling off pitches, forcing the defense to make plays by having base runners take extra bases, by delayed and double steals, bluff bunts, hit-and-run and bunt-and-run plays, and by any other means of gaining the advantage. In *Our Game*, baseball historian Charles Alexander offers this definition of the term: "Accurately defined by one commentator as merely the outguessing of one team by another, Inside Baseball featured the manager's signaling from the bench, on the coaching box for particular plays; base stealing attempts, pitchouts to keep opponents from stealing, sacrifice bunts, squeeze and hit-and-run plays, even what one's pitcher should throw or whether one's batter should swing."[23]

This style of baseball meant that every base runner was precious, and each and every advance on the base paths was valuable. For the defense, Inside Baseball meant there was a premium on the fielding abilities of catchers, first and third basemen, and to some extent pitchers.

This is not meant to denigrate the importance of the up-the-middle positions of shortstop, second base, and centerfield. However, the frequent use of the bunt as a strategic ploy placed special emphasis on the defensive abilities of players at the corners.

It can be argued that the Cubs did not jell as a team until Harry Steinfeldt anchored the Tinker-Evers-Chance infield at third base. Defensive requirements at the corners could account in part for the tolerance of Hal Chase, who was as famous as a slick-fielding first baseman as he was infamous as a crook who threw games. Finally, the requirement for defensive ability is the only plausible explanation for the eleven-year career of catcher Bill Bergen, who chalked up a career .170 batting average in 941 games for Cincinnati and Brooklyn, the lowest average for a position player with over ten years' service and over five thousand at bats. No contending team in 1908 lacked a quality defensive catcher, whether or not he could hit.

Pitching in the Dead Ball Era was also different. With few roster spots available, relief pitchers were rarely used. Starters were required to go the distance. Today we see pitchers work as hard as they can for as far as they can go. A reason for this strategy is simple. With the lively ball, nearly all hitters are long ball threats. Other contributing factors to this all-out effort are larger rosters, more frequent use of pinch hitters, and of course, the designated hitter rule. During the Dead Ball Era, pitchers would pick their spots to work hard. For instance, a pitcher would work harder against a hard-hitting Honus Wagner than against a featherweight hitter like Bill Bergen. The absence of the threat of the long ball meant pitchers could coast and bear down when they had to.

Managing a ball club during the Dead Ball Era took many of the same attributes that make good modern managers. Among these are ability to work with players and use their talents to the maximum, an eye for strategy, and the resiliency to withstand the daily pressures of winning and losing. Curiously, managers of the era were not blamed for their teams' on-field performance by the press, which often attacked players and held them accountable for their individual failings. Fred Merkle bore the brunt of the criticism for his base-running blunder. As we will see, Giants skipper John McGraw should have shared the blame, but he was not criticized by the media.

The vast majority of modern era managers are bench managers; the modern player-manager is a throwback and more of a novelty than anything else. Player-managers were more common during the Dead

Ball Era, primarily as a money-saving venture. In 1908 they were not especially numerous, but they were mostly successful. In the American League, Nap Lajoie of second-place Cleveland and Fielder Jones of the third-place White Sox were the only two player-managers. In the senior circuit, four teams were run by player-managers; the World Champion Cubs by Frank Chance, Fred Clarke of the second-place Pirates, John Ganzel of the Reds, and Joe Kelley of the Boston Doves. Note that Lajoie, Chance, Clarke, and Kelley are all in the Hall of Fame.

Whether player-managers were more effective than bench managers is a question that sparked debate during the first two decades of the century. Before you get too excited about player-managers, John McGraw and Connie Mack were bench managing in 1908, and Hughie Jennings of the Tigers was working on the second of three consecutive pennants from the bench. In his overlooked classic *Touching Second*, Johnny Evers discusses from a player's perspective the virtues of playing versus bench managers. He notes that the ideal bench manager had to be a leader with superior knowledge of the game, and that the key to success was being able to appoint competent field captains.

Evers, who wrote his book in 1910 and played a significant portion of his career under Chance's field leadership, stated that the player-manager would be successful only as long as he was a successful player: "The moment he reaches the stage where he cannot execute and demonstrate the plays he commands his men to make, they will turn on him."[24] Evers summed up his analysis with the observation that both types of managers were under a great deal of pressure because of their responsibilities for their players, on and off the field.

Other aspects of the game of Inside Baseball were less attractive and constituted primary psychological war weapons: umpire baiting and bench jockeying. Teasing from the bench was a way to get an edge on an opponent, and some managers kept players solely for that contribution to the team. Baiting of umpires was a more serious game. More than half the games played in 1908 were officiated by one umpire, a system that would change the next season. A single-umpire system left great latitude for mischief and outright cheating. Calling balls and strikes can tax an umpire to the limit, let alone covering plays involving multiple base runners, tag plays, catches deep in the outfield, double steals, and any number of situations involving simultaneous movement of fielder and runner.

Umpire baiting or kicking had a simple goal: get the edge by getting under the umpire's skin. One of the most practiced proponents in baseball history was John McGraw, who noted the importance of working the umpire: "The fact is the only teams that ever won pennants were those that had good coaches and good kickers. And by good kickers I don't mean rowdy ball players; I mean men who play aggressive ball and know when to enter a protest. I have never been of the opinion that the 'kill the umpire' style of play was advisable, and have always believed that kicking with the mouth is the only kind of kicking in which to indulge. There are men who can get all that is coming to them by calling the umpire's attention to plays at critical times."[25]

UMPIRING

Some of the most overlooked heroes of the age were the umpires. Early umpires were more than simple officials. They were pathfinders and pioneers. They established many of the traditions, techniques, signals, and mechanics that modern umpires use at all levels of the game.

While baseball was maturing as a game and as a business, umpiring was only beginning to earn respect as a profession and as a necessary part of the game. Despite the rhetoric against rowdyism, umpires were still working under very hostile conditions in 1908. Because of the tight pennant races, the umpires worked in a high-pressure environment where each call could determine the outcome of a game and possibly the pennant race itself.

The pressure on the umpires began upon arrival at the ballpark. Today's private, secure dressing facilities were unheard of during the early days of baseball, and as a result, umpires arrived at the park in uniform. The small, intimate wooden ballparks contributed to the tension. The arrangement with most if not all permanent seating close to the infield presented an ideal situation for those fans who believed it was their God-given right to abuse umpires. Traditionally, Americans are deeply ambivalent about authority figures, and nowhere is that attitude borne out more than on the ball diamond, at any level of play.

Umpires faced another obstacle to doing the job. It bears repeating that a significant part of Dead Ball Era strategy was to bait the umpire. For some clubs the tactic was as useful as the bunt or stolen base. Use of this strategy would vary from team to team and from umpire to umpire, but the goal was the same: gain the edge over the opposition. Hall of Fame umpire Bill Klem's career spanned both the Dead Ball and so-called modern or lively ball eras. He noted that umpire baiting was intended to make the umpire angry enough to lose judgment and common sense — to intimidate or frighten him into making favorable calls. Klem added another very compelling reason for umpire baiting: bad calls by an umpire could be an alibi for poor performance, errors, or losing a game.[26]

The answer to this state of affairs was not easily found. Individual umpires had to develop a style and, with it, self-confidence and competence. All of this was done on the job, for the days of umpire schools and formal evaluations were still far off. Klem stated tersely a way to cope: "Any umpire who does not think he is the best in the world is not a good umpire."[27]

To cope with umpire baiting and kicking, umpires had to be strong individuals with thick skins and no small measure of physical bravery. Early umps were held in contempt by players, managers, and even sportswriters. Klem related how sportswriters were sometimes rabble-rousers and told of a piece of advice fellow umpire Jack Sheridan had given him: "Be careful what newspapers you read around the country. The sportswriters blame everything on the umpire, including their wives' cooking." The next morning, Klem continued, "I saw my name in a newspaper headlines: 'Umpire Klem Kills Innocent Fan.' And the newspaper went on seriously to attribute a fan's fatal heart attack to my 'bad' decision."[28]

Not all sportswriters were unsympathetic to umpires. In the pages of his paper, I. E. Sanborn of the *Chicago Tribune* constantly defended the men in blue. At one point he researched the issue, questioning players and umpires about close controversial plays, and he found that "the umpires averaged about .970 percent right and that even then some of the decisions scored against them might have been given either way without injustice."[29]

During the 1908 preseason, Sanborn devoted an entire column to responding to a fan who had suggested how umpires could improve. Sanborn warned fans that complaints over ball and strike calls were more a result of "kicking" by players than of umpire incompetence and rhetorically asked how a fan could call plays from a greater distance. Sanborn asserted that the game would be improved if fans would "realize the umpire is right much more often than they are in decisions of all kinds," and that most player disputes with umpires were intended only to rile spectators and cover up failure and not to protest an injustice.[30]

It is fair to say that the umpires of 1908 did the best they could under the circumstances. It would also be fair to note that the quality of officiating was not up to present-day standards. A reason for this had much to do with the lack of formal training and instructional schools, forcing would-be umpires to learn the trade while working at it, in a crucible that combined the worst aspects of on-the-job training and trial-and-error learning.

Sam Crane of the *New York Evening Journal* was a proponent of spring training for umpires to "get cob webs off their think tanks, as well [as] to limber up their anatomical departments. Ball players get charley horses of the legs, but umpires can get the same charley horse in the head."[31]

A major problem facing big league baseball was recruiting and keeping umpires. Differing league policies caused more turnover in the National League than in the American. Recruiting major league umpires soon became a top priority because two-man crews were to become the norm within a few years. The year 1908 was the last during which more than half the regular major league games were officiated by one umpire. In 1909 the majority of games were officiated by two umpires. In the 1908 World Series, four umpires would be used to call games, in alternating two-man crews. During the 1909 Fall Classic, four umpires were used for the first time in game three. Four-man crews remained a World Series standard until foul-line umpires were added in 1947. In 1933 the three-umpire system was instituted in the major leagues for regular season games. Finally, in 1952 the standard four-man big league crew became the norm for all official play.[32]

No doubt 1908 was a significant year in the evolution of umpiring, but with most games still overseen by one umpire, it is important to examine how a game was officiated during this tumultuous season. Under a one-man system, there is no way the umpire can be in the optimal position to call all plays, so the proper procedure consisted of a series of compromises and moves to be in the best position to make a call.

Typically, the single umpire would stay behind the plate to call balls and strikes until there was a base runner. At that point, the arbiter could choose to move to a position behind the pitcher, the better to call steals and pickoffs, and would only return to the plate when a runner or runners were in scoring position. This middle infield position would sacrifice position on foul ball calls down the first and third base lines and would pose a challenge in accurately calling balls and strikes. In the case of multiple base runners, the single umpire would have to depend upon experience and a measure of luck to get himself into the proper position to make the call. It is no surprise that in the single-umpire system, some players said the best thing to do was to keep one eye on the ball and the other on the umpire!

The two-man system would always keep one umpire behind the plate, while his partner would station himself on the first base line or in the infield, according to the number of men on base. Two umpires working in concert can cover even the most difficult game without serious problems. Mechanics for a two-man system evolved over the years as umpires learned from experience. Two-man mechanics are still in the process of evolving at the college, high school, and lower minor league levels today.

Umpires would take turns behind the plate, alternating games with partners, if they had them. Their stamina must be admired. A one-man doubleheader in August in St. Louis or Cincinnati in the days before air conditioning was a feat of endurance, even though a 1908 double-header would usually be over in the time it takes to play a single game today.

The use of a single umpire is not all that unusual; indeed, many amateur umpires learn to call games today by working alone. The rule book still gives the single umpire the option of positioning behind the plate or the pitcher. Working alone may not be a huge burden on a Little League diamond with its sixty-foot base paths. Other levels with regulation base paths — high school and Babe Ruth — pose a different challenge. Use of single umpires at these levels of youth leagues is driven by the same motive that drove Dead Ball Era baseball executives: economics. It is cheaper to hire and pay one official than it is to hire and pay two.

One area where umpires did not suffer was pay. Unlike late-twentieth-century standards, early umpire and player salaries were almost on a par. Umpire salaries averaged about twenty-five hundred dollars a year, or about the same as the average major league player. Superstars such as Wagner and Cobb commanded higher sums, but on the whole, umpires and players were on an equal financial footing in 1908.

TRAVEL CONDITIONS

There was a mathematical symmetry to baseball in 1908. Sixteen teams competed in the two eight-team leagues. The St. Louis teams were the only ones based west of the Mississippi River. St. Louis, Chicago, Philadelphia, and Boston each had teams in both leagues. The New York metro area had three teams, including the one in Brooklyn. Each league was informally divided into western and eastern teams. Much was made of these divisions by the contemporary press, even though there was only one ultimate winner per league.

The western ball clubs were in St. Louis, Chicago, Detroit, Cleveland, Cincinnati, and Pittsburgh, while the eastern teams were located in Philadelphia, Washington, New York, Brooklyn, and Boston. Major league baseball would remain confined to these cities until 1953, when the Boston Braves moved to Milwaukee, which had been an American League city in 1901.

The commercial aviation and population growth in the South and West that were to make coast-to-coast baseball feasible were decades away. In the first decade after 1900, many of the great southern and western cities were small or practically nonexistent. Arizona and New Mexico were not admitted to statehood until 1912.

Scheduling was itself relatively simple. The eastern and western teams would exchange visits, making four stops on the long road trips, playing three or four games per city. The western or eastern swings would occur four times during the season. The scheduled road trips were highly structured, and if games were postponed because of rain or halted due to darkness, doubleheaders would be scheduled. In many instances, postponements or suspended games would be made up as quickly as possible in order to avoid an avalanche of doubleheaders at the end of the season.

Some writers have made much of the romance of train travel versus flight, and as applies to many romantic notions, there is just enough truth in this one to compel the gullible to ignore the hard facts. Being on the road was strenuous during the Dead Ball Era, despite the amenities of rail travel. Riding on trains did encourage interaction among players and coaches and, at times, sportswriters. But although the trips were planned to be as short as possible and trains made good time, averaging more than sixty miles an hour, by modern standards rail travel in 1908 fell under the category of roughing it.

On hot summer nights without air conditioning, the choice was to open the windows and risk getting sooty or to close the windows and roast. A ride on a sticky summer night through southern Illinois, Indiana, and Ohio would be more than enough to erase any romantic notions about early-twentieth-century rail travel. The getaway trip between Cleveland and St. Louis was not popular among American Leaguers. Passenger trains could be sidetracked because freight trains had priority, which would result in delays.[33]

Travel expenses were a major item on the team's cost ledgers. During 1908, National League teams logged over 92,000 rail miles while the junior circuit rode the rails for a total of just under 96,000 miles. Rail fares averaged about two cents per person per mile, not including berths, meals, and other incidentals.[34] Travel conditions for each ball club depended upon the generosity of the owner and what deal could be cut with the railroads.

Rail travel also had its dangers. While no major league club was involved in a large-scale train incident in 1908, one American League game was postponed because the visiting club was delayed due to a derailment. The postponement involved a game between St. Louis and Cleveland. Browns owner R. L. Hedges complained bitterly over the matter and the loss of revenue from a game that could have been seen by twelve to fifteen thousand fans. The cause of the delay was a freight wreck just outside Terre Haute, Indiana. Hedges's complaint over the long ride from Cleveland to St. Louis was valid. The trip was the longest in the league, and the road team playing upon arrival was at a disadvantage. Ironically enough, it was St. Louis complaining, not Cleveland, the team that had to make this trip most often.[35]

Tragically, "Wild Bill" Donovan, whose pitching was a key factor in Detroit's 1908 pennant, was killed in a train wreck in 1923. As manager of his minor league team, Donovan claimed the more desirable lower berth. The passenger in the upper berth escaped without injury. The uninjured party was team business manager George Weiss, who would go on to a Hall of Fame career as general manager of the New York Yankees during their glory years from 1947 to 1960.[36]

RULES OF INTEREST

Among the enigmas of baseball are the rules differences between the National and American leagues. These differences are a vestige of the separate origins of the leagues. The designated hitter rule adopted by the American League in 1973 stands as a most recognizable example of this situation. How organized baseball has handled the designated hitter rule in postseason only serves to place further emphasis on the question. Even the umpires in each league have differing rules regarding conduct on and off the field.

The rules differences stem primarily from the separate births of the leagues and the subsequent competition between them. In 1908, league constitutions contained significant differences, which had an impact on the outcome of each pennant race. During the February preseason meetings, the National League adopted a motion proposed by Cincinnati owner Garry Herrmann with the intent of allowing doubleheaders to be more evenly distributed throughout the year, to ensure that critical games were rescheduled and to give owners all the home games, and related revenue, on their respective schedules:

> Each club shall play twenty-two or more championship games with every other club in the league. A tie or drawn game, or games which are prevented by rain or other causes, shall be played off on the same grounds as it was scheduled for during the same or any subsequent series, the date to be optional with the home club. If, however, all the series of games scheduled have been ended and any such games remain unplayed then such games shall, if possible be played off on the grounds of the opposing club on a date to be determined by said club.[37]

Had the American League adopted such a rule, a postseason controversy could have been averted. The Tigers finished a half game ahead of Cleveland, having played only 153 games as of the last day of the season. Cleveland had played all 154 games, but could only watch while Detroit and Chicago determined the American League victor. If the National League rule had been in effect, Detroit would have had to play the seventh-place Washington Nationals in a game where a win meant the pennant and a loss meant a play-off with Cleveland. In addition, the White Sox played only 152 games and needed to play makeup games with the Nationals and fourth-place St. Louis Browns. Understandably, there was a great deal of unhappiness in Cleveland at the end of the 1908 season. A new rule requiring all games with a bearing on the pennant race to be played would provide a belated and inadequate answer to Cleveland's complaint.

The question remains—what would or could have happened had those games been made up? The results range from Detroit winning outright, by beating Washington, to a three-way tie among the Tigers,

White Sox, and Naps, the nickname for the Cleveland franchise at the time. An intriguing question involves who would have pitched for Washington in these games. Remember, the Nationals had the great Walter Johnson, a pitcher capable of beating any team on earth on any given day. The decision on who would have started that game could have had a huge impact on the outcome of the pennant race.

A reason for this odd state of affairs in the American League was explained by the secretary of big league baseball's ruling body, the National Commission, John E. Bruce. In 1907 the Tigers and Athletics went down to the wire with Detroit winning by a game and a half during the last week of the season. Bruce was adamant in his support of the notion that a tie would be avoided by determining the pennant winner by arithmetic rather than on the field: "In figuring the final standings of the teams the decimals will be run out four or five figures, if necessary, to determine the winner."[38] This case of tunnel vision determined the 1908 American League race. The National League had arrived at the proper and just answer before the 1908 season began.

The two leagues also could not agree on how to deal with rain delays and postponements. Both shared the same rule, which required at least a half-hour wait before calling the game. But the league presidents Johnson and Pulliam had their own ways of dealing with the situation. Johnson left it up to the umpire or umpires to order a resumption of play if the full game could be played before dark. Pulliam, unmatched in his knack for creating problems with his decisions, laid the groundwork for rhubarbs by allowing play to resume after thirty minutes only if both managers agreed.[39]

The American League allowed for the postponed game to be made up at the first open date of the same or the subsequent series. While this policy did not require a makeup game, it provided structure for teams to work with. The National League rain-out policy succeeded in creating chaos. While the National League required teams to play all games, the scheduling of makeup games was solely up to the home team. The policy resulted in a protest involving Pittsburgh and Chicago over a makeup game that could have resulted in a Cub forfeit and decided the pennant race. This rule difference between leagues caused the bunching up of doubleheaders at the close of the National League campaign. *Sporting Life* editorially expressed a preference for the American League way of doing things: "Of the two methods of playing off postponed games that of the American League is to be preferred be-

3 The Teams of 1908 A Look at the Players

The teams of 1908 were as colorful and competent as any in the Dead Ball Era. Each team had its characters and eccentrics, key players, troublemakers, leaders, and followers, both on and off the field. Baseball's Hall of Fame, not established until the 1930s, was well represented on the diamond in 1908. Nearly every team boasted at least one immortal during this season, except the Philadelphia Phillies and the truly awful Brooklyn Superbas and St. Louis Cardinals of the National League.

Among the teams of 1908 were some of the best to take the field. As we have seen, this season was the midpoint of the heyday of the great Cubs dynasty. It can be argued that the 1908 Cubs were the best of those great Cubs teams of 1906–10. The Giants and Pirates missed immortality by an eyelash, and both teams would be pennant winners within the next three years with largely the same players who played in 1908.

In the American League, the Detroit Tigers were in the second year of their three-year dynastic run. The second- and third-place teams, the Cleveland Naps and Chicago White Sox, fell painfully short of winning the flag. For both of these squads, the next shot at the golden ring was over a decade away. The White Sox won their next pennant and last World Championship in 1917. With a new nickname, the Indians took their first flag and world title in 1920. The St. Louis Browns finished fourth in the American League, one of the best finishes in the history of the franchise. During the Dead Ball Era, the Browns finished in the first division on only one other occasion, at second in 1902. The Boston Red Sox and Philadelphia Athletics were building teams that would dominate the league during the next decade.

Preseason 1908 was just like any other preseason prior to free agency. The so-called Hot Stove League, or coverage and discussion of off-season baseball news, was at full boil, with stories about contract negotiations, holdouts, signings, trades, and other news and information to keep fans informed. These subjects dominated the sports pages during the winter months simply because there were no other professional sports such as football or basketball to cover. This dominance of coverage led to baseball becoming the national pastime and dominant professional sport for more than half of the twentieth century.

Unlike in present-day baseball, teams operated under the reserve clause, a contract clause that bound a player to a particular team until that team either released or traded him. Thus contract holdouts were big news. Even then it was acknowledged that the reserve clause would never stand up in court, provided you found a judge friendly to the player's interest. The political connections of the owners prevented any serious challenge to the clause. Johnny Evers called the situation a form of slavery: "Legally, the baseball player is a slave held in bondage, but he is the best treated, most pampered slave of history."[1]

Because of the reserve clause, the only leverage a player had was to hold out for more money or better contract provisions — hence the Hot Stove League and the newspaper and fan interest in the give and take of contract negotiations, holdouts, threatened retirements, trades, and eventual signings. Free agency and competition from other sports have made this coverage and the Hot Stove League a thing of the past. Prominent holdouts of 1908 were Detroit's young phenomenon Ty Cobb and Pirates legend Honus Wagner. Cobb's holdout involved money and a provision for payment of the contract in case of injury. Wagner indicated strong interest in retirement and it took the personal entreaties of Pirates owner Barney Dreyfuss to persuade the Flying Dutchman to return to the diamond.

The Chicago press was largely preoccupied with the negotiations between player-manager Fielder Jones and Charles Comiskey, as the owner tried to persuade his reluctant field general to give it a go for one more year. The Cubs coverage dealt mainly with the health of its player-manager Frank Chance and whether an injured foot would require surgery or a special shoe. Fortunately for the Cubs, neither option materialized. The signing of players on both teams occupied large quantities of column inches, along with unsolicited opinions and stories about the holdouts.

Before detailing the teams of 1908, a further explanation is due. In most cases, the familiar team nicknames were in place in 1908. Newspapers were picking up on using them, but there were exceptions. In the interest of understanding and simplicity, the teams are referred to throughout this narrative as they were in 1908. The modern nickname, if needed, is given in parentheses. Hall of Fame members are noted on each squad, along with the year of induction of the player, manager, or club executive. Team managers have their lifetime records noted and team owners, or where applicable presidents, are named, as some of them figure in the story of the 1908 season.

AMERICAN LEAGUE

DETROIT TIGERS
1st place / 90–63 .588
Ballpark: Bennett Park. Located at the site of the current Tiger Stadium,
    making it the oldest continuously used location in big league baseball.
Hall of Famers: Ty Cobb, OF *(1936); Sam Crawford,* OF *(1957);*
    Hughie Jennings, Mgr. (1945)
Owner: Frank Navin
Manager: Hughie Jennings (Career — 15 yrs, 1,163–984 .542;
    Pennants 3; World Championships 0)

Had the American League Manager of the Year award existed in 1908, Tigers manager Hughie Jennings would have been the leading candidate, if not the hands-down winner. That year marked the second of three pennants in a row for the Tigers. The half-game margin over Cleveland in 1908 was barely an improvement over the game-and-a-half margin over Philadelphia in 1907. The hard-fought, narrowly won 1908 pennant was a morale booster for Detroit, especially in light of the Cubs' sweep in the 1907 World Series. Overcoming a poor start and injuries to key infielders and pitchers, which kept the lineup in flux, this pennant was as much Jennings's achievement as it was that of his players.

Jennings's greatest asset as a manager was to get every bit of ability out of every player nearly all the time. Having the league's best offense didn't hurt either. Detroit led the league in runs scored (645), batting average (.264), and slugging percentage (.347).

Jennings came to the Tigers in 1907 after a playing career at shortstop and first base for the National League's Baltimore and Brooklyn teams and as player-manager for Baltimore's Eastern League entry. He had been a teammate of John McGraw's on those great Orioles teams of the 1890s and was unique among his managerial colleagues. He had a college degree and was a lawyer by profession. McGraw rooted for his old friend and teammate during the 1908 season, saying on a number of occasions that he looked forward to locking horns with the Tigers in the World Series.

Nicknamed "Ee Yah" after his patented battle cry, Jennings was as much a cheerleader as a field leader. His enthusiasm often aroused the ire of American League President Ban Johnson, who was compelled to ban Jennings's use of a police whistle as a noisemaker before play began in 1908. In response, the resourceful Jennings learned how to whistle by putting his fingers to his mouth.

His greatest managerial achievement was keeping the Tigers together as a team in the face of feuding between Ty Cobb and nearly all of his teammates. In payback for what some would describe as unjustified special treatment, Cobb admired Jennings, and Cobb's autobiography showed that ingratitude was not among his many shortcomings as a person. Cobb wrote that Jennings "kept us eager to conquer at all times, maintaining our spirit and fight and imparting a tremendous urgency into what can easily become a dull task. On the coaching line, Hughie's wild cry of 'Ee Yah!' and his shrill whistles let us know he was with us and on top of every play. He'd dance with glee at a good play and tear up grass."[2]

The Detroit Tigers were built around a stout hitting attack featuring aggressive baserunning. They also boasted one of the better and deeper pitching staffs in the American League. The 1908 team was almost identical to the 1907 squad, with the exception of two key additions from the state of Indiana, pitcher "Kickapoo Ed" Summers and shortstop Donie Bush. Summers, a rookie, paced the Tigers staff with twenty-four wins. The Society for American Baseball Research recognized Summers as 1908 American League Rookie of the Year in one of its publications in 1986.[3] The Ladoga, Indiana, native won nineteen games for the Tigers in 1909, but he spent only three more years in the majors before retiring. Bush came to the team in mid-September. Appearing in only twenty games, Bush stabilized an infield situation that had been uncertain due to injuries. Bush became a superb leadoff man and spent sixteen years in the majors. He and Cobb presented opponents with a potent base-stealing attack. Bush also managed in the major leagues for seven years and led the Pittsburgh Pirates to the National League pennant in 1927. The Bucs were swept in the World Series by the great Ruth-Gehrig Yankees. Bush went on to have a successful minor league managing career and was recognized for his contributions to the game on and off the field in having the minor league Indianapolis Indians' stadium named for him.

The Tigers of the Dead Ball Era and Ty Cobb are almost synonymous. Cobb spent all but two years of his twenty-four-year career in the Motor City. But what makes fascinating speculation is how close Cobb came to being traded on at least three occasions in 1907. Cobb's abrasive personality and aggressive style of play led many baseball people to believe that he would burn out. Because of fights with teammates, Jennings wanted to be rid of him and shopped Cobb to Cleveland, New York, and St. Louis. The Tigers received a few offers, but they weren't good enough, and Cobb remained a fixture in Detroit.

One of the more intriguing of these potential trades involved Cobb and Cleveland star outfielder Elmer Flick in 1907. Flick suffered from a stomach ailment in 1908, a malady that ended his effectiveness as a player and curtailed his 1908 playing time. Had the trade been consummated, there is little doubt that the outcome of the 1908 American League race would have been different.[4]

Cobb also figured in one of those incidents that could only have occurred in 1908. He left the Tigers in August, in the midst of the pennant race, to get married! The twenty-one-year-old Cobb was leading the league in hitting and the Tigers had a two-game lead over the Browns when he left. Cobb did not seek advance permission but left the team on August 3 and returned on August 8, missing three games. During his absence, the Bengals posted a 2–1 record and remained two games up. The leave of absence set a precedent of special treatment for Cobb and added to his reputation as a player more interested in himself than in the team. In 1908 Cobb led the league in hitting (.324) and runs batted in (108), and — an aspect of his play often overlooked and underappreciated — in outfield assists (23).

If Cobb wasn't enough to give pitchers and teammates fits, center fielder and cleanup man Sam Crawford might put the opposing pitchers over the edge. Crawford was known as a slugger. He's the all-time triples leader with 312 over a nineteen-year career. "Wahoo" Sam led the American League in home runs in 1908 with seven. Crawford, like many of his colleagues, despised Cobb, but that did not keep him from teamwork with Cobb when the need arose. A favorite stratagem was with Cobb at third: if Crawford were walked, Crawford would trot to first and, on a signal from Cobb, run full speed for second while Cobb broke for home. Crawford recalled, "Sometimes they'd get him, sometimes they'd get me, and sometimes they wouldn't get either of us."[5] Despite the unpleasantness between them, Cobb respected Crawford's ability and lobbied to get him into the Hall of Fame. The Veterans Committee tapped Sam Crawford in 1957.

Filling out the Tigers' outfield were two strong leadoff men, Davy Jones and Matty McIntyre. Jones played 126 games in 1907, but injuries limited his playing time in 1908. McIntyre filled in admirably, having his best year in the majors, batting .295 and leading the team in runs scored with 105. McIntyre's status with the team was complicated due to his negative relationship with Cobb. McIntyre hated Cobb's guts; that's the only way to put it. The enmity was so strong that Jennings moved Cobb from center to right field. New center fielder Crawford was a buffer between the feuding pair and the Tigers' outfield could function effectively on defense, while fighting off the diamond. Prior to the shift, some Tigers players believed that McIntyre tried to distract Cobb in order to make the fiery Cobb look bad.

The Tigers' infield was solid, if injury prone, throughout 1908. Claude Rossman anchored first, hitting .294. He was a superb bunter and, like Crawford, he would pull off plays with Cobb. Their favorite was a bunt and run. Rossman would place the ball down the third base line and Cobb, already on the run for second, took off for third when, or if, the defense played on Rossman. Over at third base, team captain Bill Coughlin managed to play only 119 games. His frequent injuries were hard felt because he was a strong defender. All other substitutes were deficient both at bat and in the field.

Shortstop and second base were other problem areas due to injury. Detroit was fortunate to have one of the great characters of the game,

Germany Schaefer, on the roster in 1908. Schaefer was a capable number two hitter in the lineup and managed a .259 mark in 1908. Versatility was his major asset. Because of injuries to others, he played sixty-eight games at short, fifty-eight at second, and twenty-nine at third. While many fans remember him as a baseball clown for his act with Al Schacht and Nick Altrock, Schaefer was an instrumental part of the 1908 Tigers and a quality player throughout his career.

Until Bush arrived in late season Red Downs, Red Killefer, and Charlie O'Leary all shared short and second with Schaefer, according to who wasn't in sick bay. None was any more than below average at bat, and they were only so-so in the field. O'Leary went on to coach in the majors and minors after his playing days were over.

Behind the plate, Charlie "Boss" Schmidt was the first stringer and played 121 games. He was noted for his physical strength and toughness. He had once boxed an exhibition with heavyweight champ Jack Johnson. Schmidt was one of the top catchers in the league and his on- and off-field leadership was particularly valued. Schmidt's backups were Ira "Chief" Thomas and Freddie Payne. Payne spent four years in the majors for the Tigers and White Sox. Thomas was sold to the Philadelphia Athletics after the season. He made an important contribution to the pennant winners for the A's in 1910–11 and 1913.

Before the year began, Jennings expressed confidence in repeating, because of the strength of his pitching staff. In 1907 Wild Bill Donovan, "Twilight Ed" Killian, and George Mullin had all won twenty or more games. But in 1908 injuries and sore arms kept the trio from repeating the feat.

Ed Summers's twenty-four wins paced the staff in his first year. Without him, Detroit's pitching would not have come close to keeping them in the chase. Wild Bill Donovan started only twenty-eight games but posted a solid 18–7 record. Donovan was a durable pitcher who tended to lose the strike zone on occasion, hence his nickname. Rounding out the Tigers staff were Killian, Mullin, and Ed Willett. Willett won fifteen, while Mullin and Killian registered seventeen and twelve wins respectively.

With the exception of Summers and his knuckleball, Tigers pitchers were known as power pitchers, relying on the fastball to win. Had there not been so many injuries to the staff, it would not have been beyond the realm of possibility that Donovan, Mullin, and Willett could have won twenty for Detroit in 1908 and breezed to the pennant. While playing just above .500 against the other first division teams, 34–32 against Cleveland, Chicago, and St. Louis; the Tigers feasted on the lowly Nats and Highlanders, winning 31 of 41 games.

CLEVELAND NAPS (INDIANS)

2nd place / 90–64 .584

Ballpark: League Park

Hall of Famers: Nap Lajoie, 2B-Mgr.(1937); Elmer Flick, OF (1963);
*   Addie Joss, P (1978)*

Owner: John F. Kilfoyle

Manager: Nap Lajoie (Career — 5 yrs, 377–309 .550 no postseason)

In 1994 Terry Pluto's *Curse of Rocky Colavito* presented the baseball world with a history of the misfortune of the Cleveland Indians. He went back only to 1960, but Pluto could have established Cleveland as a snake-bit franchise much earlier than 1960. During the first decade of the twentieth century, Cleveland finished only six games above .500 (719–713 .501) and second place in 1908 was the team's best finish during that time span.

Inconsistency was the trademark of the early days of the Cleveland team. It seemed that when the pitching was working, the hitters would be off, and vice versa. Or they'd start fast and finish flat or play steadily then have a horrible, season-destroying slump. Until the pennant and World Championship in 1920, 1908 remained the year of could-have-beens and what-ifs for the Cleveland faithful.

The team leader was playing manager Napoleon "Larry" Lajoie, arguably one of the game's earliest superstars and one of its finest hitters. During 1908, Lajoie smacked his two thousandth hit. Lajoie was a steady .300 hitter, but his offense suffered due to the strain of managing, and he hit only .289 in 1908. Like other playing managers, Lajoie led by example. While not among the league leaders in offense, in 1908 he led Cleveland in hits (168), runs scored (77), doubles (32), and runs batted in (74). Lajoie would not hit .300 again until he relinquished the managerial reins. The Cleveland team was nicknamed the Naps in honor of Lajoie and would not become the Indians until after his departure in 1915.

Cleveland's strength was its pitching staff. Leading the league with an earned run average of 2.02, the Naps boasted three starters with

ERAS under 2.00—Addie Joss, Bob Rhoades, and Charlie Chech. Joss was the class of the trio and among the best pitchers in baseball. Standing six feet, three inches tall and with long arms, Joss possessed an imposing physical appearance and produced a sharp curve and a fastball with control. That potent combination made him a threat to win every time he took the mound. If his accuracy weren't enough, Joss's delivery would drive hitters to distraction: "Standing straight up, he rested his arms just below his waist. He would then rock on his left foot, while turning his right foot clockwise. Taking a full windup, he raised his arms completely above his head, while turning his body to face second base. Beginning his delivery plateward, Addie kicked his left leg high into the air while hiding the baseball behind his thigh until the last possible instant."[6]

During his brief career of nine years, Joss pitched two no-hitters and six one-hitters. Joss was cut down in his prime by illness, dying of tubercular meningitis in 1911. In 1908 he went 24–11 with a 1.16 ERA, including a late perfect game against the White Sox. The biggest question was: How did he lose that many games? It is clear that Joss at times suffered from a lack of support, and he often started against the opposition's best pitcher.

While Joss and his achievements are well known, the rest of the Cleveland staff were journeymen who all chose to have good to great years in 1908. Right-hander Bob Rhoades turned his curve and screwball into an 18–12 record, including a no-hitter. Charlie Chech had his best year ever at 11–7. Chech's claim to fame would be that he was traded to the Red Sox for Cy Young. Spitballer Heinie Berger was 13–8 and Glenn Liebhardt was a hard-luck 15–16. The won-lost records of Joss and Liebhardt as pitchers reflected the Naps' weakness: an inconsistent offense, with a team batting average of .239, ranking fourth in the league.

The Naps' infield was anchored at first by George Stovall and at third by Bill Bradley. Both were above average at bat and outstanding on defense. Stovall led Cleveland with a .292 average and batted third in front of Lajoie; he also led the league's first basemen in fielding. Bradley was one of the game's early sluggers, but by 1908 his power had been eroded by age and chronic injury. It was Bradley's defensive gem with two out in the ninth that sealed Joss's crucial late-season perfect-game win over the White Sox. In a memoir of that game, Bradley said he recalled that Sox pinch hitter John Anderson was a pull hitter, and he shifted toward the line, getting into perfect position to make the play.[7]

Lajoie anchored the infield at second, but it was shortstop that caused most of the headaches. No fewer than eight players tried their hand at the position during the season. George Perring had won the job in preseason, but injuries limited him to only eighty-nine games. Outfielder Bill Hinchman turned in fifty-one games at short, and Terry "Cotton" Turner would split his duties between outfield and short as well.

Outfield was another problem area for Lajoie due to injuries. The biggest disappointment was the illness of Elmer Flick. The hard-hitting Flick could have made the difference for the 1908 Naps, but a stomach ailment limited him to nine games and all but ended his career. Flick's absence meant the outfield lineup would have to be juggled. Joe Birmingham, Josh Clarke, Hinchman, Turner, Charlie "Piano Legs" Hickman, Wilbur Good, Dave Altizer, and Denny Sullivan each saw duty in the outfield.

Birmingham was best of the lot in terms of all around play. He had one of the strongest arms in the game and turned in twenty assists in 1908, several in critical, game-saving situations. Clarke, brother of Pittsburgh player-manager Fred, was a capable leadoff man and an above average base stealer. The remaining outfielders were journeymen, good backup players but hardly starters.

The Naps were in capable hands behind the plate. Justin Jay "Nig" Clarke was one of the first Canadian-born major leaguers and in 1996 was selected to the Canadian Baseball Hall of Fame.[8] Clarke enjoyed a reputation as a steady defender with an above average arm and as an excellent handler of pitchers. Staff ace Joss claimed Clarke as his personal catcher whenever possible. Clarke's claim to fame was being among the first catchers to use shin guards. However, he is often overlooked for this distinction because they were not worn externally. Betraying his familiarity with another sport, Clarke used soccer shin guards worn under his socks. Veteran catcher Harry Bemis filled in for Clarke and appeared in seventy-six games.

The Naps were a formidable team when they were on, ranking first in pitching and third in defense. They dominated the season series against Detroit and Chicago, winning twenty-seven of forty-four games. During the season Lajoie's charges started well and were in the fight from April through June. But like all other Cleveland teams before them, they had a midseason slump. The 1908 funk happened in July when Cleveland won twelve and lost seventeen. That performance put them eight games off the pace.

The Naps stormed back in August, winning fifteen of eighteen, but fell a half game short. In typical cursed Cleveland fashion, they came up against Detroit's not being required to play its 154th game, which would either have forced a play-off or have given the Tigers the pennant outright. The game Detroit would have played was against Washington, a team the Naps couldn't beat when it counted. Cleveland was 8–14 on the year against the lowly Nationals; that sad record sealed the fate of an otherwise fine baseball team.

CHICAGO WHITE SOX
3rd / 88–64 .579
Ballpark: South Side Park (located four blocks south of current Comiskey Park)
Hall of Famers: Big Ed Walsh, P (1946); Charles Comiskey, owner (1939); George Davis, IF (1998)
Owner: Charles Comiskey
Manager: Fielder Jones (Career — 10 yrs. 683–582 .540; Pennant: 1; World Championship: 1)

The 1908 White Sox represented the last hurrah for the old Hitless Wonders of 1906. The conquerors of the mighty Cubs were aging none too gracefully. The South Siders had one of the oldest teams in the majors. With a team batting average of .224, the Sox again relied on brains, conditioning, pitching, and the best defense in the league to make a gallant run at the flag. They fell short because they couldn't consistently beat the Tigers and Naps, going 9–13 against Detroit and winning 8 and losing 14 to Cleveland, for a composite 17–27 mark against the teams they had to beat.

The heart and soul of the White Sox was player-manager Fielder Jones, one of the most overlooked managers in baseball history. His managing career was short, ten years, including two seasons in the Federal League. During his five years with the Sox, Jones always had his club in the midst of a pennant race, running the team from his position in center field. A strict disciplinarian, he was intolerant of players drinking or being out of condition. He demanded total mental attention to the game and was credited with inventing the motion infield or wheel play to deal with bunts, and with positioning his outfielders according to the hitter.[9]

Jones was also one of the few players to be independently wealthy. He and his brother had oil and forest land holdings in the northwestern United States. An economic slump in the region was among the reasons Jones decided to stay with the Sox in 1908, his last year with the team. He left in controversy, losing the last game of the season after deciding to start a worn-out Doc White over the well-rested Frank Smith, whom Jones disliked intensely. Jones's willingness to call it quits could also be attributed to penny-pinching by owner Charles Comiskey. Jones was often the sole buffer between the owner and unhappy players; by the end of 1908, he had grown tired of the role.

The 1908 White Sox pitchers ranked third in the league in ERA but threw twenty-three shutouts to tie with the Athletics for the league lead in that department. At times the Sox staff seemed to consist entirely of Big Ed Walsh, a spitballer, who had the year of years for the Sox. Appearing in sixty-six games, Walsh won forty, lost fifteen, saved six, and threw eleven shutouts, accounting for just over half the team's victories and pitching a staggering 464 innings. Some believed Walsh ruined his arm from overuse in 1908. He posted good years after 1908, but it was true he wasn't the same pitcher again as during his career year.

Walsh was one of the most effective spitball pitchers to play the game. He would often fake the spitter for effect. Hall of Famer Sam Crawford described the Walsh delivery aptly: "I think the ball disintegrated on the way to the plate and the catcher put it back together again; I swear, when it went past the plate it was just the spit went by."[10]

After Walsh, the rest of the Sox staff suffered in comparison. The next two pitchers were Doc White and the controversial Frank Smith. White, who prided himself in his control, spent the off season in his dental practice. He went 18–13 and threw five shutouts in 1908. White was what would today be called a junk ball pitcher. He used a curve and off-speed pitches to great effect during his career.

Frank "Piano Mover" Smith posted a 17–16 mark, including a no-hitter, but he had an attitude. Tiring of early morning practices and complaining of overwork, Smith left the Sox in June. His month-long absence strained a thin pitching staff and has to be considered a major factor in why the Sox lost the pennant. It also earned him the enmity of

Fielder Jones. Interestingly, after Jones left the team, Smith had his best season for the Sox in 1909 with a 25–17 mark.

After Walsh, White, and Smith, no other Sox pitcher won more than six games. Frank "Yip" Owen and Nick Altrock suffered from arm troubles and were major disappointments. Owen and Altrock were the mainstays of the 1906 Hitless Wonders but were at the end of their effective careers in 1908. Owen became a doctor after retiring in 1909. Altrock, an excellent pitcher and skillful defensive player in his prime, remained active until 1924 but won only two more games in the big leagues after his 3–7 1908 performance. His major claim to fame was his clowning with Germany Schaefer and Al Schacht while with the Washington Senators. The trio built a tradition of baseball clowning, which could still be seen in the person of Max Patkin in minor league parks as recently as the early 1990s.

The 1908 White Sox infield was one of the lightest-hitting units among pennant contenders in baseball history. No regular hit over .250. Jiggs Donahue (.204) held down first and Lee Tannehill (.216) started at third. Both Sox cornermen were excellent with the glove, justifying their presence in the lineup. When Donahue was injured, 1906 series hero Frank Isbell (.247) filled in. At second, George Davis (.217) was winding down a twenty-year career. Davis had starred as a member of the New York Giants in the 1890s, figured in the player wars at the turn of the century, and been an integral part of the Hitless Wonders. Davis's Hall of Fame numbers finally got him into Cooperstown in 1998. By 1908 age had eroded his talents and thus it was an off year for this quality player. Many fans probably did not recognize his name when the Veterans Committee selected him. The figures say it best. Davis had better offensive numbers than two Hall of Fame shortstops, Bobby Wallace and Rabbit Maranville, and his .295 career batting average is thirty points better than that of Cubs shortstop Joe Tinker.[11]

The problem area for the Sox was shortstop. While Davis filled in when needed, the two regulars were Freddy Parent (.207) and Jake Atz (.194). Both were above-average glove men, but their inability to hit was a major weakness. Parent had been a member of the Red Sox 1903 World Champions and was considered tough in the clutch, but age had weakened his skills.

Shoring up the Sox defense behind the plate was Billy Sullivan, one of the finest defensive catchers of the era. His weakness? You guessed it; he couldn't hit. Sullivan's .212 lifetime batting average ranks him next to last in all-time batting, last belonging to another Dead Ball Era catcher, the previously mentioned Bill Bergen of Brooklyn. Sullivan was inventive, patenting a chest protector with an inflatable pad. A master of all defensive aspects of the game, Sullivan was described by no less than Ty Cobb as the best catcher "ever to wear shoe leather."[12]

Sullivan's backups were inadequate. When Sullivan was injured late in the year, Sox owner Charles Comiskey bought Ossie Schreckengost from the Athletics. Schreckengost, or Shreck as he is referred to in many of the contemporary accounts and box scores, was an excellent defensive catcher and among the first to use a one-handed style. His last year in the majors was 1908, and his claim to fame was as catcher for the A's and Rube Waddell. During his days in Philadelphia, according to the well-known story, Schreckengost had arranged for the eccentric Waddell's contract to contain a provision preventing the lefty from eating crackers in bed when they roomed together on the road.[13]

White Sox offensive productivity came primarily from the outfield. Only four players—Jones, Eddie Hahn, Patsy Dougherty, and one of the few native Norwegians to play in the majors, "Honest John" Anderson—were used in the outfield. Jones led the team in runs scored with ninety-two. The fleet-footed Hahn used a sharp batting eye to be one of the league's best leadoff hitters. Dougherty was a scrappy player who led the team in hitting (.278) and the league in stolen bases with forty-seven. Anderson spoke with a thick accent, much to the amusement of sportswriters, was among the team leaders in RBI, and was a tough hitter; 1908 was his last year in the majors.

The departure of Fielder Jones at the end of the season was the beginning of the end of one of the most interesting teams of all time. The Hitless Wonders had demolished the '06 Cubs and had come within an ace of another flag and a rematch with the West Siders. In many ways they were a prototype of the Go Go Sox of the 1950s, as both teams won with speed, pitching, defense, and brains. After a sixth-place finish in 1910, Comiskey rebuilt his team. This time there would be more offense. The 1917 Sox brought another pennant and world title to Chicago. The same contingent disgraced themselves—and the game itself—two years later, by throwing the World Series. The Black Sox Scandal, according to some historians, ended the Dead Ball Era, and 1921 witnessed the beginning of the another era, on which Babe Ruth left his indelible mark.

ST. LOUIS BROWNS

4th / 83–69 .547
Ballpark: Sportsman's Park
Hall of Famers: Rube Waddell, P (1946); Bobby Wallace, SS (1953)
Owner: Robert L. Hedges
Manager: Jimmy McAleer (Career — 11 yrs. 736–889 .453; no postseason)

Some teams build contenders by luck, some by having good scouts and insightful front office support. Some teams try to do it with trades and purchases as a shortcut to success. For the Browns, 1908 was to be the year and owner Robert L. Hedges was dealing. Trades and a purchase were made in an attempt to win the pennant for a franchise that had finished over .500 only once since the American League was formed in 1901. Indeed, 1908 would be one of the better years in Browns history. After contending most of the year, they faded in September and finished fourth. The Browns were among the most exciting teams of 1908, despite their ultimate failure.

One of the blockbuster trades of the year came in February when the New York Highlanders and the Browns swapped five players. St. Louis sent pitcher Fred Glade and outfielder Charlie Hemphill to New York for infielders Hobe Ferris and Jimmy "Buttons" Williams and outfielder Danny Hoffman. Those three players gave the Browns the offense required to contend. Excitement grew when the Browns bought star left-hander Rube Waddell from the Athletics. The addition of Waddell gave the Browns the pitching depth required of a contender.

Waddell was one of the superstar pitchers of the Dead Ball Era. When he was on his game, he was an overwhelming fastballer, but his eccentric behavior, coupled with and probably caused by a drinking problem, was eventually too much for any manager to handle. Connie Mack sold him to the Browns because he believed Waddell was past his prime and harmful to team unity. While Waddell's 19–14 record led Browns pitchers, 1908 was his last impact year. It was a season marred by stories of marital problems, troubles with landlords, and teammates unhappy with his unreliability and frequent absences from the team.

Waddell had a reputation as a strikeout artist in an era when the strikeout was not as frequent as it is now. He fanned 232 hitters during the season and appeared in forty-three games. However, 1908 marked the first year he failed to lead the American League in strikeouts since joining it in 1902, losing the crown to Walsh of the White Sox. In 1914, Waddell died of tuberculosis at the age of thirty-seven, only four years after he left the majors.

Three other Browns pitchers won more than ten games — "Handsome Harry" Howell, Jack Powell and Big Bill Dinneen. Howell was 18–18 and his 1.89 earned run average matched that of Waddell. His out pitch was a spitball and he was known as a strong, steady pitcher who avoided injury and took his turn when called, in sharp contrast to Waddell.

Like Waddell's however, Howell's baseball career ended under a cloud. Late in 1910 Howell was implicated the scandal involving the Browns and Napoleon Lajoie's race for the batting title with Ty Cobb. Howell was fired from his front office job for encouraging and pressuring the official scorer to award base hits to Lajoie, thus throwing the batting title to the more likable and popular Frenchman.

Veteran sidearmer Jack Powell won sixteen games for St. Louis and led the team in shutouts with six. Dinneen was winding down his career with a strong finish, going 14–7. Dinneen had starred in the 1903 World Series, winning three and losing one for the Red Sox. After retirement, he stayed in baseball and enjoyed a twenty-nine year career as an American League umpire.

The Browns' roster had one other pitcher of note, Barney Pelty. A native Missourian, Pelty was an average pitcher during his ten-year career, posting a 91–116 record. Despite seeing limited action, 1908 was one of his best seasons. Pelty notched a 7–4 record and 1.99 ERA. His claim to fame in 1908 was two big wins against Cleveland, the Browns' opener and a late-season shutout.

One of the weaknesses of the Browns was the catching corps. The primary backstop was Tubby Spencer, who was competent at bat and in the field when sober. His battle with the bottle hindered his effectiveness. Backups Jim Stephens and Syd Smith were unable to hit over .200 and were not strong defensively. Such weakness was nearly always fatal to a team's chances during the Dead Ball Era.

The strength of the Browns was in the infield. As a unit, Brown infielders managed to avoid serious injury and played superb defense when the need arose. The Browns led the league in double plays with ninety-seven. Tom Jones capably held down first base, leading the league in double plays and putouts. He was a skilled base runner but a below average hitter. The addition of Hobe Ferris at third immediately shored up the infield. Not only did he lead the league in fielding for his position, but his seventy-four RBI led the team, while he hit a solid .270. Shortstop was held down by Hall of Famer Bobby Wallace. Like Ferris, he led the league in fielding for his position, and his .253 batting average and sixty RBI was nothing to be ashamed of in a year when pitching dominated. Wallace's keystone mate was newcomer Jimmy "Buttons" Williams. Williams was above average in the field, but his reputation as a slugger did not follow him from New York. He managed to hit only .243 with four homers, as age was catching up with him.

The Browns' outfield corps was a more troublesome unit. Consistency was the problem. Browns outfielders were a collection of good hit, no field players; no hit, good field players; and those playing out their string. The primary outfield was George Stone in left, Danny Hoffman in center, and Roy Hartzell in right. Stone hit well (.281) but committed sixteen errors. Hoffman was a good base runner but had to be platooned against left-handers. Hartzell battled injuries and missed almost a fourth of the season. Reserve outfielders Emmet Heidrick, Charlie "Casey" Jones, and Al Schweitzer made positive contributions, but the chemistry that makes a team click was absent.

One other Browns player deserves mention, Dode Criss. His tale is a classic of a quality player without a position. He hit .341, better than the league-leading Cobb. But Criss made only eighty-two trips to the plate, primarily as a pinch hitter. Manager Jimmy McAleer said he was a better hitter than Cobb, then promptly used him as a pitcher in nine games, in the outfield in seven, and at first base in one game. During his four years in the majors, Criss was the best pinch hitter in the American League. In a way, he was the first designated hitter. But the question remains, if he was that good, why wasn't he a regular?

Perhaps Criss served as a metaphor for the Browns. If Criss was a player without a permanent position, perhaps the Browns also managed not to find their place, lacking the chemistry required of a winner. Finishing a disappointing fourth, six and a half games out, the Browns were third in the league in hitting, and second in fielding and pitching. Those team numbers could and should have resulted in a better finish. The Browns remained in competition until fading in September. In Criss, Waddell, and others, St. Louis had good individuals, but they just didn't jell as a team. Perhaps the biggest reason for their finish was their mediocre record against Detroit, Cleveland, and Chicago. Splitting the twenty-two-game season series with the Naps, the Browns were 10–12 versus Detroit and had a 10–11 mark with the Sox, a performance that helps prove the baseball truism that you must beat the teams ahead of you if you want to succeed.

BOSTON RED SOX

5th / 75–79 .487
Ballpark: Huntington Avenue Grounds
Hall of Famers: Cy Young, P (1937); Tris Speaker, OF (1937)
Owner: John I. Taylor
Manager: Deacon McGuire (Career 6 yrs. 210–287 .423; no postseason)
and Fred Lake (Career 3 yrs. 163–180 .475; no postseason)

Despite lineup changes, a late season managerial shift, and inconsistency on defense, the Red Sox managed to improve two slots over their 1907 finish. After a World Championship in 1903 and a pennant in 1904, the Red Sox declined quickly due to disagreements between the front office and field management. By 1908 Boston was in a rebuilding mode. It was little noted at the time, but Tris Speaker and "Smokey Joe" Wood, stars of the great Boston teams of the teens, made brief appearances during the 1908 season.

The major and only star for the Red Sox of 1908 was the immortal Cy Young. At the age of forty-one, Young went 21–11 with a 1.26 ERA. He threw three shutouts, including a no-hitter, during this season, which marked his record-setting fifteenth season of twenty or more wins. He took his turn every fourth day and was a marvel. Contemporary news accounts constantly discussed how and why Young had lasted so long. Young credited off-season farm work with keeping him in playing shape. In terms of devotion to conditioning and longevity, Nolan Ryan is one of the few contemporary pitchers to compare with Young. It is no exaggeration to say that Boston's 1908 season would have been a nightmare if Young had not been part of the team.

Only one other Boston pitcher could be considered a household name, Eddie Cicotte. Cicotte, working his first full year in the majors, relied on a newly developed knuckleball to garner an 11–12 record. He spent another three and a half years with Boston before being sold to the White Sox, where he was a star and one of the primary figures in the Black Sox scandal.

Cy Morgan, Fred Burchell, and George Winter rounded out the staff. Morgan was 13–13, Burchell 10–8, and Winter 4–14 before being sold to the Tigers at midseason to bolster Detroit's injury-riddled pitching staff. Cy Morgan played a key supporting role for the Athletics when they were pennant winners and World Champions in 1910–11.

One of the other strengths of the Bosox was their catching corps, with both starter and substitute among the top receivers in the game. Cy Young won 511 games, the most of all time. Like many fine pitchers, Young had a personal catcher, Lou Criger. From 1896 through 1908, Young and Criger were teammates. A lifetime .221 hitter, Criger was known as a capable receiver who would express his opinion to umpires on every ball or strike call. Criger could handle Young and his fastball, a talent which made him valuable. His backup was Bill "Rough" Carrigan, who was a strong leader on the field and in the dugout. As playing manager, Carrigan led Boston to World Championships in 1915 and 1916.

One of the reasons Boston couldn't win consistently was their sixth-place ranking in fielding. Two of their regular infielders, second baseman Amby McConnell and third baseman Harry Lord, led the league in errors at their respective positions. Shortstop Heinie Wagner held his own at the position throughout the year. The addition of Jake Stahl at midseason stabilized the first base situation.

The outfield was the scene of most of the experimentation due to inconsistent offense and defense. Journeyman Jack Thoney logged the most games, playing center and left. Denny Sullivan received a great deal of playing time before being dealt to Cleveland at midseason. Former Cub Doc Gessler, "Cactus Gavvy" Cravath, Jim McHale, and future Hall of Famer Tris Speaker logged time in the outfield as well.

Gessler was more than adequate at the plate (.308) but lacked range in the field. Cravath became the home run king of the National League in the next decade. His twenty-four homers in 1915 for the Philadelphia Phillies set the major league record until Babe Ruth hit twenty-nine for the Red Sox in 1919.

In 1908 Cravath hit only .256, and he was dealt to the White Sox in 1909. McHale appeared in twenty-one games in his only season in the big leagues. As for Speaker, he hit only .220 but impressed those around the league with his fielding, handling sixty-five chances without an error.

At year's end, Boston fans had to be content with the team's improvement and its gameness. The Red Sox split the season series with the pennant-winning Tigers and went 10–12 against second-place

Cleveland. The record against the other first division teams revealed Boston's weakness, inconsistent play at bat and in the field. The White Sox took 16 of 22 from Boston. But the Red Sox lorded it over the Browns to the tune of a 15–7 season mark.

PHILADELPHIA ATHLETICS
6th / 68–85 .444
Ballpark: Columbia Avenue Grounds
Hall of Famers: Connie Mack, Mgr. (1937); Eddie Collins, 2B (1939);
* Jimmy Collins, 3B (1945); Charles "Chief" Bender, P (1953);*
* Eddie Plank, P (1946); Frank Baker, 3B (1955)*
Owner: Benjamin F. Shibe
Manager: Connie Mack (Career — 53 yrs. 3,731–3,948 .486;
* Pennants 8; World Championships 4)*

One of the most disappointing finishes in the early history of the Athletics was that of 1908. After finishing a strong second in 1907 one and a half games behind Detroit, the A's sagged to sixth. Victims of injuries, poor hitting (last in the league), and the inability to replace Rube Waddell and retired shortstop Monte Cross, they could have finished much worse.

Philadelphia loyalists may have agonized over their team's problems in 1908, but Connie Mack had the nucleus of his first great dynasty on the roster. With many of his 1908 players Mack won pennants in 1910–11 and 1913–14 and three World Series during those years. Some baseball historians consider the Athletics teams of the early teens one of the great dynasties in the sport.

One of the few bright spots among the Athletics was pitching. Philadelphia ranked seventh in pitching, but its hurlers threw twenty-three shutouts to tie the White Sox for first and led the league in strikeouts with 740. However, wildness hurt the team as over four hundred walks were issued.

The only pitcher with a winning record was "Colby Jack" Coombs with a 7–5 mark. One of the handful of major leaguers to come up without minor league experience, Coombs was an excellent hitter splitting his time between the mound and outfield. Relying on a curveball, Coombs was a key member of the great A's teams of 1910 and 1911 with fifty-nine wins. After retirement Coombs, who was among the many college players signed by Mack, coached baseball at Duke and Princeton.

The two Hall of Famers on the staff, Chief Bender and Gettysburg Eddie Plank, had decidedly un-Cooperstown-like off years. The Athletics' chances were hurt in that these two stars bunched their bad years. Bender was hampered by injuries, posting an 8–9 record. Plank chose 1908 to have one of only two of his career losing seasons with a 14–16 mark, a record indicating a lack of support more than a lack or loss of ability. The other pitchers on the staff, Rube Vickers (18–19), spitballer Jimmy Dygert (11–15), and Biff Schlitzer (6–8), were journeymen whose careers were not only short but undistinguished.

Philadelphia was in capable hands behind the plate. Doc Powers and Ossie Schreckengost split most of the duties. Powers was known as Plank's personal catcher and an excellent handler of pitchers. Tragically, he would die of an intestinal disorder shortly after the start of the 1909 season due to an injury suffered during the inaugural game at Shibe Park. Schreckengost played sixty-six games at catcher until his sale to Chicago. Neither player figured strongly in the team's offense.

The Athletics' infield was unstable for most of the year due to injuries and lineup juggling. Harry Davis with his five homers, sixty-two RBI, and team-leading sixty-five runs scored anchored things at first base. Second was shared by Eddie Collins in his first full year in the majors and Danny Murphy. Murphy split duties between infield and outfield because the lineup needed his bat (.265, 4 HR, and 66 RBI). Future Hall of Famer Collins led the team in hitting with a .273 mark.

The shortstop situation was simply a search for a replacement for Cross. Simon Nicholls played the most games at the position, but fifty-six errors and a .216 batting mark led Mack to take a hard late-season look at Jack Barry. He saw limited action in 1908 but starred for A's pennant winners in later years as a member of the so-called hundred-thousand-dollar infield.

Aging star Jimmy Collins was in the last year of his fourteen-year Hall of Fame career in 1908. An excellent defensive third baseman who appears on many all-time Dead Ball Era teams, Collins appeared in only 115 games and hit only .215. A rookie named Frank Baker appeared in only nine games but would be a regular at the hot corner for the Athletics for the next six years of his Hall of Fame career. He earned the nickname "Home Run" for his performance during the 1911 World Series.

The injury and illness bug bit the Athletics particularly hard in the outfield. Two regulars, Socks Seybold and Rube Oldring, missed significant action. Seybold's injury was a particularly hard blow. He was one of the few power hitters of the Dead Ball Era and held the American League home run record (16) and until Babe Ruth came along. Seybold played only thirty-four games in 1908 and then retired. Oldring's long illness deprived the A's of a reliable second-place hitter and an effective center fielder for a third of the season. Chaos in the outfield meant pitcher Coombs and infielders Murphy and even Eddie Collins saw significant action there. Leadoff man Topsy Hartsell and Oldring were the only two players to appear in more than one hundred games as outfielders for the 1908 Athletics.

Another outfielder of note debuted in late 1908, "Shoeless Joe" Jackson. Jackson was miserable in Philadelphia. He was teased mercilessly by teammates, many of whom were college players. Mack always had high praise for his more educated players, saying, "These boys, who knew their Greek and Latin and their algebra and geometry and trigonometry, put intelligence into the game."[14] Intelligence can also breed intolerance and snobbery. Jackson's illiteracy, pride, and rural southern upbringing worked against him among his more sophisticated colleagues. As a result, Mack had to deal Jackson to Cleveland, losing one of the greatest hitters in the game. Jackson's career ended in disgrace, a result of the Black Sox scandal.

With a lineup that at times seemed a mix of has-beens, green rookies, and walking wounded, it was miraculous that the A's actually were in first place for a day in 1908. It's a tribute to the managing ability of Connie Mack that the team was as competitive as it was. Ominously for the rest of the league, a dynasty was forming. Thirteen of the 1908 Athletics would be members of the World Champion 1910 club and would form the core of the powerful 1911 team. Though fans could not have known it at the time, the 1908 edition of the A's provided an example of the grain of truth embedded in the baseball fan's motto of eternal optimism, "Wait 'til next year!"

WASHINGTON NATIONALS (SENATORS)
7th / 67–85 .441
Ballpark: League Park
Hall of Famers: Walter Johnson, P (1936)
Owner: Thomas Noyes, president
Manager: Joe Cantillon (Career — 3 yrs. 158–297 .347; no postseason)

When you have at best an ordinary lineup and your star pitcher comes down with a mastoid infection in the days before antibiotics and misses a third of the season, you have the recipe for a poor finish. An optimist could note that the Nationals finished one place better than in 1907. A realist or cynic would argue that there is little difference between seventh and eighth in an eight-team league.

Washington's best pitcher was the incomparable Walter Johnson, who wowed the American League in his rookie year in 1907 with a 1.87 ERA while posting an ordinary 5–9 record with an inferior team. Johnson did not start his first game of 1908 until June 11. Because illness kept him out of spring training, he was forced to pitch himself into shape. Johnson was 14–14 with a 1.65 ERA and threw six shutouts, including an astonishing three in five days against the last-place Highlanders late in the season. Johnson was continually matched against the opponent's top pitchers. When you consider how illness had drained him of strength, it must be concluded that Johnson's 1908 season record was indeed remarkable, setting the tone for the remainder of this career.

Johnson was one of the greatest pitchers ever. Like Cleveland's Addie Joss, he had long arms and used this physical attribute to great advantage. Johnson's delivery was described by his biographer and grandson Henry W. Thomas. The "Big Train" would use a short windmill windup, "then swept the arm behind his back as far as it would go before whipping it forward in a smooth sidearm-underarm arc"[15] This simple mechanic made Johnson a durable and devastating pitcher, in that the almost effortless delivery appeared to make him faster than he was, and he remained strong throughout the game.

Until Johnson came along, Long Tom Hughes, who had been a twenty-game winner with the pennant-winning Red Sox in 1903, held down the fort. Fortunately for the Nats, in 1908 Hughes had the second best year of his thirteen-year career with an 18–15 mark.

After Johnson and Hughes, no other Washington pitcher won more than eight games. Charlie Smith was 8–13; "Sleepy Bill" Burns and Burt Keeley matched 6–11 marks. The best of the lot was Cy Falkenburg, who posted a 6–2 record before being sold to Cleveland. Burns and Keeley both are notable for deeds on and off the field. Burns's feat is more one of infamy than anything else. His season and career with Washington ended when his ribs were broken during a fight with a teammate. In 1919 Sleepy Bill used his connections as a former player to make contacts between Ed Cicotte and gamblers, which led to the Black Sox scandal. The diminutive Keeley's deed was more honorable. The five-foot, nine-inch hurler was the first pitcher in 1908 to start both games of a doubleheader. He did it on September 14 against the Athletics. His feat is largely overlooked because he won the opener and lost the second game, which went only eight innings. He was out of major league baseball before the end of the 1909 season.

Washington's catching duties were shared by "Gabby" Street, Mike Kahoe, and John Warner. Street was the best of a light-hitting lot. Nicknamed Gabby because of his talkative nature, Street had a successful playing and managerial career that was somewhat over shadowed by a stunt. In August 1908, Street caught a ball dropped from the Washington Monument. The grab came after fourteen tries. However, Street wasn't the first to do it. Old-time catcher Pop Schriver did it on his first try in 1894. Such grandstanding aside, Street was a capable baseball man and managed the Cardinals in their pennant years of 1930 and 1931. His Cards won a World Championship in 1931.

The Nats infield was known as a fleet-footed, generally sure-handed, but only average offensive unit. Jerry Freeman and George McBride held down first and shortstop. Freeman logged a respectable .253 batting average. McBride hit well in the clutch and added to his reputation as the one of the top defensive players by leading the league in double plays with fifty-eight.

The problem areas were second and third. Second baseman Jim Delahanty, of the hard-hitting Delahanty clan, hit a robust .317 but appeared in only half the Nats games due to illness and a lengthy suspension by American League President Ban Johnson for abusing an umpire. At third, Bill Shipke and Bob Unglaub shared duties. Unglaub hit .308 for the year and came to Washington in a July trade with Boston. Unglaub's bat relegated Shipke to the bench and utility duty.

As a unit, the Washington outfield of Clyde "Deerfoot" Milan, Bob Ganley, Ollie Pickering, and Otis Clymer was average to below average. Milan was a fine defensive center fielder, noted for his base-stealing ability; he and the great Johnson spent their entire careers with the Nats. Milan's talents have been largely forgotten, but contemporaries considered him Cobb's equal as a base stealer and in the field. Ganley was a fair hitter and fielder in left. Pickering and Clymer shared right field but were on the whole unsatisfactory.

The poorest franchise in the American League, year in and year out, the Nats were a perennial second division team and were destined to finish dead last in 1909, losing 110 games. Despite their mediocrity, they played an interesting and decisive role in the pennant race. As it was said back then, they had the hoodoo over the Cleveland Naps, winning fourteen of twenty-two games, while managing to win only five over Detroit and six from the White Sox.

This sharply contrasting record against the top three contenders led to accusations that Washington did not try to beat Detroit during their last trip west. Nothing came of the reports, as even a partisan observer would have had to concede that Cleveland played rather poorly against Washington.[16] There was no immediate investigation by league president Ban Johnson. It appears that the reports may have come from a player unhappy with Manager Joe Cantillon. Cantillon's conduct was passionately defended by *Sporting Life*'s Washington writer J. Ed Grillo: "He did everything in his power to win these games and if the team did not put up a strong game against Detroit it was not his fault, and subsequent events proved that he was more chagrined over the team's failure against the Tigers than were the members of the Cleveland team, who thereby lost the pennant."[17]

Even though Cantillon was apparently cleared, questions surrounding the 1908 season eventually led to a split between Cantillon and Ban Johnson. After the 1909 season, Cantillon was fired as Washington manager and former Highlander manager Clark Griffith was named skipper, all of this happening at the behest of Johnson, who wanted his old friend as an owner in his league.[18]

NEW YORK HIGHLANDERS (YANKEES)
8th / 51–103 .331
Ballpark: Hilltop Park
Hall of Famers: Wee Willie Keeler, OF (1939); Clark Griffith, Mgr. (1946);
  Jack Chesbro, P (1946)
Owners: Frank J. Farrell and William Devery
Manager: Clark Griffith (Career — 20 yrs. 1,491–1,367 .522; Pennant 1;
  no postseason); Kid Elberfeld (Career — 1 yr. 27–71 .276;
  no postseason)

Like a cheap skyrocket, the Highlanders started with a flash, soared high, and then sputtered like a dud in what the 1909 *Reach Guide* called "the signal failure of the year, for no apparent reason but mismanagement."[19] New York led the league from the start of the season until early June. Manager Clark Griffith was fired or had already resigned when New York was fading and fading fast, with a 24–32 mark. From then on they were 27–71 under the guidance of Kid Elberfeld. His only year managing in the majors convinced him to return to being a full-time player in 1909.

On paper, the Highlanders looked like a contender. Successful teams often win because their players have great years. The Highlanders were a failure because many of their key people had bad years, and the team itself was racked with dissension. Griffith's departure from the Highlanders was typically controversial. No one was neutral about the matter of whether he quit or was fired. Some charged that he quit because things got rough. Others claimed that unhappiness with Griffith among some players drove him off the team. No matter the cause, in this particular case, the manager took the heat.

Griffith's departure created a stir because he always seemed to attract attention and controversy. He had been one of the moving forces behind establishing the American League and is among those credited with developing the idea of using a relief pitcher as a strategic ploy, not a dire necessity. Griffith's 1908 experience left him with a lifetime dislike of the New York club, whether it was named Highlanders or Yankees.

If you subscribe to the evil man theory of history, some of the Highlanders' problems could be placed at the feet of Hal Chase. Chase was a brilliant fielder and a solid hitter; his problem was purely moral. A California native, Chase hopped between the majors and the Pacific Coast League, chasing the money. He constantly complained of being underpaid and was often suspected of padding his wallet by throwing games. When publicly suspected of such behavior in 1908, Chase expressed outrage and jumped the team. He returned to New York in 1909 and actually managed the Highlanders in 1910–11. His managerial ambitions and other activities are believed to have contributed to Griffith's demise. Chase was finally banned from baseball in 1919 in the wake of the Black Sox scandal. Chase's impact on baseball has been capsulized thus: "possibly the shadiest professional ball player after the turn of the century, as crooked off the field as he was talented on it."[20]

When he decided to play, Chase was the one of the best defensive first basemen in the game. Early baseball all-star teams often featured him at first. But in New York he was playing for an infield that was porous at best. It was a state of affairs that makes it difficult to move beyond strong suspicion of Chase's honesty. Chase's ability and notoriety aside, the rest of the Highlander infield were an ordinary to subordinary bunch.

Shortstop Neal Ball committed eighty errors, fielding at a horrid .898 rate; Ball replaced Elberfeld after the latter was severely spiked and put out for the season. Second was held down by journeymen players Harry Niles and Frank LaPorte. "Wid" Conroy played most of the year at third but also chipped in at second. George Moriarty, a future American League umpire, was a utility player. As a team, New York made 337 errors, the infielders as a unit chipping in 223 or fully two thirds of team's miscues.

Outfield duties were split among Wee Willie Keeler, Charlie Hemphill, Jake Stahl, Irish McIlveen, and Frank Delahanty. This unit was in turmoil most of the year because of poor performance. Keeler's Hall of Fame talents were in clear decline, but he hung on until 1910, despite threatening to retire at the end of 1908. Charles "Eagle Eye" Hemphill hit .297, but twenty errors cut his effectiveness. Jake Stahl was released, a casualty of the dissension on the team. McIlveen and Delahanty were barely adequate fill-ins. Delahanty was famous as being one of the five brothers to play in the majors. Three Delahantys played in 1908.

At catcher, veteran Red Kleinow provided excellent defense but hit only .168. His substitutes Walter Blair and Jeff Sweeney also filled in at first and in the outfield. Like Kleinow, both failed to break the .200 mark at the plate.

The extent of New York's collapse was nowhere more apparent than on the mound. No pitcher had a winning record, and Jack Chesbro and Joe Lake had the dubious distinction of losing twenty and twenty-two games respectively. Rube Manning, "Buffalo Bill" Hogg, and Al Orth were also in double digits on the loss side. All of the hurlers shared the characteristic of being just plain ineffective. Highlanders pitchers had the highest staff ERA in the American League at 3.16 and allowed the most walks (457). Opponents scored a league-high 713 runs against one of the worst teams in franchise history.

New York was decidedly inferior to the crosstown Giants and would remain that way until the arrival of Babe Ruth a decade later. The 1908 collapse was indicative of management problems, which were proven beyond doubt when the owners allowed Chase to return in 1909 and hired him as manager a year later. The Highlanders wouldn't get on the right track until Frank Ferrell and William Devery sold the team to Jacob Ruppert and Tillinghast L'Hommedieu Huston.

Many baseball historians have wondered how and why a player like Chase could be tolerated. Ferrell and Devery may have tolerated him because of their own moral blind spots. Ferrell made his fortune from gambling. Devery, a former New York City police chief, used gambling and prostitution payoffs to fund his real estate fortune. They could hardly be expected to take a hard line against Chase, and they could be relied upon to look the other way in matters of against gambling and game fixing.

NATIONAL LEAGUE

CHICAGO CUBS
1st / 98–55 .643
Ballpark: West Side Grounds
Hall of Famers: Johnny Evers, 2B (1946); Frank Chance, 1B-Mgr. (1946);
 Joe Tinker, SS (1946); Mordecai "Three Finger" Brown, P (1949)
Owner: Charles W. Murphy
Manager: Frank Chance (Career — 11 yrs. 946–648 .593; Pennants 4;
 World Championships 2)

The 1908 Cubs will be the darlings of Cub fans as long as they draw breath or until the franchise wins another World Championship. It is unfortunate that the achievements of this ball club have been forgotten. This team, mainly built by Frank Selee and managed by Frank Chance, was one of the finest, if not the best, in franchise history. Like the Oakland A's of the 1970s, they were a quarrelsome bunch. Second baseman Johnny Evers and shortstop Joe Tinker did not speak to each other, and there were confirmed reports of postgame fights that caused some injuries.

Playing manager Frank Chance operated under a philosophy of "do it my way or see me after the game under the stands." There is no doubt that the 1908 Cubs were a tough team. They had to be. They beat McGraw's Giants and Wagner's Pirates by a single game with a roster that saw only two players play in more than 129 games, Tinker and third baseman Harry Steinfeldt. Absence of many of the starters was due to injuries and suspensions resulting from ejections and, in a few cases, fights among teammates.

As if to emphasize the team play of the club, the 1908 Cubs did not lead the league in either hitting or pitching. The pitching staff managed to lead the league in strikeouts and shutouts. Big Ed Reulbach took the only individual title, his 24–7 .774 mark being the league's top winning percentage. The Cubs led the league in only two offensive categories, doubles and stolen bases, and had no league leader in any individual category. The team strength was defense. Cubs fielders committed a major league low 206 errors to lead the league in fielding percentage at .969.

The Cubs' overall strength was that they were a team in every sense of the word. They resembled a quarrelsome family. They fought among themselves but unified against all outsiders. It could be argued that Mathewson was the Giants and Wagner was the Pirates, but there was no single Cubs player who could take overall credit for the team's success. The Cubs proved that they could perform as a team without their starters, but this is not to say they lacked outstanding performers.

One key player was catcher John Kling, a largely overlooked member of the Cubs dynasty but one of the most respected backstops of his day. He drove in fifty-nine runs in 1908. But his offense was overshadowed by his defense. Kling's importance to the Cubs is perhaps illustrated by this: the only year the Cubs did not win the pennant between 1906 and 1910 was 1909, the year Kling retired from baseball to pursue a professional billiards career. He was an acknowledged master of working umpires to get close calls and worked well with his pitchers and infielders. A contemporary said, "I would catch for half the salary I am getting if I had that infield to throw to and work with."[21]

That infield played together for only 123 games in 1908. The Cubs' starting infield was formidable, if not impregnable. Manager Frank Chance and Harry Steinfeldt held the corners at first and third. Up the middle were Johnny Evers at second and Joe Tinker at short. Steinfeldt and Tinker went through the year without serious injury. Utility men Heinie Zimmerman and "Circus Solly" Hofman filled in when needed and when they were healthy. Hofman was a natural outfielder, but pressed into service he did an above average job at second. He also contributed several key hits during the stretch run. Zimmerman hit

.292 in his cameo appearances. He won a triple crown while with the Cubs in 1912. In 1919 Zimmerman was banned from baseball for trying to bribe a New York Giants teammate.

The leader of the group in terms of playing time was Joe Tinker, who led the league in fielding percentage, batted .266, hit six home runs, and drove in sixty-eight runs to lead the team. Tinker was a dangerous clutch hitter and was one of the toughest outs Christy Mathewson ever faced. In 1908 the normally light-hitting Tinker was 8 for 19 against the Giants ace, including two clutch homers and a game-winning triple in the final game of the season against the Giants. His .421 average against Mathewson was 155 points higher than his average against the rest of the league.

Tinker's success had to do with a characteristic of all successful professional athletes, the ability to adjust. In an interview in 1911, Mathewson noted that Tinker was an easy out when given a steady diet of low outside curveballs. Mathewson said that changed when Tinker made adjustments to his approach to batting: "He [Tinker] got a nice long bat and took his stand at least a foot farther from the plate, and then he had me. If I kept the ball on the inside edge of the plate he was in splendid position to meet it, and if I tried to keep my offerings on the outside, he had plenty of time to 'step into 'em.' From that day on, Tinker became one of the most dangerous batters I have ever faced."[22] Tinker was a warrior and relished the competition of the Dead Ball Era. He told interviewers that Chance and McGraw were born to battle on the diamond, and any game between the Cubs and Giants was all-out war. We have already read of his feeling that true Cubs honestly and furiously hated the Giants.[23]

Steinfeldt was an iron man, playing in 150 of the team's 158 games. Hitting only .241, Steinfeldt drove in sixty-two runs and played steady defense. He came into his prime under Chance's tutelage and was a key, if unacknowledged, part of the Cubs dynasty. Some believe Steinfeldt has been ignored because his name would not scan poetically and thus was left out of the poem "Tinker to Evers to Chance."

Johnny "Crab" Evers at second was one of those players who got more out of his ability than anyone could expect. Despite his reputation as a light hitter, Evers led the team with a .300 average in 1908. He was tough, aggressive, and always in search of the edge needed to win. Evers's aggressiveness was not limited to the opposition. Chance was uncomfortable with Evers, who often did not get along with teammates, notably his keystone mate Tinker. Evers played a vital role in the 1908 season because of his attention to the rules and desire to find the edge needed to win. It was his insistence on enforcement of the rule barring runs from scoring when the third out is a force-out that resulted in the most famous controversy in baseball history when Fred Merkle did not touch second base after an apparent game-winning hit.

Two observations about Evers made by those who knew him reveal much about the man and player. Umpire Bill Klem described him as "the toughest and meanest man I ever saw on a ball field."[24] In Evers's book *Touching Second,* his co-author Hugh Fullerton won the debate over whether to publish this description: "All there is to Evers is a bundle of nerves, a lot of woven wire muscles, and the quickest brain in baseball. He has invented and thought out more plays than any man of recent years."[25]

Frank Chance led his team from first base and for thirty-two games from the bench in 1908. His managerial philosophy evolved from that of his mentor, Frank Selee, stressing team work, inside play, and base-running. Nicknamed "Husk" for his size and "Peerless Leader" for his managerial abilities, he led by example and, if necessary, by force. Chance batted in fifty-five runs and was among the top defensive first basemen in 1908. He was a perfect complement to John McGraw. Games between these two turned the diamond into a battlefield as they matched and countered strategies.

Injuries and mishaps hampered the Cubs' outfield. As a unit, the first stringers played together in only 102 games. Called the Sigmas by Chicago writers, Wildfire Schulte, Jimmy Slagle, and Jimmy Sheckard formed one of the better outfields in the game, but poor health held down their offensive production in 1908. Hofman and Del Howard filled in ably when needed. Schulte was known as one of the better power hitters in baseball but hit only .236 due to injury, while leading the league's right fielders in defense. Slagle covered center skillfully but hit only .222. Sheckard chipped in with a .231 mark, while playing a key role in the Cubs dynasty. Hofman's clutch hitting down the stretch helped take pressure off a team depleted by injuries. Howard was a journeyman player and, after retiring as an active player, enjoyed a successful career as an executive and manager in the Pacific Coast League in the teens and '20s.

Cubs pitchers, who were the team's strength in '06 and '07, came through again in the hard-fought season of 1908. The staff's leader carried a somewhat melodious name, Mordecai Peter Centennial Brown. Nicknamed "Miner" by teammates because he had worked in west-central Indiana coal mines before signing a baseball contract, he was better known as "Three Finger." A farm accident had rendered Brown's right hand a mangled mess, which gave him a wicked, jug-handle curve that took a huge dip before reaching the hitter. Brown posted a 29–9 record in 1908 and, like Cy Young, was known for his attention to conditioning. Brown also was a pitcher who would pitch to a hitter's weaknesses by working against his stance: "If a batter had a straight-up stance, close to the plate, I'd pitch inside to him. If he crouched, I'd try to keep the pitch a little high, and a fellow who stood away from the plate was fed outside pitches. The main objective is to take the power away from the hitter — keep him from putting much wood against the ball."[26]

The other pitching stalwart was Big Ed Reulbach. One of many college players brought to the Cubs by George Huff, a one-time athletic director at the University of Illinois, Reulbach developed his reputation pitching for the University of Notre Dame in nearby South Bend, Indiana. His 24–7 mark was the best won-lost record in the league. He was plagued by wildness at times, but Reulbach was steady and durable. Those traits were shown when he started and won both ends of a doubleheader against Brooklyn in late September. In eight years with the Cubs from 1905 to 1912, he never had a losing season and posted wins in the double digits.

Other Cubs pitchers had ordinary years due to injury or illness. Orvall Overall, twenty-game winner for the 1907 team, started well, but a hand injury hampered him and he finished 15–11. He returned to form late in the year and won two World Series games. Jack Pfiester's 12–10 is not exciting at all, but he picked his spots well. During the glory years of the Cubs-Giants rivalry, the left-handed Pfiester was 15–5 against New York, earning him the nickname "Jack the Giant Killer." He won several key games down the stretch and, as we will see, turned in a gutty performance in the Merkle game.

Carl Lundgren, another Huff and University of Illinois product, had seen his best years; his 6–9 mark was a huge disappointment. Following his retirement, Lundgren succeeded Branch Rickey as head baseball coach at the University of Michigan.

Because of injuries and a lack of depth, the Cubs acquired Andy

Coakley from the Reds in September. His 1908 Cubs record was 2–0. He never won another big league game after this season, but he left an indelible mark on baseball. He was Lou Gehrig's coach at Columbia University, and the ball field at the school is named for the man who won two critical games in one of the tightest pennant races in history.

The 1908 edition of the Cubs tends to be overlooked by those who rate the great teams of baseball history. The '06 unit won more games than any in history but lost the World Series. The '07 club was dominant and won a World Championship, so that club could arguably stake a claim to greatness. But the 1908 Cubs should not take a back seat to any team. They won the pennant by a game in a race where each pitch, at bat, fielding play, run, stolen base, and out could determine the outcome. In winning the pennant by a single game, this team gamely assembled a 38–8 (.826) record for the September and October stretch run. If they were not the greatest Cubs team ever to take the field, they certainly were the toughest in the clutch.

NEW YORK GIANTS
2nd (tied) / 98–56 .636
Ballpark: Polo Grounds
Hall of Famers: Christy Mathewson, P (1936); John McGraw, Mgr.
   (1937); Roger Bresnahan, C (1945); Rube Marquard, P (1971)
Owner: John T. Brush
Manager: John McGraw (Career — 33 yrs. 2,784–1,959 .587;
   Pennants 9; World Championships 3)

John McGraw went to his grave believing that his 1908 Giants had been robbed of the pennant. Galling as the decisions by the National League office on the Merkle play were, McGraw never blamed Merkle for not touching second in the September 23 game against the Cubs that turned a Giants win into a tie. Perhaps most frustrating to McGraw was that the Merkle incident negated one of his finest managing jobs.

No one seriously predicted that the 1908 Giants would make the pennant run they did, but McGraw drove his mixture of youngsters and hardened veterans to within an ace of glory. The 1909 *Reach Guide* described the Giants team as "unpromising, but under McGraw's skillful management and (Turkey Mike) Donlin's efficient captaincy it soon became welded into a harmonious and efficient base ball machine, gradually made its presence felt in the race, ultimately became the sensation and the storm center of the season and the leader of the race, and made one of the gamest fights on record."[27]

Age had caught up with the nucleus of McGraw's '04 and '05 teams. The 1907 edition finished a below-par fourth. The Giants did a total rebuilding job during the 1908 preseason, using a mixture of home-grown talent, a big trade, and the return of a star of the past. By bringing up Merkle, Larry Doyle, and Buck Herzog, the Giants started a youth movement that would become a key element in a Giants dynasty just three years later.

In a blockbuster trade, the Giants acquired first baseman Fred Tenney, infielder Al Bridwell, and backup catcher Tom Needham from the Braves for aging shortstop Bill Dahlen, outfielder George Browne, pitcher George Ferguson, and catcher Frank Bowerman. In one of the most one-sided deals ever, the Giants shored up weaknesses in their infield in return for veteran players who had seen their best years — and in fact who had represented those infield weaknesses. An added bonus was the return of slugger "Turkey Mike" Donlin after his 1907 absence. Donlin was a leader and he worked well with the newcomers.

Had McGraw owned a crystal ball, he might have tried to get another pitcher. His staff was woefully thin at times. You could argue that the Giants fell a game and a pitcher short of winning it all in 1908. The pitcher who carried the Giants all year was the incomparable Christy Mathewson, and 1908 was Matty's greatest single year. He was 37–11 and threw twelve shutouts. His earned run average was a microscopic league-leading 1.43. He struck out 259 and walked only forty-two in his 391 innings pitched. A master of the screwball, termed the fadeaway back then, Mathewson had pinpoint control. He saved his strength by throwing as few pitches as possible. Matty could and would strike out hitters when needed, but according to his pitching philosophy, a groundout or pop-up on one pitch was just as efficient.

New York's only other consistent pitcher was George "Hooks" Wiltse. He was an above average pitcher for the time and his 23–14 record was a pleasant surprise. He enjoyed the distinction of winning in double digits for his first eight years with the Giants, and 1908 was his first twenty-win season. On July Fourth, he came within a pitch of a perfect game against Philadelphia. His nickname had nothing to do with his curveball or the shape of his nose; instead it reflected his ability to snag liners and ground balls coming through the box, giving him the reputation of being the best defensive pitcher in the game.

The rest of the Giants staff was in comparison disappointing. Doc Crandall managed a 12–12 mark. Known as one of the first pure relief pitchers, Crandall was also used as a pinch hitter and infielder when need be. The three remaining pitchers, "Iron Man" McGinnity, "Dummy" Taylor, and Leon "Red" Ames, were effective when used. Each had a win percentage of over .600. But only McGinnity had wins in double digits (11). The trio totaled forty-five starts, one fewer than Mathewson. Ames was slowed by illness. McGinnity and Taylor stayed healthy but remained underutilized by McGraw for reasons known only to himself.

In an attempt to reinforce his pitching, McGraw brought up Rube Marquard in late season. Unlike the Cubs' experience with their late-season acquisition, Andy Coakley, Marquard failed to win a game. His introduction to the big leagues was a rude one. He lost his only start in 1908, the first step in an eighteen-year, Hall of Fame career.

Another Hall of Famer, Roger Bresnahan, stood behind the plate for the Giants. Unlike many catchers of the era, Bresnahan was an offensive as well as defensive star. He batted third in the order, a spot usually assigned to a team's best hitter. In the year of the pitcher, he hit a credible .283, scoring seventy runs and driving in fifty-four. Combative and pugnacious, Bresnahan was a McGraw clone on the field. Aside from his ability as a player, the Duke of Tralee had another major claim to fame.

He innovated at least two forms of protective equipment, the batting helmet and shin guards, and has been credited with changing the padding in the catcher's mask.[28] His batting helmet idea did not catch on, despite the frequency of bean balls. His modification of cricket shin guards did find favor eventually. These pads were external, as opposed to the soccer equipment worn by Cleveland's Nig Clarke. The gear apparently worked; Bresnahan appeared in 140 games, second in the majors in 1908. In the hard-nosed days of the Dead Ball Era, Bresnahan had to endure ridicule until players realized that protection from career-threatening injury made better sense than taking unnecessary risks.

As the result of Bresnahan's durability, his backup, Tom Needham, played a mop-up role, seeing action when Bresnahan needed a rest or when a game was well in hand. Needham was a capable defensive backstop but provided little offense. Needham was an aggressive player who enjoyed fighting as much as he did baseball. He was the kind of player McGraw liked to have around when a punch would be just as effective as a well-placed bunt.

Of some interest was the Giants' third catcher, Fred Snodgrass. He debuted in 1908, appearing in only six games. He went on to a fine career as an outfielder and an undeserved place in the Giants Hall of Infamy for a dropped fly ball during the deciding game of the 1912 World Series.

The Giants saw substantial improvement in both infield and outfield play, primarily due to two players who had not been around the year before. They were the aforementioned Donlin, who sat out the bulk of 1907 to pursue an acting career, and first baseman Fred Tenney, who came over in the big trade with the Braves.

Donlin's return to action bolstered the outfield as he hit .334, drove in 106 runs, and provided the kind of leadership needed on a serious pennant contender. Importantly, Donlin missed only two games. Center field was in the capable hands of Cy Seymour, who missed only one contest. He led the league in assists with twenty-nine and hit five homers, second on the team to Donlin's six. Left field was the weakness of the Giants, as "Spike" Shannon did not come up to McGraw's expectations. "Moose" McCormick was purchased from the Phillies in June and became the regular, hitting a robust .302. Shannon was sold off to the Pirates in July and Shad Barry was acquired from St. Louis in July as a backup.

Tenney was the infield stalwart, leading the league in putouts, and was edged by Cincinnati's John Ganzel for the overall fielding crown. An ideal leadoff man, Tenney drew seventy-two walks, second only to Bresnahan in the National League. Tenney missed only one game all year, and it was a big one. His sole absence gave Fred Merkle the start in that infamous September 23 game against the Cubs. Besides his offensive talent, Tenney was one of the top fielding first basemen in the game.

Third was occupied by Art Devlin, one of the best defensive third sackers in the league, with the best fielding percentage while making the most putouts and assists. Devlin hit only .253, but his speed and base-stealing ability made him an ideal fit with the Inside Baseball strategy of McGraw.

Defensively strong at the corners, the Giants' middle infield was strong at bat and weak in the field. "Laughing Larry" Doyle saw most of the duty at second and led the league in errors at the position with thirty-three. He made up for the defensive lapse by hitting .308. Doyle, in his second year, became a key member of Giants as pennant winners in 1911–12 and 1912–13. His primary replacement was Buck Herzog, who hit .300 but would never be accused of playing consistent defense. Al Bridwell hit a solid .285 but led the league in errors at shortstop with fifty-five. Bridwell was the man who made the hit that set up the Merkle play. Years later, Bridwell told anyone who would listen that he regretted making the hit that had set off the controversy.

A primary substitute was the nineteen-year-old Merkle. Plagued by injuries — blood poisoning nearly killed him during the season — Merkle filled in at first, third, second, and in the outfield. He hit .268 and his .439 slugging percentage was among the best in the league. Merkle was a victim of circumstance and fate. He was not a stupid player. He had a solid career with the Giants and Dodgers and, ironically, with the Cubs. He was a gamer, playing on five pennant winners. But none of his World Series teams won the title. Guilty only of following a convention that was clearly contrary to the rules, Merkle unfairly carried for all his life the burden of what happened on the afternoon of September 23, 1908.

The 1908 Giants remain a team that could have been. Most members went on to form McGraw's second great dynasty of the early teens. This dynasty was a star-crossed one. Perhaps it was a hangover from the Merkle incident, or perhaps merely ill fate, but those great Giants teams of 1911–13 did not win a World Series. Those teams, like the 1908 contingent, would always be called near great because they fell just short of the ultimate prize.

PITTSBURGH PIRATES
2nd (tied) / 98–56 .636
Ballpark: Exposition Park (on site of present-day Three Rivers Stadium)
Hall of Famers: Honus Wagner, ss (1936); Fred Clarke, OF-Mgr. (1945);
  Vic Willis, P (1995)
Owner: Barney Dreyfuss
Manager: Fred Clarke (Career — 19 yrs. 1,602–1,181 .576; Pennants 2;
  World Championship 1)

Some say baseball is a team game and no one player can ever carry a team all by himself. Those who believe this have not paid much attention to the Pittsburgh Pirates of 1908, who finished in a tie for second with the Giants. It would be hard to believe that the team from the Steel City would have fared as well had they had to go without the immortal Honus Wagner. But that is what nearly happened.

Wagner declared his retirement several times during the preseason, and his puzzling over retirement was fuel for Hot Stove League fires in all big league cities. In various communications with the Pirates organization, Wagner mentioned his health, a desire to become a chicken farmer, and just being too tired as reasons for not returning. Losing the National League's greatest power hitter of the day from a team designed around his power hitting spelled disaster to owner Barney Dreyfuss. Dreyfuss opened his wallet and persuaded the Dutchman to return to the fold for the then princely sum of ten thousand dollars. Wagner signed after opening day and joined the team in Cincinnati. Ironically, Wagner's first day of action on the field also marked the Pirates' first loss of the season.

Just how important was Wagner to the Pirates? In 1908 he led the league in batting and slugging average, total bases, runs batted in, stolen bases, total hits, doubles, and triples. He missed the home run title and a triple crown by two homers. In the field, he led National League short-stops in putouts with 354. In summation, he was the heart of the team and arguably the best all-around player in the game. McGraw of the Giants paid his diamond foe the ultimate compliment: "While Wagner was the greatest shortstop, I believe he could have been the number one player at any position he might have selected. That's why I vote him baseball's foremost all-time player."[29]

Joining Wagner at third base was one of the outstanding players to play the position during the Dead Ball Era, Tommy Leach. Known for his speed and bat control, Leach batted second and scored ninety-three runs, second on the team only to Wagner's one hundred. Leach was also a big extra base hitter and was second only to Wagner in production of doubles, triples, and home runs; but though Leach was above average in the field, clearly his value to Pittsburgh was at bat.

One of the first Italian-American stars of the game, Ed Abbaticchio, occupied second base. A glove man who led the league in fielding percentage for his position, Abbaticchio hit a respectable .250 in 1908 and made several key hits in clutch situations. His value to the Pirates was overshadowed by Wagner.

The problem position for the Pirates was first base. Four players— Harry Swacina, Alan Storke, Jim Kane, and Warren "Doc" Gill—all saw action at first, as player-manager Fred Clarke desperately sought a solution to a season-long weakness that robbed the infield of consistency. The foursome played a total of ten years in the big leagues, including Swacina's two years in the Federal League. Kane and Gill saw their only major league action in 1908, and Gill figured in a Merkle-like incident against the Cubs in August. Fortunately for him, the Pirates' win was preserved despite protests. Storke was considered the answer but didn't report to the team until late season. If the Giants fell a pitcher short of winning the flag, it could be said that the Pirates could have won it all if first base had been occupied by a quality or even an average player all season.

The Pirates' outfield was above average primarily because of the presence of Fred Clarke, a player-manager who, like Chance of the Cubs, led by example. A fierce competitor, Clarke had an approach to baseball that was akin to warfare. His passion contrasted with the cool competence of Wagner. Together they were formidable. Clarke played left field. Right field was held down by rookie Owen "Chief" Wilson, a speedy customer who holds one of those records that may never be broken, for the most triples in a year. Wilson hit thirty-six three-baggers in 1912. Triples were more common during the Dead Ball Era due to the depth of some of the outfields in the old wooden ballparks and a willingness by runners to take an all-important extra base. Today's symmetrical parks and modern player attitudes do not lend themselves to one of the game's exciting plays. Wilson would be a mainstay for the Pirates in later years but hit only .227 in 1908.

Center field was a problem area all season long. Roy Thomas, Spike Shannon, Danny Moeller, and even Leach toiled there. Leach's move to center was entirely experimental and was scrapped when no one stepped in to replace him at third. Thomas and Shannon came from Philadelphia and New York as stopgaps and were merely adequate.

"Adequate" would never describe catcher George Gibson. Although a light hitter, Gibson was regular backstop for Pittsburgh from 1905 to 1916. He was one of the first Canadians to come south to play big league ball. His contribution was steady defense and durability; he was seldom injured, and that helped in the pitching department. Eddie Phelps and Paddy O'Connor were Gibson's subs, but they did not see much action because the durable Gibson caught 140 games.

Pitching had been a Pirates strength for years, and 1908 would be no different. The staff was an even mix of youngsters and veterans. Consistency was the staff trait, as five Pittsburgh pitchers won fifteen or more games. Nick Maddox and Vic Willis paced the mound corps with twenty-three wins each. Willis with his 23–11 mark notched the third of four consecutive twenty-win seasons in a 248-win career, which won him a belated spot in the Hall of Fame in 1995. Maddox's 23–8 was his best mark in a four-year career ended by arm trouble.

Howie Camnitz (16–9), Sam "The Goshen Schoolmaster" Leever (15–7), and Lefty Leifield (15–14) rounded out a staff that finished second in team-earned run average. Camnitz and Leever performed to expectations and Leifield was a disappointment, coming off a twenty-win season in 1907.

Preseason predictions gave Pittsburgh a shot at beating the Cubs. The Pirates would have turned the trick had first base and center field been stable. Pittsburgh chalked up one of the most unusual team statistics in any pennant race during the 1908 season. On the road the Pirates were 56–21 for a scorching .727 winning percentage. At home, the won-loss record was a more pedestrian 42–35 (.545). Ironically, it was a road loss to Chicago in the last game of the season that ended the Pirates' pennant run a game short. The loss was particularly heartbreaking for the Pittsburgh faithful, as the Pirates managed a winning 23–21 record against the Cubs and Giants.

PHILADELPHIA PHILLIES
4th / 83–71 .539
Ballpark: National League Park
Hall of Famers: none
Owner: William Shetsline, president
Manager: Billy Murray (Career — 3 yrs. 240–214 .529; no postseason)

The Phillies were one of the those teams that would not and could not easily be figured out. The Phils led the league in pitching and won 13 of 22 from the Cubs. They had a middling 24–20 record against lowly Boston and Cincinnati, and were only 6 and 16 against high-and-mighty New York. A pitcher named Harry Coveleski won three of those games, playing a critical role in the outcome of the pennant race. Hopes for a flag in Philadelphia faded quickly in the face of inconsistent hitting, despite the strong pitching.

The best of the Philadelphia pitchers was George Washington Mc-Quillan, who posted a 23–17 mark and a fine 1.52 earned run average.

Named National League Rookie of the Year by SABR in a poll of members in 1986, McQuillan had debuted in 1907 with a 4–0 mark.[30] His best season in a ten-year career was that of 1908. The other two Phil pitchers who registered wins in double digits were Tully Sparks (16–15) and Frank "Fiddler" Corridon (14–10). Sparks was known as a power pitcher and had won twenty-two games in '07 but was on the downside of a twelve-year career. Corridon spent only six years in the big leagues, and his personal claim to fame was his assertion that he invented the spitball; he was one of many pitchers to make such a statement in a bid for immortality.

Three other pitchers who would see major action were Lew Moren (8–9), Bill Foxen (7–7), and Lew Richie (7–10). Moren was dubbed the "Million Dollar Kid" because his well-to-do father would pay him a hundred dollars for each win. Dad would have been out forty-eight hundred dollars if he ponied up for each of Moren's career wins.

Meanwhile Foxen and Richie should have sued for nonsupport by the Phillie offense. Both notched earned run averages under two points. Their records embody the frustration Philadelphia fans must have felt: their pitching was good enough to win a pennant, but the offense was barely that of a first division team. Richie was known for his sense of humor and was a source of many classic Ring Lardner stories. The tribulations of 1908 must have tested that aspect of his personality severely.

One of the surprise stars of the year was twenty-two-year-old Harry Coveleski, son of Polish immigrants. He was 1–0 in 1907 but was sent back to the minors. In 1908, Coveleski was bombed in an early-season start against the Giants and demoted to the minors again. He returned to the Phils in September and made an indelible mark on the National League race. In a five-day stretch in late September, Coveleski earned the nickname "Giant Killer" by defeating New York three times.

McGraw never forgot Coveleski and vowed revenge. Fred Snodgrass claimed that the Giants avenged themselves by running him out of the league using psychological warfare. The Giants exploited his habit of carrying sausage in his pocket and eating it during a game. "McGraw saw to it that some of us players would always meet Coveleski as he was going to and from the pitcher's box whenever he pitched against us. We'd stop him and say, 'Hey, give us a chew of that bologna, will you?' Well, this so upset this fellow that he couldn't pitch against us to save his life."[31]

Whether the story is true or not, Coveleski was 6–10 in 1909 and went back to the minors in 1910. In 1914 he returned to the majors with the Detroit Tigers and rang up three consecutive twenty-win seasons. His brother, Stanley, won 215 games in a Hall of Fame career with Cleveland. Harry's 1908 feat was a source of pride among members of the coal-mining clan, and according to Stanley the bologna story was untrue. His denial was a blunt one: "What a lot of bull that story is."[32]

If most Phillies pitchers were a hard-luck lot, it couldn't be blamed on their catcher, Red Dooin. A .248 hitter in 1908, Dooin was statistically among the best defensive backstops, leading the league in assists and double plays. He was known as an aggressive, fiery, and hardworking player. His contemporaries noted that he was always talking, smiling, or fighting. Dooin's backup was veteran Fred Jacklitsch, a reliable defensive replacement with an above average bat.

The infield was like the team, good but not outstanding. "Kitty" Bransfield, one of the top hitting stars of the game, held down first. He hit .304 and was a strong defender. At the end of his playing days he became a major league umpire. At second was a player as tough as his name sounded, Otto Knabe. Known as a rough and physical player, he hit only .218 but led the league in putouts and assists for second basemen. Team captain Mickey Doolan played adequate shortstop but, like his keystone mate, was a weak hitter. Doolan put up a .234 average.

At third was one of the interesting and tragic figures of the Dead Ball Era, "Harvard Eddie" Grant. Grant was a strong fielder with good speed on the bases and was a reliable clutch-hitting leadoff man. Grant was distinguished among the college players: he was one of the few who actually graduated before playing pro ball. Grant was a genuine American hero too. He was the only major league player to be killed in action during World War I. Grant lost his life while leading his unit during an attempt to rescue the "Lost Battalion," which had been trapped behind German lines during the Argonne Forest campaign. He died on October 5, 1918, just five weeks before the Armistice that ended the war. Grant was laid to rest in the Meuse-Argonne Cemetery in France.[33]

Philadelphia's outfield was one of the few in the game to go through the season without major injury. John Titus, Sherry Magee, and Fred Osborne played as a unit for 142 games, quite a feat in a year when injury to starters was common. Osborne's .267 was his best year in a short three-year career. Titus was in the middle of a solid career and hit a respectable .286. Magee was among the finest outfielders of the day.

A Phil regular for ten years, Magee was an intelligent and aggressive player who was among the best all-around players in the game, possessing speed, excellent defensive skills, and a strong bat.

The Philadelphia Phillies of 1908 were no great success, but they weren't the spectacular failures that would make the franchise infamous in later years. A lack of hitting kept them from doing better. The Phils were a contingent of good but not great players, evidenced by the cold hard fact that the Phillies were one of three teams not to have a member of baseball's Hall of Fame on their 1908 roster.

CINCINNATI REDS
5th / 73–81 .474
Ballpark: Palace of the Fans
Hall of Famers: Miller Huggins, 2B (1964 elected as Mgr.)
Owner: Garry Herrmann
Manager: John Ganzel (Career — 2 yrs. 90–99 .476; no postseason)

Cincinnati was one of those franchises that had its on-field performance overshadowed by the personality of its owner and chief executive, team president August Garibaldi "Garry" Herrmann. Herrmann served as the swing vote on the three-member National Commission, which governed the game until Kenesaw Mountain Landis was named commissioner in 1920. Herrmann was an agreeable, sociable man who had a nose for good food and the business of baseball. He shook the baseball world late in the 1908 season by announcing that he would experiment with night baseball the next year. News of this experiment briefly diverted attention away from the tight pennant races and the Reds' so-so year.

The year began optimistically with the appointment of John Ganzel as player-manager. The Reds got out of the box strong and faded with the heat of summer, but they still ended the season with the moral victory of finishing atop the second division.

Ganzel's National League managing career began and ended in 1908. He managed the Brooklyn team of the Federal League in 1915 with indifferent results. His biggest problem was material. The '08 Reds ranked sixth in hitting, fourth in team pitching, and seventh in team defense, a formula for mediocrity if ever there was one. Weak hitting hurt the team profoundly. Ganzel and third baseman Hans Lobert were the only starters to hit over .250. A leaky defense constantly pressured the pitching, which collapsed under the weight of it all as another summer descended upon the Ohio River valley.

Ganzel was the leader of the infield and was the best defensive first baseman in the league; his last season as a player was 1908. Lobert held down third and was one of the most feared hitters in the game. He spent his entire seventeen-year career in the National League and is famous for his rather uncanny facial and physical resemblance to the great Wagner. Because he so strongly resembled the Flying Dutchman, Lobert, whose given name was John Bernard, was often referred to as "Hans," "Honus," and even the "Little Dutchman."

The diminutive but scrappy Miller Huggins played second. He was a good fielder but a weak hitter. His batting eye and ability to coax walks made him a valued leadoff man. He was fast on the bases and a threat to steal at any time. Huggins learned baseball from the school of hard knocks, playing in mediocre clubs and beginning his managing career as a player-manager for some stunningly average St. Louis Cardinals teams. As manager of the Yankees in the Ruth-Gehrig era, Huggins won six pennants and three World Championships, resulting in his election to the Hall of Fame. His managerial career was tragically cut short in 1929 when he died of blood poisoning at the age of fifty.

At shortstop, Rudy Hulswitt was a major disappointment. A .228 batting average and forty-two errors earned him a transfer to St. Louis after the season. Mike Mowrey and Dick Egan were the infield reserves. They were merely okay in the field and undistinguished at bat. Dick Hoblitzel, who was a rookie in 1908, filled in at first when needed. He was a key player for those great Red Sox champions in 1915–16.

The Cincinnati outfield was troubled by injury and inconsistency all year. The starting unit of Mike Mitchell, John Kane, and Dode Paskert played together for fewer than 120 games. Mitchell and Kane suffered under the influence of a season-long hitting slump, hitting .222 and .213 respectively. Paskert, who had a reputation for being an excellent defender and underrated hitter, struggled at the plate with a .243 mark. A quality player, Paskert played in two World Series for the Phillies and Cubs during his fifteen-year career.

Behind the plate, George "Admiral" Schlei and Larry McLean split duties. Both were solid big league catchers with longer than average careers; Schlei spent eight years and McLean thirteen in the majors. McLean had a reputation as a heavy drinker and was shot to death during a brawl in 1921. Neither had a batting average exceeding .220 in 1908.

The pitching staff should have raised concerns during the preseason. The four top hurlers were all older than thirty-one, which was old in an era when few players remained in the game after the age of thirty-five. Bob Spade (17–12) and Bob Ewing (17–15) were the aces of the staff. Spade was developing a reputation for being difficult to work with in the second year of a four-year career. Ewing was a durable workhorse and one of the better spitball pitchers in the game.

Bill Campbell, Jake Weimer, Andy Coakley, and Jean Dubuc rounded out the staff. Campbell logged a 12–13 record, Weimer was 8–7, Coakley 8–18, and Dubuc a disappointing 5–6. Campbell would be out of baseball after 1909. Weimer had been a twenty-game winner with the Cubs earlier in the decade but was past his prime when Chicago traded him to the Reds for Harry Steinfeldt. Coakley had a miserable time in Cincinnati and was probably the happiest man in baseball when he was sold to the Cubs in September.

Jean Dubuc came off a college campus as a reinforcement. He later developed into an above average pitcher in the American League with the Detroit Tigers. His career ended in banishment from the game when organized baseball finally got serious about the influence of gambling in the wake of the Black Sox scandal in 1919. Dubuc's crime was that his association with Sleepy Bill Burns gave him prior knowledge of the fix.

The Reds would remain a below-par team throughout most of the Dead Ball Era. Their first modern era pennant and World Championship in 1919 were blemished by scandal. Despite a poor performance during the Dead Ball Era, Cincinnati remained a strong baseball town loyal to the oldest professional franchise in the sport, though the on-field performance seldom earned the devoted following the team enjoyed.

BOSTON DOVES (BRAVES)
6th / 63–91 .409
Ballpark: South End Grounds
Hall of Famers: Joe Kelley, OF-Mgr. (1971)
Owner: George B. Dovey
Manager: Joe Kelley (Career — 5 yrs. 338–321 .513; no postseason)

Had a prize been handed out for the most unpleasant atmosphere in big league baseball in 1908, Boston's National League franchise would have won hands down. Owner George Dovey was openly disappointed that his trades and purchases failed to produce a winner. Player-manager Joe Kelley was leading a team fractured by dissent. Late in the year the team ownership was reduced to complaining about umpires as another losing season unfolded before them.

The trade with the Giants that brought pitcher George Ferguson, catcher Frank Bowerman, outfielder George Browne, and shortstop Bill Dahlen to Boston was one-sided. It strengthened the Giants by plugging their leaks, while weakening the Doves in critical areas and sowing within the team the seeds of dissension.

Throughout the history of sports, successful teams seem to have had two qualities: consistency and avoidance of injury. The 1908 Boston Doves lacked both. Thirty-eight-year-old Bill Dahlen played the most games, 144. For a good part of the season, Boston's lineup was a makeshift affair. Another circumstance hurting this team was age: Boston had the oldest lineup in the majors, and there were times when it showed.

The most senior player was catcher Frank Bowerman. At thirty-nine years old, he was near the end of a fifteen-year career as a backstop. He had a reputation as a fighter and his aggressiveness led him to undermine Kelley's managerial authority. Some contemporary accounts blame Bowerman's June hand injury for the team's demise, but that is being overly polite. Bowerman wanted to be a major league manager. He could not in New York because of McGraw's presence. He replaced Kelley in 1909, but was out of baseball at the end of the year. Peaches Graham was the stand-in backstop. He hit well (.274) but the pitching suffered because he was neither a particularly talented defender nor a good handler of pitchers.

There's a saying that you can't make chicken salad out of feathers. Blaming the worst pitching staff in the National League on a substitute catcher is a stretch at best, and perhaps even a cheap shot. The 1908 Boston staff were an undistinguished lot. The only pitcher with a winning record was former Giant George Ferguson (12–11) and his year was hampered by arm troubles. Ferguson won only thirty-one games in his six-year career. In fact, none of the top pitchers on the team won more than a hundred games in his career.

The winningest of them all, Patsy Flaherty, won sixty-six games in nine years. He was 12–18 in 1908, which was the last year he would win a game in a career that ended in 1910. The left-handed Flaherty had a wild streak, which left him pitching constantly with base runners or behind in the count.

Right-hander Vive Lindaman had a hard-luck 12–16 mark. He went 1–6 with Boston in 1909 and retired to Iowa, where he was more successful as a postman. The staff was rounded out with Gus Dorner, who was an ineffective 8–19 as he was winding down his career. The only pitcher on the staff who was a household name was Irv "Young Cy" Young. In 1905, he won twenty games with Boston and was 4–8 with the Doves before being traded to Pittsburgh in June, where he logged a respectable 4–3 mark with the second-place Pirates.

Boston's keystone combo, Claude Ritchey and "Bad Bill" Dahlen, led the league in double plays. That achievement is a dubious distinction among serious fans. Lots of double plays means base runners, and allowing many opposing hitters on base usually spells trouble. Ritchey led regulars with a .273 average and was known as one of the better offensive and defensive players in the game. Dahlen was a player well past his prime. He hit .239 in 1908 and was nowhere near the player he had been when he was one of the leading run producers for New York Giants pennant winners of 1904–5.

Dan McGann, another former 1904–5 Giant and Baltimore Orioles teammate of John McGraw's, spent his last year in the majors in 1908 at first base. In his prime, McGann was fast, aggressive, and a key part of the early Giants dynasty. By 1908 he had lost most of his speed but remained a fierce competitor. He was among the leading first basemen in the field but hit only .240.

Bill Sweeney and Jack Hannifin split duties at third and didn't make much of an impression. They committed fifty-three errors between them. Both, better known as utility infielders, were forced into regular duty because the team lacked depth.

The top outfielder of the team, "Ginger" Beaumont, is the answer to one of the better baseball trivia questions. Beaumont was the first batter in the first World Series game for Pittsburgh in 1903. He was a key part of the Pirates' attack for the 1901–3 pennant winners. Usually a leadoff man, he batted second or third for the Doves simply because he had lost a step on the bases.

Another Giants castoff, George Browne, played right field as though he was in a fog in 1908. He hit an anemic .228, almost a hundred points under his production with the 1904–5 Giants. Johnny Bates and Joe Kelley were the remaining outfielders. Bates was a journeyman player and filled in adequately, hitting .259. Kelley hit .258 in his last year as a player and manager.

The year 1908 was a difficult one for Kelley, who had tasted glory with the Orioles of the 1890s. All but one of Boston's regulars had seen World Series action with other teams. Owner George Dovey's emphasis on experience and veteran ball players who had played on winners earlier in the decade didn't take. Instead the pressures of losing got the best of this group of players, most of whom had seen better days. The trade with the Giants was a disaster. It turned a year of optimism into one of failure and frustration for a team that finished in the first division only once during the first decade of the Dead Ball Era.

BROOKLYN SUPERBAS (DODGERS)
7th / 53–101 .344
Ballpark: Washington Park
Hall of Famers: none
Owner: Charles W. Ebbets Sr.
Manager: Patsy Donovan (Career — 11 yrs. 684–879 .438; no postseason)

If you write a history of this storied franchise, there is a strong temptation to refer to the first decade of the Dead Ball Era as the dark ages for Brooklyn. It was downhill all the way for Brooklyn after winning the National League flag in 1900. The 1908 version of the Superbas enjoyed the distinction of hitting .213, one of the lowest team batting averages in big league history. Poor hitting offset an above average defense, and as a result, Brooklyn pitchers came within one loss of having four twenty-game losers on the staff.

The fortunate soul who escaped that collar was Nap Rucker, whose 17–19 mark, six shutouts, and one no-hitter made him the bright spot in an otherwise dismal staff. Rucker spent ten years in the big leagues and an entire career with Brooklyn, including a two-inning stint in the 1916 World Series. While his numbers fell well short of constituting a Hall of Fame career, many of his contemporaries maintain that he was one of the best pitchers of his time. His absence from the Hall was a result of being with poor teams, not a function of lacking talent.[34] Evidence of his ability lies in the fact that during his career, he never won fewer than thirteen games in any season with poor ball clubs.

While few argued Rucker was not ace of the staff, in reality he had little competition. His mates, "Kaiser" Wilhelm (16–22), Harry McIntire (11–20), and the hapless Jim Pastorius (4–20), lost a total of sixty-two of the team's 101 losses. All could be generously considered journeymen. McIntire pitched for the Cubs in the 1910 series and lost a game in relief. Wilhelm was 57–108 in his nine-year career and managed the Phillies for two years, putting seventh- and eighth-place finishes on his record. The Kaiser was also an umpire in the Federal League in 1915. Pastorius was plagued with terrible luck; he lost fourteen consecutive games in 1908, went on to win one game in 1909, and then retired.

If Brooklyn's pitchers were setting records for futility, their battery mates were in a class by themselves as well. Bill Bergen was the starter. An outstanding defensive catcher, Bergen enjoys the dubious distinction of having the lowest lifetime batting average (.170) among all major leaguers with at least ten years' experience. Bergen hit .175 in 1908 but led National League catchers in fielding percentage. He played in only ninety-nine games due to injury and the rigors of the job. Replacements Lew Ritter, Joe Dunn, and Alex Farmer all failed to hit .200, and Ritter and Farmer had short and undistinguished major league careers. Ritter was Bergen's primary backup for nine years and was one of the few big leaguers born in Great Britain.

If Rucker was the bright spot on the pitching staff, slugger Tim Jordan easily eclipsed his mates at bat. His .247 average was the best on the team, and he was the National League home run champion with twelve. Jordan won two home run crowns in a short seven-year career. He was plagued by bad knees, which cut into his effectiveness and ultimately shortened his playing career.

None of the other infielders hit above .220. Third baseman Tommy Sheehan was a good bunter and 1908 was his first year as a regular and the last of his four-year big league career. Harry Pattee and Phil Lewis held down second and short; as with Sheehan, the 1908 season was their last year in the majors. For Pattee it was his only year. John Hummell and Whitey Alperman rounded out the infielders. Both saw significant action as reserves. Alperman broke his ankle and was unavailable for half the season. Hummell was also an outfield reserve, playing in 154 games in a utility role that saw him play all infield positions but third base. His forty-one RBI was second on the team, behind Jordan.

Good field, no hit was an apt description of the Brooklyn outfield. Slugger Harry Lumley won a home run crown in 1904 but managed only four homers and a meager .216 batting average while battling injuries in 1908. Al Burch and Billy Maloney rounded out the lineup. Neither distinguished himself on a team that struggled for most of the year to stay out of last place.

The *Reach Guide* called Brooklyn the greatest disappointment of the season. Looking at the lineup, one wonders about the source of the optimism that would have resulted in disappointment. Perhaps it was the pitching that gave so much hope, but not even immortals can win with an offense that hits .213 and scores 2.4 runs per game. Brooklyn was never in the race and was pounded to the tune of 4–18 by the Cubs, 6–16 by the Giants, and 9–13 by Pittsburgh. The only team Brooklyn got the better of was the Cardinals.

ST. LOUIS CARDINALS
8th / 49–105 .318
Ballpark: National League Park (Robison Field)
Hall of Famers: none
Owner: Matthew Stanley Robison
Manager: John McCloskey (Career — 5 yrs. 190–417 .313; no postseason)

The *Reach* and *Spalding's* guides had a charming way of mincing words when describing a bad team. The word is *experimental.* Dealing with a variety of lineups out of necessity due to injury and poor performance, the Cards' experiment managed to score 371 runs — six fewer than Brooklyn; they committed 348 errors — 111 more than Brooklyn — and had a team-earned run average of 2.47, good enough for seventh place. The Cardinals would remain mired in the second division for most of the Dead Ball Era and wouldn't taste the glory of a pennant until 1926.

The strength of the Cardinals, if there was one, centered on the strong right arm of Arthur "Bugs" Raymond. Raymond's weakness for booze was already legendary, and between hangovers he parlayed his spitball into a 15–25 record. Raymond threw five shutouts during the year and without him, St. Louis would have redefined the word *awful.* Raymond was traded to the Giants in December 1908, a move that brought Roger Bresnahan to the Cardinals as a player-manager and gave John McGraw another rehabilitation project. Despite McGraw's therapy, Raymond drank himself into a short career and an early grave.

The only other St. Louis pitcher to win more than ten games was

Johnny Lush, whose name stood in ironic complement to Raymond. His 11–18 mark was as good a job of pitching as you would see in the league. He threw a no-hitter for the Phillies in 1906 and an officially unrecognized one against Brooklyn in 1908 in a rain-shortened six-inning contest. Lush never toiled for a winning team in his seven-year stint in the big leagues.

No other Cardinals pitcher won more than five games. Fred Beebe and Art Fromme posted 5–13 marks, Ed Karger was 4–9, while "Slim" Sallee and Irv Higginbotham shared 3–8 records. Of this group, only Sallee had a long career. His rookie year was 1908, and Slim would toil on the mound for another thirteen seasons. He pitched for the pennant-winning Giants in 1917 and the World Champion Reds in 1919.

Unlike Brooklyn, the Cardinals had some quality players who would play key roles with future pennant winners in other cities. Third baseman Bobby Byrne hit a pathetic .191 and led the league in errors at the hot corner. Byrne would be traded to Pittsburgh in 1909 and would become an important part of that great Pittsburgh World Champion team. Power-hitting "Big Ed" Konetchy played most of his fifteen years in St. Louis and hit .248 in 1908. In the twilight of his career, Konetchy played first for Brooklyn's pennant winner in 1920. The other quality player was Red Murray, who led the Cards in hitting with a .282 average, seven homers, and sixty-two RBI. Murray went to New York in the Bresnahan trade and became a key part of McGraw's pennant winners in 1911–12 and 1912–13.

Under other circumstances Byrne, Konetchy, Murray, and even Raymond could have formed the nucleus for a contender. But St. Louis was caught in a dreadful cycle. As quality players came up, weaknesses emerged. As a result, good players were traded in hopes of plugging weaknesses. This cycle was the Cardinals' way for most of the Dead Ball Era.

Second baseman Billy Gilbert (.214) and shortstop Patsy O'Rourke (.195) rounded out the Cardinals' infield. Neither played more than ninety games. Chappy Charles and Champ Osteen saw significant action as utility players. O'Rourke's career lasted one year. Besides his poor hitting, he also committed forty-one errors in fifty-three games, etching an .860 fielding percentage into the record book.

In the outfield Albert Shaw and Joe Delahanty were better than could be expected. Shaw was a speedy leadoff man with a good bat but was shaky in the field. Delahanty was yet another of the five Delahanty brothers to play in the majors. He hit .255 and played for only one more year. Shad Barry filled in as a sub until he was sold to New York in July.

Catching was handled primarily by Bill Ludwig, Art Hoelskoetter, and Jack Bliss. This trio had combined major league service of ten years and were below par at bat and in the field. Catching was a Cardinals weakness, a fatal flaw in an era when a premium was placed upon a catcher's ability to handle pitchers and to play strong defense against the bunt and stolen base.

The Cardinals were 13–52 against the Cubs, Giants, and Pirates. Like Brooklyn, they were never in contention. The Bresnahan trade would eventually bring a first division finish. But the glory years for this storied franchise were still long way off. When the pennant finally flew for the Cardinals in 1926, it marked the first time a National League flag had flown over St. Louis and finally allowed the faithful to lay to rest the failures of the past.

4 The Men in Blue The Umpires of 1908

Though few in number, the umpires of 1908 had a profound impact on the game of baseball. Like pioneers in other professions, these arbiters helped establish the traditions, rules, and procedures under which participants in the game function today. Also like some pioneers, they caught arrows, in the form of criticism and outright aggression from fans, players, coaches, managers, owners, and sportswriters — and, of course, they were not perfect. But they were strong men, even those who weren't successful, because they had to stand up to a great deal of criticism, both justified and unjustified.

Their contribution to the game is fact, but the passage of time has hidden their accomplishments. Not the least of these was the ability to oversee a complex game featuring the bunt, stolen base, and hit and run as common offensive strategy. This talent, exercised both alone and with a partner, required judgment, knowledge of the game, and mental and physical courage.

The umpires of 1908 were among those who had introduced the use of hand signals to communicate calls to a partner, the players, the bench, and the fans. Umpire signals had been in practice prior to the 1908 season, and their use was becoming standard. The *Reach* and *Spalding's* guidebooks called the signals the umpire's semaphore system. Signaling strike, safe, and out calls was an important means of adding to enjoyment of the game, noted *Spalding's Guide*. The signal system had been "invaluable assistance" to the umpires in "making their decisions understood when the size of the crowd is such that it is impossible to make the human voice carry distinctly to all parts of the field."[1] Many of the signals used in the early twentieth century are still in use today.

Besides signals, these umpires also introduced use of safety equipment and pioneered many of the mechanics used by present-day umpires behind the plate and on the bases. They established the traditions governing ejections and other matters covering the often uneasy relationship umpires had with players and managers. By 1908, umpire authority was getting more support from the game's leadership. Respect for the signal callers was growing to the point where "even addressing an umpire by anything other than Mr. (last name) was grounds for ejection or fine."[2]

During the 1908 season, seventeen men umpired over twelve hundred games, including 135 doubleheaders (see appendixes D and E for umpiring statistics). Of these seventeen individuals, three — Bill Klem, Tom Connolly, and Billy Evans — have received baseball's ultimate honor, election to the Hall of Fame. As earlier noted, more than half of the games played in 1908 were contests officiated by one umpire, and this would be a source of controversy and debate during the year. Indeed, as also noted, 1908 was the last year during which games overseen by single umpires were in the majority. While modern fans accustomed to multiple-umpire crews may express surprise at this, adopting a double-umpire system was debated throughout the season.

Oddly, umpires themselves were not of one voice when it came to the issue of umpire staffing. One of the better known voices in favor of multiple umpires was Klem himself. Having done his share of one-man games, he noted that a maturing game demanded quality officiating: "Any game that attracts huge crowds that fill baseball's coffers deserves four umpires to assume the fans just that little extra. Three umpires can handle a game very nicely, of course. Two can be used with safety in an emergency. But I insist that no one man can umpire a baseball game."[3]

Among the umpires of the era who preferred to work alone, Tommy Connolly of the American League and the misanthropic Hank O'Day in the National stand as examples of the breed, each conceding nothing on the question of whether two umpires were better than one.

O'Day simply did not like a two-man system. You could argue he did not like people all that much either, but O'Day believed it was more trouble working with another man: "in many cases he has not only had to give his own decisions, but sometimes his mate's as well."[4] Ironically, it was O'Day who made the controversial call in the Merkle game, after his partner, Bob Emslie, admitted he had not seen the play. Because Emslie was on the bases, it was initially his call.

American League umpires Jack Sheridan and Silk O'Loughlin were strong proponents of the two-man system. *Sporting Life* weighed in with an opinion recognizing that the days of one-man umpiring were numbered, "With batting cut down to a minimum, the slightest error by an umpire often deprives a team of victory. There is really too much for one man to watch in a ball game."[5] Two-man crews were already standard for World Series play by 1908. As we shall see, nearly all of the decisive games of the 1908 pennant races were overseen by two umpires. The game was outgrowing the ability of a single umpire to do the job. Concerns about the credibility of the game contributed to the movement toward adding more umpires to league staffs.

The umpires of 1908 faced other challenges, the rigor of travel schedules and living on the road. Teams on the road stayed in one town three to four days and then moved on. As in many areas governing the life of umpires and baseball, there was a difference between the leagues regarding umpire travel. In the American League, umpires would generally remain in a single town, or area such as between Philadelphia and Washington or New York and Boston, for a longer period of time. Tracing the travels of Billy Evans of the American League, he would stay in the same city for at least two series before moving on to a different city. National League umpires tended to officiate a series in one city and then move on, often following one of the teams that had played in the previous series. In other words, in the senior circuit, umpires did not get any special travel breaks.

As could be inferred from how each league handled rainouts, scheduling of doubleheaders was a haphazard affair. The 1908 season had several instances of umpires working back to back doubleheaders alone. Generally the umpires would work a couple of weeks alone and then double up with a partner. Also, new umpires were often paired with veterans to give them game experience during the late season.

While some umpires might have had it better in terms of not having to pack their bags as often, they were away from the their homes for extended periods during the season. Players were assured of being home for at least half the year, but the same could not be said for the umpires.

Life on the road was lonely. It could be very lonely if your calls were not supported by league leadership. Both league presidents supported their umpires, but there were differences in the details of how the executives handled matters.

American League President Ban Johnson was a strong supporter of umpires and was not shy about handing out suspensions to those players and managers who were overly abusive of the men in blue. As we have seen, Johnson was a leader in the fight against rowdyism, and his support of umpires was a large part of that campaign. John McGraw hated Johnson, mainly because Johnson did not like McGraw's umpire baiting. McGraw's ouster from the American League was a source of animosity between the two. But it was a move McGraw did not fight because he had the Giants job. The whole affair gave McGraw an excuse to maintain a high level of hostility against the junior circuit.

Johnson was, in the words of today, proactive about rules interpretations. His support of umpires was total, as long as they were correct. If they weren't correct, Johnson was prone to issuing clarifications of rules to avoid conflicts in the future. A noted example of this policy occurred in the April 29, 1908, game between the Tigers and White Sox. The play in question involved an attempted squeeze play and the question of whether the Detroit pitcher balked or the Tigers catcher interfered with the batter. The play centered on the issue of whether the pitcher made a pitch to the batter or a throw to play on the runner. No formal protest was lodged because the White Sox won the game. Fortunately, the umpire's decision did not change the outcome of the pennant race.

Umpire Silk O'Loughlin ruled that pitcher Ed Siever and catcher Freddie Payne had acted within the rules because Siever had not begun his windup before making a play on a base runner breaking for the plate. The play was described thus: "When (Patsy) Dougherty started to steal home in the third inning Siever was standing on the rubber ready to deliver the ball to the plate, and as soon as Pat started in Payne ran in front of (George) Davis and caught the ball, preventing George from taking a swing at it."[6]

Sox manager Fielder Jones contended that O'Loughlin's ruling would negate the use of the suicide squeeze play by allowing the pitcher to balk and a catcher to interfere with the hitter. He claimed that Payne committed catcher's interference by catching the pitch before the Sox hitter was able to swing at the ball. Johnson became aware of the play because of the very public complaining of Jones. After studying the play and talking to witnesses, Johnson overruled O'Loughlin. Johnson stated that a pitcher must step off the rubber before attempting to throw out a runner attempting to steal home. If the pitcher remained on the rubber and threw, the ball was a pitch with the batter having the right to swing at the pitch before the catcher could make a play. To make the play properly, the pitcher must step backward off the rubber and throw home or otherwise make the play.[7] This ruling did not have to be made because there was no protest. It was Johnson's response to questions about the ruling on the play in question, and his recognition of the impact it could have on play due to the importance of squeeze plays during the Dead Ball Era.

Johnson's action contrasted sharply with the blanket policy of National League head Harry Pulliam. Pulliam, like his counterpart Johnson, was an avowed opponent of rowdyism. During the 1908 season he issued periodic statements as to how behavior in the league was improving. When encountering protests, Pulliam's stock response was to support the umpires, no matter what and despite evidence to the contrary, without any clarification. His attitude was tersely stated: "When I believe they are right they shall have my hearty support."[8]

Pulliam's policy cost him dearly late in the 1908 season when he did not look beyond support of an umpire on a critical play involving Pittsburgh and Chicago on September 4. In a carbon copy of the more famous Merkle play just a few weeks later, the Pirates rookie Warren "Doc" Gill failed to touch second when the game-winning run was scored against the Cubs. The Cubs protested that the run should not have counted, even though umpire Hank O'Day declared the game over with Pittsburgh the victor. Chicago cited supporting witnesses and stated that the run could not score if the third out of an inning was a force. Pulliam stated his support of the umpire's original decision, ignoring the eyewitness evidence.

While he could and should have been expected to uphold O'Day's decision, Pulliam lost a golden opportunity to issue a clarification of the rule in the Gill play — the same rule O'Day would enforce against Merkle and the Giants just a couple of weeks later. Had Pulliam been as proactive as Johnson about rules interpretations, the Merkle play might not have occurred. Pulliam cannot take all the blame for what happened, but he must shoulder a large share of it. Clarifying the rule stating that no run can score during a play when the third out of an inning is made by a force-out would have saved everyone a lot of grief.

All baseball seasons include controversy over umpires and their judgments. Contemporary journalists' accounts of Dead Ball Era games are often suspect due to partisanship and a lack of the modern tools of film and video tape. As a result it is difficult to determine the competence of umpires and how they may have affected the outcomes of games. To a great degree we have to recognize their devotion to the game and give the umpires the benefit of the doubt, assuming that they did the best they could. Baseball and the umpires themselves could ask for nothing less.

The following introduction to the umpires of 1908 includes their years of service in their respective leagues and, where applicable, dates of induction to the Hall of Fame.

AMERICAN LEAGUE UMPIRES

BILLY EVANS (1906–27) / Hall of Fame 1973
Called "Big Boy Blue" or "The Boy Umpire" as terms of endearment, Evans began his major league career at the age of twenty-two. He quit college in 1903 to combine sportswriting with umpiring to support his family, and he joined the American League in 1906. Known as a diplomat among the men in blue, he urged his colleagues to shun confrontation whenever possible. He is credited with developing the technique of walking away from close plays after making a call to give everyone a chance to cool off. He tried to avoid ejections by appealing to players' pride and their obligation to the fans. When players such as Cobb and Ruth grew combative, Evans told them: "Fifty thousand people in the stands, every one out here to see you, not a single one interested in who is umpiring, yet you are going to force me to put you out of the game much against my better judgment, but the game must go on and that seems to be the only solution."[9]

But Evans had his limits, proving that even the most tactful of diplomats must sometimes resort to warfare. He and Ty Cobb once settled differences with a fight under the stands in 1921. Evans did not win the fight; Cobb had to be pulled off the beaten umpire.[10]

Evans's *Umpiring from the Inside* stands as a classic handbook for umpires at any level. He worked as a front office executive for Cleveland, Detroit, and Boston after he retired from umpiring. His reputation for fairness and integrity set an example for the profession, and his advice of "run your ball game, but don't overrun it," is a motto all umpires can live by today. [11]

TOM CONNOLLY (NL 1898–1900; AL 1901–31) / Hall of Fame 1953

English immigrant Tom Connolly and Bill Klem share the honor of being the first umpires inducted into the Baseball Hall of Fame. Connolly's was a career of firsts, umpiring the first American League game in 1901, serving with Hank O'Day in the first World Series, and umpiring inaugural games at Comiskey, Shibe, and Fenway Parks and Yankee Stadium.

During his thirty-year career, Connolly had a reputation of expert knowledge of the rules and of not hesitating to eject players to keep order on the field. He also preferred to work alone. He usually led American League umps in contests officiated alone, before the days of the two-man standard. He worked alone during the regular season through 1907.

When he retired at the age of sixty, Connolly became umpire-in-chief of the American League and remained in that capacity until 1953. His career included a stint on the rules committee during the last years of his life; he died in 1961. It is said that many of Connolly's on-field calls are now rules, and that they are as much part of the game as hot dogs, peanuts, Cracker Jack, and the national anthem.

FRANK "SILK" O'LOUGHLIN (1902–18)

O'Loughlin holds an interesting record: he was behind the plate for seven no-hitters, a feat no other umpire has come close to equaling. He also was the first umpire to eject the fiery Ty Cobb from a game. On May 2, 1908, Cobb objected to O'Loughlin calling him out as the Georgia Peach tried to stretch a triple into a home run against the White Sox.

O'Loughlin owned a distinctive speaking voice, with which he loudly announced called strikes for all to hear. The press of the day constantly referred to his call, "Strike Tuh!" But it was his long curly hair that gave him his nickname. O'Loughlin is known for one of the better baseball quotations in reply to an upset batter: "I have never missed one in my life and it's too late to start now. The Pope for religion, O'Loughlin for baseball. Both infallible."[12]

Unfortunately, O'Loughlin was all too mortal. His voice was stilled in December 1918, when he fell victim to the post–World War I influenza epidemic. He was at the height of his career and baseball was left the poorer with the loss of one of its most colorful participants and skilled umpires.

JOHN SHERIDAN (NL 1892–93, 1896–97; AL 1901–14)

Big Jack Sheridan is one of the few umpires to have served in both the American and National leagues. It was said that a game called by Sheridan would be marked by consistency and fairness, and contemporaries considered him a model for young umpires. Sheridan was senior umpire for the American League during his tenure. During the 1908 season, he was noticed asking hotels in big league cities for used register books. The huge leather-bound volumes became makeshift chest protectors for the inventive Sheridan. He held the books under his coat. As a result of this protection, Sheridan was able to assume a crouch behind the catcher in order to get a closer look at pitches. A National League colleague, Cy Rigler, also used this mode of protection.[13]

Most of his other colleagues used the external, or balloon or raft, protector until manufacturers came up with an internal one. Ironically, Sheridan's efforts did not lead to American League adoption of the internal protector. Junior circuit umpires kept using the external protector long after National League arbiters adopted the internal vest.

In Evans's book, two pieces of advice from Sheridan are cited. They are good advice for any umpire: "Don't see or hear the things that you shouldn't see or hear. Always hear or see the things that you should," and "Keep your eye on the ball and you will keep out of trouble."[14] In the late season Sheridan would often be paired with new umpires so that they could gain from his experience.

JOHN EGAN (1901, 1907–14)

Nicknamed "Rip," Egan began his baseball career as a pitcher in the International League, and after retiring as an umpire, he managed in the minor leagues. Known for his love of the game, Egan was a fine umpire who often told friends that his greatest thrills in the game occurred while umpiring and witnessing the feats of the stars of the day. In 1908 he was the target of extreme criticism in the Cleveland press for a controversial call at first base in a key late-season game between Cleveland and St. Louis. Despite demands for his dismissal, which included signed petitions from fans, Egan remained with the American League for another six years and was highly regarded.

TIM HURST (NL 1891–98, 1900, 1903–4; AL 1905–9)

Many early umpires were known as much as fighters as they were for their ability to call games. Timothy Hurst would lead any list of arbiter/fighters. Hurst was also one of the most colorful storytellers of the time. He enjoys the dubious distinction of having been fired by both major leagues as a result of on-field incidents. Because of his pugnacious nature, Hurst rarely worked alone in 1908.

One story Hurst was reportedly fond of telling involved the Baltimore Orioles of the 1890s, a team noted for bad behavior.

[Hurst was] working alone behind the plate in Baltimore, the visitors had a runner on first who started to steal. As the runner left the bag, he spiked first baseman Dan McGann who retaliated by tripping him. Undaunted, the runner recovered, dashed for second, and tried to spike shortstop Hughie Jennings. Meanwhile, the batter hit the catcher, Wilbert Robinson, on the hand with his bat in an effort to prevent the throw. Robinson tramped on Hurst's toes with his spikes and shoved his glove into Tim's face so he couldn't see the play. When Hurst was asked what decision he made, he said: "Well, I punched Robbie in the ribs, called it a foul, and sent the runner back to first."[15]

Such incidents gave Hurst a well-earned reputation of resorting to fists or other physical means rather than reason. He was dismissed by the National League in 1898 for throwing a beer stein at a fan who had thrown the container at Hurst. Hurst's problem was that he hit the wrong spectator.

His umpiring career came to an abrupt end in August 1909 at the hands of American League President Ban Johnson. During an argument with Athletics second baseman Eddie Collins, Hurst spat in the future Hall of Famer's face. Johnson, a staunch supporter of the men in blue, had no choice but to fire him. Reportedly, Hurst was dismissed when he refused to apologize for his behavior because of his dislike for college players, such as Collins.[16]

Hurst went on to referee professional boxing and became events manager at Madison Square Garden in New York City. Despite his decidedly aggressive nature and bad end, Hurst enjoyed umpiring and is known for a classic quote that sums up his attitude toward the profession: "You can't beat the hours."[17]

As with many quotations, Hurst's statement reportedly came in response to a lengthy, self-pitying soliloquy by Silk O'Loughlin:

> An umpire's life is worse than a murderer's. He is an Ishmaelite, an outcast, a thing despised, loathed and hated. He must hide from his fellow men; he dares not talk to anyone; he has no friends; he can not speak to the players; he must hide in obscure hotels; conceal his identity; endure abuse, insult, and even assault. Who there that is his friend — that will stand by him when thousands are shouting 'Thief!' and 'Robber!' and thirsting for his blood? Who, I say? Why the worst criminal in the world gets more consideration and kindness; the umpire, hated, abused, insulted, and often hunted, stands alone with twenty thousand people shouting every insult, taunt, and vilification known at him. From three o'clock in the afternoon until five he must —

At that point Hurst interrupted with his observation about the working hours.[18]

JOHN KERIN (1908–10)

Kerin's brief career as an umpire was marked chiefly by his being the victim of a sucker punch at the hands of an irate White Sox fan at the end of a game late in the 1908 season. In 1908, he worked ten games during which he paired up with O'Loughlin, Sheridan, and, in the game after which he was assaulted, Connolly.

JOHN WARNER (1908)

Warner had a brief career solely as a substitute umpire. Warner called his only game in 1908 with Hurst on October 3 in New York. Warner was a reserve catcher with the Washington Nationals but had been idled by a knee injury. In the box score Warner's name is listed first, a convention used by *Sporting Life* to indicate the plate umpire. If so, he was behind the plate against his teammates in this contest.[19] While playing in the National League, Warner served as a substitute umpire during games in 1896, 1897, 1901, and 1903.

NATIONAL LEAGUE UMPIRES

BILL KLEM (1905–41) / Hall of Fame 1953

One of the most famous of all umpires in 1908, Bill Klem was in the fourth year of a thirty-seven-year career as a National League arbiter, a career during which he which witnessed the development of baseball into the national pastime. With a reputation as a superior judge of the strike zone, Klem spent the bulk of his career exclusively behind the plate, the result of his seniority. During the 1908 season he worked a number of one-man games, sharing plate and base duties with his partners when assigned to two-man duty. Because of his work behind the plate, Klem is credited with two innovations: use of the inside chest protector and working from the slot. The early inside protector was nothing more than a catcher's chest protector with shoulder pads added.[20] With this protection, the umpire could work closer to the catcher. By positioning himself in the slot, or behind the catcher in the space between the batter and catcher, the plate umpire could get a better look at pitches. Because of Klem's status within the National League, the inside protector was adopted long before American League umpires discarded the outside or balloon protector.

Among those credited with using signals to signify strikes and outs, Klem made another major contribution to the profession with the force of his personality. He was known for his honesty and integrity, and his ability to control a game. Klem also waged an often lonely campaign to raise the working and economic conditions of his colleagues.

During his career Klem umpired in eighteen World Series and officiated many important games, including the deciding 1908 Cubs-Giants contest. He served as chief of National League umpires from his retirement in 1941 until his death ten years later. The story of how he came to his decision to retire provides an interesting measure of the man and umpire.

Most sources say Klem's umpiring career ended in 1940, but it didn't. He described the last time he wore the blue in his 1951 *Collier's Magazine* interview just months before his death.

In 1941, I worked a few games. Toward the season's end, St. Louis and Brooklyn were in a crucial series and I joined a three man umpiring team as a fourth man. I was working at second base and I played a little deep as an experiment. I was out of position and I knew it. And I was uncomfortable.

A St. Louis man attempted to steal second. Billy Herman took the throw and put the ball on the runner. I called him out. The runner jumped up and protested, 'He didn't touch me. He never tagged me,' he yelled. I walked away from the beefing ballplayer, saying to myself, 'I am almost certain Herman tagged him.' Then it came to me and I almost wept. For the first time in my career I only 'thought' a man was tagged."[21]

HANK O'DAY (1888–94, 1895–1911, 1913, 1915–26)

If medals were awarded for entries in the most categories in the Baseball Encyclopedia, Hank O'Day would win hands down. From 1884 until 1926, O'Day was a major league player, umpire, and/or manager. As a batter, he hit .190 and one homer. On the mound, he chalked up a 70–110 record, including one twenty-win season and three of twenty losses. As a manager he led the Cincinnati Reds and the Chicago Cubs to fourth-place finishes in 1912 and 1914 with an ordinary 153–154 record.

While his record as a player and manager is average, O'Day was anything but average when it came to umpiring. That he is not in the Hall of Fame is an oversight. This is partly a function of the fact that he never married; baseball was his love, and he had no family to lobby for him. Conspiracy buffs may believe the oversight to be a measure of revenge by New York sportswriters for O'Day's the decision in the infamous Merkle game, but more likely it is because O'Day was not known as a particularly friendly person.

He began umpiring while pitching for the National League Washington Statesmen during the 1880s. He umpired games he wasn't pitching and, as accounts of the day put it, became addicted to umpiring.[22] During his career in blue, O'Day umpired ten World Series, second to Klem's mark. O'Day and his close friend Bob Emslie were second only to Klem in career longevity as well.

O'Day was a quiet, private man who let his actions stand for themselves. His personality led many to believe he was a misanthrope as a result of the pressures of umpiring. This is understandable, in that O'Day preferred to work alone. He was respected as a competent, honest umpire who had a thorough knowledge of the rules. It was this knowledge of the rules and their application that led him to call Fred

Merkle out for not touching second base. Unfortunately, there is no record of O'Day's thinking on that fateful day, other than a letter he wrote to National League offices explaining his decision, in which he made no reference to any previous incidents or rulings.[23] Following his retirement as a field umpire, O'Day served as an umpire scout for the big leagues.

National League President John Heydler praised O'Day with these words: "He is a wonderful character and a wonderful umpire, doubtless the best the game has known on balls and strikes. He always was a stickler for the rules. He was an umpire and nothing else. He spent his winters getting ready for the summer work of his life. He was always in shape. He did not want to quit when he was retired from active service."[24]

BOB EMSLIE (1891–1924)

O'Day's closest associate on and off the field was Bob Emslie, who matched O'Day's longevity record as an umpire. Like O'Day, the Canadian-born Emslie was a pitcher. In 1884 for the American Association Baltimore Orioles, he notched a gaudy 32–17 record. A bad arm ended his playing days.

Little has been written about Emslie as an umpire, except that he was on the bases with O'Day during the Merkle game. He had to be tough, umpiring in the rowdy National League in the 1890s, and he had numerous close calls and scrapes with fans.

Giants manager John McGraw called him "Blind Bob" because of his role in the Merkle game. Emslie was base umpire and the force-out should have been his call. When he admitted that he had not seen the play, O'Day made the call. If a popular story is true, Emslie may have got the last word on McGraw's opinion of his eyesight. Reportedly, Emslie went to a Giants practice with a rifle, placed a dime on the pitcher's mound, went to home plate, shot at, and hit the dime. The coin went spinning, and McGraw reportedly never challenged Emslie's eyesight again.[25]

JAMES JOHNSTONE (AL 1902 ; NL 1903–12)

James Johnstone's umpiring career was short, but he enjoyed the distinction of umpiring three different major leagues. His production was low in 1908 due to appendicitis. His first game was in late May. Johnstone was limited to working with a partner until he recovered fully.

His two claims to fame both involve McGraw's Giants and Chance's Cubs. In 1906 his calls angered the Giants so much during one game that the club barred him from the ballpark for a game the next day. His partner that day was Emslie, who refused to work without Johnstone. Emslie refused to start the game and forfeited the contest to the Cubs. That game was one of Chicago's record 116 wins.[26] Johnstone and Klem called the 1908 Cubs-Giants "play-off" tiebreaker game, and Johnstone was first to report to league offices the attempt to bribe them before the game. He wrapped up career in the big leagues serving as an umpire in the Federal League in 1915.

CHARLES "CY" RIGLER (1905–22, 1924–35)

Cy Rigler was a big man and a quality umpire. He umpired ten World Series and was among those chosen to officiate at the first All-Star game. Valued as an instructor of young umpires, he often worked with younger colleagues. On retirement, he was appointed the first National League chief of umpires.

He is credited by some sources as the originator, during a brief stint in the minor leagues, of the right arm raised to signify a strike. By the time he reached the majors, the strike sign and other signals were already common practice.

JOHN E. RUDDERHAM (1908)

John Rudderham did not finish the 1908 season. In Fleming's *Unforgettable Season*, Rudderham is seen as the target of a steady stream of criticism from players and sportswriters alike. The rookie umpire was often paired with veterans and worked the fewest one-man games of any umpire in 1908. Rudderham was frequently involved in controversy, and Brooklyn owner Charles Ebbets called for his dismissal at midseason. Rudderham did not umpire in the majors after August 1908; he was dismissed in early September by National League President Harry Pulliam without comment from either Pulliam or sportswriters.

CLARENCE B. "BRICK" OWENS (NL 1908, 1912–13; AL 1916–37)

A rookie umpire in 1908 who saw limited late-season duty, Owens possesses a classic nickname that speaks of his toughness and perhaps his sense of humor. He was dubbed "Brick" after irate minor league fans hit him in the head with a thrown brick.

Owens was a capable signal caller who would not take a whole lot of grief. One of his ejections is prominent in baseball history. In 1917 he tossed Red Sox lefty Babe Ruth after the Bambino angrily protested four consecutive called balls and rushed the combative Owens. According to eyewitness accounts, Ruth swung at and hit Owens. Reports vary only on the landing place of the punch. But it was the first assault on an American League umpire during a game. Ruth was fined one hundred dollars and suspended for ten days.[27] Following the ejection, Ernie Shore entered the game, the base runner was thrown out trying to steal, and Shore retired the next twenty-six hitters for a perfect game.

CHARLES LANIGAN (1908)

Charles Lanigan had a brief and practically anonymous career. He umpired four games that had no bearing on the National League race. The Philadelphia at Brooklyn series was the entire body of Lanigan's major league umpiring career.

AFTERWORD: UMPIRING IN 1908

Of all the facets of baseball history that have been studied over the years, an overlooked area has been umpires and umpiring. It is a field of study where a great deal can be learned and one where much work remains to be done. The study of umpires and umpiring reveals a lot about the state of the game. The evolution of baseball as the national pastime can be directly traced by examining the attention paid to the quality of umpiring, both on the field and in training.

By 1908 it was clear that the days of single umpires were numbered. Two umpires had been assigned to World Series games since 1905. In 1905 through 1907, one umpire from each league officiated the games. The 1908 World Series was the first in which two umpires from each league were appointed to officiate games in crews of two.

As we have seen, 1908 witnessed an almost even split between one-man and two-man games in the American League. In the National the margin was strongly on the side of one-man games, mainly due to the illness of Johnstone. Of 619 games played in the American League, 319 or 51.5 percent were officiated by two umpires, while 300 were overseen by a single umpire. The National League put 628 games on the books and 371 or 59.1 percent were one-man games, while 257 were officiated by two umpires.

During the preseason of 1908, both leagues hired six umpires. In a perfect world this arrangement would result in an even split between one- and two-man games. With eight-team leagues, there would be a maximum of four game sites to staff. Thus with six umpires, two could be assigned to work alone at two game sites, and four could be assigned to the other two sites. Illness, injury, and other absences interrupted the otherwise perfect world. Johnstone, for instance, missed the first month of the National League season and worked only two games alone until early July. An illness in late July sidelined O'Day for two weeks. Over in the American League, the umpires stayed healthy and in service, except for Egan, who missed a week's action in late April after being struck by a foul tip. That injury confined him to bases for a few days after his return.

Umpire scheduling was handled by the respective league offices, American League in Chicago and National League in New York. How and why umpires were assigned is an interesting question, with no obvious answer. Umpire assignments are a sensitive issue in any league or organization. In most cases they are best handled on a random or availability basis, with the exception of playoffs and World Series play, where assignments are usually, or should be, granted by merit.

Contemporary accounts ignore the topic, but it appears from raw data obtained from study of 1908 box scores that umpires in both leagues were scheduled on criteria based on attendance, crowd and security concerns, importance of contests to the pennant race, competitive considerations between the two leagues, travel considerations, and in some cases, the experience and health of the umpire. It appears that attendance and security were prime criteria during the early and middle parts of the season, and in the case of late-season 1908, the close pennant races dictated two-man assignments for most games involving contenders from September onward.

While some umpires worked together a lot — Hurst/Evans fifty-six games and Sheridan/Egan fifty-three games in the American League, and Johnstone/Klem forty games in the National — it appears that two-man scheduling was done to ensure that all umpires worked with one another at least once during the season.

The assignment of umpires to one-man duty in 1908 reflects tacit recognition that the more people witnessing a game, the larger the concern over the quality of officiating. This position seems to be underscored by the fact that Chicago and St. Louis had the fewest one-man games and that these cities ranked first and second in overall attendance in the American League. That New York and Philadelphia ranked third and fourth in one-man games was more of a reflection of the importance of those cities to the American League in its competition with the National League for fans. Clearly Cleveland's and Detroit's rankings in this category reflected relatively poor attendance and absence of National League competition in these cities, rather than the on-field performance early in the season. The Naps and Tigers saw more two-man crews as the season wore on and it became clear both clubs were contending for the pennant.

In the National League, the relationship between attendance and officiating held as well, with New York and Chicago ranking 1–2 in the fewest one-man games and most two-man contests. Pittsburgh and Philadelphia were third and fourth in one-man games, and this ranking was reversed in games officiated by two umpires.

In the heat of the extremely close pennant races in both leagues, the attendance, public relations, and security criteria meshed with the use of two officials in games directly involving the contending teams. In the American League, 65.9 percent or 91 of 138 games among the Tigers, Naps, White Sox, and Browns were officiated by two umpires, compared to a league average of just over 51 percent. In the National League 82.4 percent or 56 of 68 games involving the Cubs, Giants, and Pirates were given two-man coverage. The National League average for two-man games was just under 41 percent. It must be noted that only a handful of games involving contenders from September onward were assigned single umpires.

During any baseball season, there will be ejections. While arguments and ejections often attract more attention than they deserve, there is still some interest in studying them, especially during the Dead Ball Era when intimidation of umpires was part of many teams' game plans.

Study of the subject is hampered by lack of data on ejections. Researchers must glean data from the *Reach* and *Spalding's* guides, newspapers, and other accounts. Contemporary accounts would note ejections only if they appeared to be significant to the outcome of the game. Such accounts, in the case of two-man umpire crews, would not mention the specific umpire who ordered the ejection. Examination of accounts from *Sporting Life* and the SABR database yielded the ejections data in appendixes F and G.

It is surprising that contemporary accounts come up with more ejections in the American League than in the reputedly rowdier National

League. To prove the futility of tracking ejections, in 1909 National League President John Heydler noted ninety-four ejections in his annual report on the 1908 campaign, compared to 112 during the 1907 season. My examination of the SABR database showed only ninety-nine total ejections in both leagues, with the American having a 51–48 lead in the category. Ejections were not always included in game accounts because writers would generally take no note of a player's or manager's ouster unless it had some influence or impact on the outcome of the contest.

The SABR database shows most ejections to have been the result of arguing ball-strike and tag plays on the bases. A number of ousters were also the result of players leaving their positions in the field to argue, a criterion supported by both leagues and strictly enforced in 1908. One constant between the Dead Ball Era and today's game is that arguing ball-strike calls or leaving your position in the field to charge an umpire would get you an early shower then as it does now.

5 **April** The Best Hopes of Fans

The eighth big league season of the modern era began amidst joy, hoopla, and cold, damp weather. After enduring sixty-nine weather-related postponements in 1907, owners were understandably concerned about foul weather. But in the days before domed stadia and teams in mild-weather southern and western cities, early-season baseball confined to the northeast quadrant of the United States was more often than not played under less than optimal conditions. The weather was a concern, but fans turned out in numbers because it was opening day, a ritual observance of the eternal optimism of the baseball fan facing a new season.

Opening day also marked a renewal of efforts to clean up the game and eliminate rowdyism. Boston Red Sox President John I. Taylor expressed deep concern over foul language used by players and urged American League President Ban Johnson to take action or at least condemn the practice.[1] Intentionally, and it must be added, ironically, the Cubs posted this sign in the dugouts of West Side Grounds: "Please Use No Profane Language."[2] In Chicago such restrictions lasted only as long as each bench was pleased with the umpires and their calls or until McGraw and his Giants came to town.

The 1908 season opened on April 14, 1908, in New York, Chicago, Boston, and Philadelphia in the American League, while the National

League started in Philadelphia, Cincinnati, and Brooklyn. The Pirates-Cardinals opener in St. Louis was postponed due to rain, and the game was played the next day. Wet weather erased all the rest of the major league schedule on April 15. That postponement was a blessing in disguise for Pittsburgh, which started the year without star shortstop Honus Wagner. Wagner's holdout continued through April 17, when to the relief of Barney Dreyfuss and Pittsburgh's faithful, the Dutchman inked a contract; he joined the team in Cincinnati on April 19.

The Giants opened the campaign with a 3–1 win over Philadelphia on the back of Christy Mathewson's four-hitter; the Cubs were also winners. Chicago's victory was a come-from-behind 6–5 win over Cincinnati. The Reds stormed to an early 5–0 lead, thanks to three Cub errors. But in a theme that would become common during the year, Three Finger Brown's clutch pitching and timely hitting by Johnny Evers and Johnny Kling won the day. On the next day, Pittsburgh defeated St. Louis, giving all three of the eventual National League contenders a successful opening day start.

The other National League opener was significant only in what occurred following the game. Boston defeated the Superbas 9–3, thanks to four Brooklyn errors. The game was played in a cold drizzle and witnessed by Henry Chadwick, editor of the *Spalding's Guide* and known among his contemporaries as the Father of Base Ball. The elderly Chadwick caught a chill at the game and died on April 21. His death was the first of many headline events during this controversial season.

Over in the American League, the eventual pennant contenders were locked in combat from the start. The Browns ruined Cleveland's opener with a 2–1 win over Naps ace Addie Joss, as surprise starter Barney Pelty got the win. It would be one of the few games Joss would lose until the dog days of summer, and he could blame only himself. In the tenth inning Tom Jones singled and took second on a wild pitch. Jimmy Williams's single drove him home for the game winner. Cleveland lost its second game of the season as well; 6–2 in ten innings thanks to an error by usually reliable outfielder Joe Birmingham. Had anyone had any way of knowing it at the time, those losses sealed the Naps' fate. The media and fans inevitably focus attention on late-season games as big games. Any manager or player, however, will tell you that games won or lost in April are just as important as those won or lost in October.

In Chicago, the Sox used a month's worth of hits and five Tigers errors to nail Detroit by an uncharacteristic 15–8 score. The poor showing in the opener was the beginning of a terrible start for the defending American League Champions, doubly so because all of the month's losses were to the White Sox, Naps, and Browns—all of the teams the Tigers had to beat. By month's end Detroit was in the cellar with a 3–9 mark and four and a half games out of the running. Tigers fans also found themselves hollering ungratefully for manager Hughie Jennings's head.

Detroit's poor start was a matter of not getting their game all together. When the pitching was on, the hitters failed. When defense failed, they were blown out. The Tigers lost three early-season games to Cleveland by 12–8, 9–2, and 11–5 scores. Symbolic of the Tigers' start was the 8–5 loss to the Browns on April 21. St. Louis committed four errors, giving Detroit a chance to win the game. In the ninth, Detroit loaded the bases with no one out, but a liner to Browns third baseman Hobe Ferris resulted in a game-ending unassisted double play. Despite the misfortune and bad luck, Jennings remained optimistic, telling writers and anyone else who would listen that his team would be there when the pitching jelled.

Detroit's month of frustration came to a head at a home game with the White Sox on the April 29. The White Sox won 6–3, as the Tigers left six runners on base against Doc White. This was the game referred to earlier, in which umpire Silk O'Loughlin allowed the Tigers' battery to bend the rules on a suicide squeeze attempt (see chapter 4). O'Loughlin failed to see pitcher Ed Siever throw the ball to the plate while on the rubber and ruled that catcher Freddie Payne's play on the ball was legal, when in fact the call should have been catcher's interference or a balk. The potential protest of O'Loughlin's call was rendered moot because of the Sox victory. In defense of O'Loughlin, who was the sole umpire, making the right call against Siever was almost impossible when behind the plate. In a two-man game, such a call would likely have been made by the base umpire.

While Detroit languished and the White Sox struggled at the .500 mark, Cleveland, St. Louis, and New York came out of the blocks fast. Cleveland's fast break was propelled by taking 5 of 6 from Detroit, behind timely hitting and the strong pitching of Addie Joss. Naps manager Napoleon Lajoie attempted to instill discipline on his team while it was hot. He banned card playing and the common practice of betting by team members. Lajoie asserted: "Gambling is detrimental to base-

TABLE 1. *American League Standings — April 30, 1908*

	W	L	Pct.	GB
New York	8	5	.615	—
Cleveland	8	5	.615	—
St. Louis	9	6	.600	—
Philadelphia	8	7	.533	1
Boston	7	7	.500	$1\frac{1}{2}$
Chicago	7	7	.500	$1\frac{1}{2}$
Washington	5	9	.357	$3\frac{1}{2}$
Detroit	3	9	.250	$4\frac{1}{2}$

ball. A player who draws to two pair at midnight is apt to hit the wind the next day, and if he has a bet down on a pony he is sure to make a costly error."[3]

St. Louis, boasting of the addition of Rube Waddell to work with Harry Howell, along with a robust hitting attack, won nine of their first fifteen games, including two out of three from the Tigers and Naps. The Browns split eight contests with the White Sox, with Waddell winning a one-hit shutout and a 2–1 win in St. Louis's home opener on April 24 against Chicago.

The surprise team was the Highlanders, who responded in equal measure to wins by the Naps and Browns. New York used tight pitching and strong defense to edge fellow eastern opponents, all of whom would be among the also-rans in 1908. The strong start ignited a huge case of pennant fever in the city. But few noted that Clark Griffith's charges were yet to face the stronger western teams. New York would collapse before the heat of summer because the team could not live up to high expectations built up by the fast start. The pitching and defense that propelled the team to the top eventually wore down, leading to dissension within the ranks led by first baseman Hal Chase.

National League standings at the end of April revealed almost a carbon copy of the eventual outcome, with Chicago leading Pittsburgh and New York. From early on, Frank Chance's Cubs took no prisoners and jumped off to an 8–3 start, reminding fans that the World Champions had won the 1907 pennant by seventeen games and swept the Tigers in four. The Cubs' start was marred by a loss to the Cardinals

1.
John "Bonesetter" Reese. A Welsh immigrant, this Youngstown, Ohio, native made his mark on early baseball history by using bone and muscle manipulation to cure ball players. His talents were so respected that the State of Ohio granted him a special license to practice. (The Mahoning Valley Historical Society, Youngstown, Ohio)

2. Outrage over umpire John Egan's call in a late-season game against St. Louis was vented by Cleveland fans in many ways. Newspapers used cartoons in sports coverage much as present-day cartoonists describe politics. In this *Cleveland Press* cartoon of October 6, 1908, umpire Egan is shown kicking the Naps off the pennant express. The porter is saying the ticket looked good enough for him. Note the military-style hat depicting the team's nickname and its manager Napoleon Lajoie. (Author's personal collection)

3. "Poor Little Old New York" was the title of a *Chicago Tribune* cartoon following the Merkle game. Note the Giant's head bandages resulting from the doubleheader loss the day before. (© Copyrighted Chicago Tribune Company. All rights reserved; used with permission)

4. National League President Harry Pulliam (left) was a sick man in early 1909. The strains of the Merkle incident and the bribery probe are here clearly etched on his face. This photo of the National Commission was taken in January, just before his nervous breakdown in February. Other members are (left to right) Garry Herrmann, American League President Ban Johnson, and J. E. Bruce. (Library of Congress)

5. Composites were the primary means of showing teams from the previous year. The 1908 Cubs are referred to as 1909 Champions in the 1909 *Reach Guide*. (1909 *Reach Guide*, reproduced from the original held by the Joyce Sports Research Collection of the University Libraries of Notre Dame)

6. Fans of the Dead Ball Era were better dressed than their contemporary counterparts, as seen in this overflow crowd at the Cubs' West Side Park. Note the proximity of players and spectators, and the lack of security presence in this 1908 photo. (Chicago Historical Society)

7. Game action at the Cubs' West Side Park shows umpire placement with a two-man crew. West Side was one of the few Dead Ball Era parks with permanent seating in the outfield. (Chicago Historical Society)

8. Umpire Hank O'Day looking dapper in civilian clothes. A respected umpire, O'Day figured in nearly every controversial game during the year. He was a Chicago native, and it is ironic that the Cubs figured in two of his biggest calls: the Gill and Merkle games. (National Baseball Hall of Fame Library and Archive, Cooperstown, New York)

9. Christy Mathewson had his greatest year in 1908. He was 37–11 with a 1.43 ERA and eleven shutouts, but his efforts fell a win and a game short. (National Baseball Hall of Fame Library and Archive, Cooperstown, New York)

10. Old Cy Young added to his legend with a 21–11 mark with the mediocre Red Sox. His no-hitter at the age of forty-one was considered a marvel by the contemporary press. (National Baseball Hall of Fame Library and Archive, Cooperstown, New York)

opposite

11. Fred Merkle was a rookie in 1908. His expression seems to show the burden of a baserunning error that unfairly marred an otherwise respectable career. (National Baseball Hall of Fame Library and Archive, Cooperstown, New York)

12. A pair of aces. Cleveland's Addie Joss (left) and Chicago's Big Ed Walsh were the American League's dominant pitchers. Together they won sixty-four games, threw twenty-one shutouts, and carried their teams. Joss's October 2 perfect game against Walsh and the Sox remains one of the greatest games ever. (National Baseball Hall of Fame Library and Archive, Cooperstown, New York)

opposite

13. Ty Cobb led the American League in batting average, RBI, total hits, and stolen bases. He left the Tigers in August to get married, displaying a self-centeredness that harmed his relationship with teammates. (National Baseball Hall of Fame Library and Archive, Cooperstown, New York)

14. Unlike Cobb, Honus Wagner was popular with his mates. Wagner (right) led the National League in hitting, RBI, stolen bases, and slugging. He is shown here with Pirates manager Fred Clarke (left) and third baseman Tommy Leach. (National Baseball Hall of Fame Library and Archive, Cooperstown, New York)

opposite

15. Walter Johnson in his rookie year. A mastoid infection delayed his 1908 debut until June. His string of three shutouts in five days over New York was one of the outstanding pitching feats in this year of the pitcher. (National Baseball Hall of Fame Library and Archive, Cooperstown, New York)

16. Cubs shortstop Joe Tinker and second baseman Johnny Evers did not talk to each other even though they formed the core of the best infield in baseball. Tinker was the team's clutch performer and would have been a strong candidate for Most Valuable Player, had the award existed in 1908. Evers was not a friendly man, but he knew baseball and was a winner. His .300 average led the Cubs in hitting, and his attention to the rules ignited the Merkle affair. (Transcendental Graphics)

17. Frank Chance was known in the press as the Peerless Leader. His bench leadership and play sparked the Cubs to the best five-year won-lost record in baseball history. (National Baseball Hall of Fame Library and Archive, Cooperstown, New York)

under circumstances involving umpire judgment, an event which recurred in later games involving Chicago and, interestingly, umpire Hank O'Day.

Some baseball historians search in close pennant races for games in which a bad call by an umpire, or another circumstance besides player effort, decides a game and a pennant race. The Cubs-Cardinals game of April 18, 1908, may have come as close as any game to fit into this dubious category. One account of the game comes from Johnny Evers's *Touching Second*.

The Cubs lost 3–2 as St. Louis took advantage of Ed Reulbach's wildness. Three Cardinals errors in the seventh allowed Chicago to tie it up. With one out in the home half of the ninth, pitcher Art Fromme was at bat with Art Hoelskoetter at third and Billy Gilbert at first. Fromme hit a smash to Evers; Evers looked Hoelskoetter back to third and tagged Gilbert. Evers said he tried to run to first to double up Fromme, when Gilbert tripped him. Evers got up and claimed he had beaten Fromme to the bag, while Hoelskoetter scored from third. Umpire Hank O'Day was apparently watching the plate and didn't see Gilbert's interference. O'Day allowed the run to score, ending the game.

In the book, written while both Evers and O'Day were still active, Evers is charitable toward O'Day: "If there had been two umpires instead of one on the field that day, Chicago probably would have won the game and ultimately the pennant without the bitter struggle they had to do it. . . . It was not O'Day's fault, except in that he did not think rapidly enough. The fault lay with the league for furnishing only one umpire."[4]

Despite Evers's claims, there are questions about this account. For example, where was Cub first baseman Frank Chance? Did he take himself out of position in trying to field the ball? Why wasn't Cubs pitcher Jack Pfiester covering first? O'Day was working alone; how could he have called Gilbert out and not seen the later interference, especially if Hoelskoetter had been looked back to third? Or did Hoelskoetter fake Evers and attract O'Day's attention by breaking for the plate? Why didn't Evers throw to the plate?

The *Chicago Tribune* account of the game, which could be expected to take the Cubs' side of things, differs significantly from Evers's account in there is no mention of contact between Evers and Gilbert during the play. *Tribune* reporter Charles Dryden described the play thus:

Fromme hit to Evers on the line. John grabbed the ball and tagged Gilbert, who made a futile effort to dodge our demon second sacker. Then, instead of tossing the sphere to the peerless leader [reference to first baseman Frank Chance], Evers engaged in a running race with the angular Fromme. In the stretch John made a high dive to dirt and stuck the ball on the bag. According to the Cubs, the speedy Evers beat Fromme a couple of feet. According to Hank O'Day, the sprinting pitcher's hoof hit the canvas before John reached the same goal. . . . Our Cubs swarmed around O'Day in loud and angry protest, but what Hank says goes and that settled the matter.[5]

Ending the game when the winning run scored, as O'Day ruled, may not always be the correct call, as we shall see later with the Gill and Merkle plays. Players and umpires alike were concerned about getting off the field once the game ended. As already noted, crowd control and security at turn-of-the-century ballparks were lax, if not downright non-existent, in the vast majority of situations. Fans would often storm the field after a game, posing security problems for player and umpire alike.

An example of this situation followed the Cubs' 1–0 win over Cincinnati on April 17: Cincinnati star Hans Lobert was escorted from the field by police because of incidents involving fans during the game. One fan claimed that Lobert spat in his face and slugged him twice. Contemporary accounts say Lobert's play was subject to strong and profane criticism by fans and the complainant was one of those critics. The incident also brought to light something nearly all players already knew — that Cincinnati's Palace of the Fans was not a pleasant place to play. Cheap beer served in a section called "Rooter's Row" was creating a nasty atmosphere for visiting and home teams alike. "From the accounts of the Lobert row in Cincinnati and the language directed at that player by the occupants of a so-called 'Rooter's Row,' it is a wonder that the Cincinnati team ever can win a home game with such 'rooters' on hand."[6] So much for early-season efforts to cure fan and player violence, at least in Cincinnati.

While Cubs fans could point to April with confidence, the followers of the Pirates could also be excused if they felt the warm glow of pennant fever. The great Wagner was back in the fold. Pittsburgh won all three games they played without their leading player, adding to the optimism. As indicated, he returned to the lineup on April 19 in Cincinnati. The Pirates promptly lost 4–3, as well as losing their next two games with the Reds, but Wagner's presence helped Pittsburgh take three of four from St. Louis. The month-ending 2–1 win over the Cubs came as the result of base hits by Paddy O'Connor and Wagner. O'Connor's game-tying hit would be one of only three he made all year. The outcome of that game was controversial in that Pittsburgh may have won as a result of a call by umpire John Rudderham. In their biography of Honus Wagner, the DeValerias claim that Rudderham missed a crucial two-out call, which could have ended the game.[7] The *Sporting Life* account of the game mentions nothing of the call.

The Giants' 8–6 start was noteworthy in that Mathewson went 4–0, with two shutouts and a one-hitter against the Boston Doves. Those two weeks in April would symbolize the Giants season. Mathewson was the sole consistent pitcher, and as he went, so went the Giants. Two of the Giants' wins were of particular interest. On April 17, New York walloped the Phillies 14–2; among the pitchers shellacked was Harry Coveleski. He allowed five runs on two hits in two and two-thirds innings of work. Coveleski earned a trip to the minors for that performance, but returned to the majors in late season to win critical games against the Giants.

The Giants' home opener win over Brooklyn raised eyebrows in some quarters and provides a measure of proof that injustice in baseball is often in the eyes of the beholder. In *Unforgettable Season*, G. H. Fleming notes that Turkey Mike Donlin's game-winning two-run homer was roundly hailed in the New York papers as the feat of a returning hero; noting that Donlin had sat out the 1907 season, the press acknowledged his overall importance to New York's fortunes.

While Donlin's home run was heroics as usual in New York, the *Chicago Tribune* account of the game was headlined, "Robbed of Game by Crowd." The lead sentence read: "Brooklyn was robbed of a well earned victory at the Polo grounds today." The Giants' opener was viewed by an overflow crowd of twenty-five thousand. The game account noted that the crowd began to intrude upon the outfield and that spectators were not removed despite Brooklyn objections. Fred Merkle's ninth-inning ground rule double, which fell into the crowd, would have been easily caught, according to the account. Instead it helped set up Donlin's home run.[8] This incident and the Cardinals' 2–1 win over the Cubs also give proof of just how difficult it is to find evidence showing beyond reasonable doubt that umpire calls and deci-

TABLE 2. *National League Standings — April 30, 1908*

	W	L	Pct.	GB
Chicago	8	3	.727	—
Pittsburgh	7	4	.636	1
New York	8	6	.571	$1\frac{1}{2}$
Philadelphia	5	5	.500	$2\frac{1}{2}$
Boston	5	5	.500	$2\frac{1}{2}$
Cincinnati	5	6	.455	3
Brooklyn	6	8	.429	$3\frac{1}{2}$
St. Louis	3	10	.281	6

sions or matters other than player performance could determine the outcome of a pennant race.

AFTERWORD: FATHER CHADWICK, R.I.P.

The death of Henry Chadwick at the age of eighty-three at the start of the 1908 campaign meant the loss of one of the founding fathers of the sport. Selected in 1938, Chadwick is the only writer elected to and enshrined in the Baseball Hall of Fame among the players. All other writers or media figures in the Hall have been honored in a separate wing.

While most modern fans would be hard pressed to identify Chadwick on a multiple-choice exam, they are familiar with his major contributions: the invention and creation of the box score and a system of scoring to keep up with the game. Those gifts have given many fans more hours of enjoyment than the on-field efforts of some overpaid present-day superstars.

Chadwick played rounders as an English schoolboy and played baseball in Brooklyn after his parents emigrated to the United States. As a *New York Times* correspondent, he wrote about cricket until seeing a baseball game. The story goes that he then decided to help promote baseball as the American national sport by writing about it and boosting it whenever he could. He was a supporter of the idea that baseball evolved from the English game of rounders and was not, as the Mills Commission asserted, a uniquely American game. But any disappointment he may have felt about the Mills Report did not dampen his enthusiasm for the sport.

Among his accomplishments were rules changes to make the game more balanced between offense and defense and between mental and physical effort. He edited the *Spalding's Guide* from 1881 until 1908, contributed articles to *Sporting Life,* and was an outspoken and influential foe of gambling and other forms of corruption in the sport.

Upon his death, tributes to Chadwick came from all quarters of the baseball world in the florid language of the day. A collection was taken from all teams and fans for a monument to him. *Sporting Life*'s tribute to the man everyone called Father Chadwick is just one example of the appreciation all associated with the sport felt for this adopted American son: "With rare singleness of purpose, without hype or sordid financial reward, and with absolute honesty, he labored from early youth to extreme age for the successful establishment and decent conduct of his beloved game of baseball."[9]

Chadwick stood for clearly written rules and honest play without influence of gamblers. Considering circumstances surrounding the end of the 1908 season, it seems ironic that Chadwick should have died that same season. Had he lived, his reaction to the Merkle situation would have been interesting. The rule is clear; it was how it was interpreted and enforced that caused the problem. Chadwick's guidance in the matter could have been instructive. More predictable would have been his reaction to attempts to fix the outcome of the National League pennant race. Chadwick would have been appalled and outraged over the bribery attempt and how National League leaders handled the subsequent investigation.

A crowning irony was that the year of the death of one of baseball's first writers marked the birth of an organization designed to provide uniform scoring guidelines and better working conditions for journalists. The Base Ball Writers Association of America (BBWAA) was organized in Detroit shortly after the end of the World Series.

As explained in a BBWAA history, the organization was founded because of the terrible working conditions reporters experienced during coverage of the World Series. Reportedly, writers from outside Chicago were compelled to sit in the last row of the grandstand at the Cubs' park. In Detroit writers had to climb a ladder to get to positions on the roof of the pavilion, overlooking the first base line. Extremes of weather added to the miserable working conditions that led to the founding of the group.[10]

While all of this sounds like a noble effort in the face of injustice,

Sporting Life noted of the founding meeting in Detroit that score keeping was the main concern. "The writers who gathered in Detroit (last week) were of one mind that uniform scoring rules be agreed upon."[11]

But in fairness to the position that unjust working conditions were the major issue, it should be noted that writers had met with National League President Pulliam in August 1908, a few weeks before on-field events overwhelmed him. Reports called the session a courtesy call to inform Pulliam of the plan to organize a writers' association. The report said the senior circuit chief executive was in favor of the goals of the group, namely that "better facilities are desired in the press boxes of certain cities, and it is also the hope of the men that the organization will do much to promote uniform scoring."[12] Discussions about organizing the group had been held by writers in New York and Cincinnati as early as 1906.[13]

The BBWAA organizational effort in 1908 was not the first attempt to get sportswriters together in a professional association. In December 1887, the Base Ball Reporters Association (BBRA) was formed in Cincinnati for two purposes: to advance the interests of baseball through the press and, interestingly, to bring about a uniform method of scoring games. Henry Chadwick was the first vice president of the group.[14]

The BBRA was a first step in the attempt to establish the importance of sports journalism to the game. It was a recognition of the mutual interests of reporters and baseball; which without each other, neither would flourish. Interest in it faded in the 1890s. The birth of the BBWAA must be considered a reincarnation of the BBRA.

The current Baseball Writers Association of America is not only involved with working conditions but also has a role in reviewing and revising the official rules of baseball. Selection of Most Valuable Players and voting for Hall of Fame nominees are the more public roles played by the organization. Though many contemporary baseball writers would be hard pressed to identify him, it is through them that the pioneering spirit of Father Chadwick lives.

6 May The Makings of a Pennant Race

A major difference between media coverage of today's game and that of yesteryear is the quality and quantity of the journalism. Modern writers with their electronic and print outlets dwell on controversy and the horse-race aspect of baseball's pennant races, with little or no attention paid to writing style or colorful prose. Modern baseball fans are inundated with information from cyberspace and broadcast and print media; their early-century counterparts were swimming in a sea of newsprint.

The sportswriters of 1908 were limited to print. Game accounts were relayed to papers by wire, and the electronic media we use today were still inventors' dreams. It is unfair to conclude, however, that early reporters were unduly restrained by the limitations of print. Often sportswriters wrote prose and verse alike. Some of the attempts to turn a phrase fell flat, while others now seem overly wordy and ostentatious. But often they struck a chord.

Poetry was written both as solo contributions and as a means to fill space. None other than the immortal sportswriter Grantland Rice contributed verse in tribute to the start of the 1908 season.

GET IN THE GAME!

On Rooters Row the Bugs arise
To cheer again the timely rap;

The base hit and the sacrifice
  Are once again upon the map.
And from afar the noisy shout
  Arises in a wild acclaim —
Springs up in catalystic rout:
  Get in the game! Get in the Game!

The events of the world flit past
  But no one bothers anymore;
The query of the day is cast:
  "Who won today?" or "What's the Score?"
T. Roosevelt and the Trusts passout —
  The umpire now gets all the blame
Amid the whirling, whooping rout —
  Get in the game! Get in the Game![1]

While Rice and his colleagues provided encouragement, terrible weather continued to take its toll on the schedule and did not let up in May. Eleven National and seven American League games were scratched because of weather. For the National League contenders, the Pirates had five games scrubbed and the Cubs four. This meant doubleheaders later in the season, when injuries and tired pitchers could determine the outcome of the pennant race. The Giants seemed favored, having only one postponement due to weather. In the American League the White Sox had four games scrubbed, Cleveland three, and there were two each for the Tigers and Browns.

If Mark Twain indeed said that everyone complains about the weather but no one does anything about it, he must never have met a contemporary of his, Pirates owner Barney Dreyfuss. Fed up with weather problems depriving him of revenues because of a field that could stay damp well into summer, Dreyfuss unveiled a tarpaulin for Exposition Park's infield. Made of brown paraffined duck canvas, the 120-by-120-foot square of fabric manufactured by the Pittsburgh Waterproof Company cost two thousand dollars. It was designed to cover the field between games to keep it dry and could also be deployed during a contest if rain threatened. Using a truck, the cover took fifteen to twenty minutes to deploy — slow by modern standards but progress for 1908. The tarp did little to affect Pirates fortunes on the field, but the baseball world took note of Dreyfuss's innovation and eventually adopted it.[2]

For Dreyfuss and the Pirates, the tarpaulin was a short-term solution. In 1909 the Pirates moved to a new home, Forbes Field. Besides being new, Forbes had the advantage over Exposition Park of being on higher ground, with better drainage, farther from the Allegheny and Ohio rivers. While Dreyfuss sought higher ground and a field cover, it must be noted that he was not the first owner to try to fight the weather. During the 1880s Chris Von der Ahe, the eccentric owner of the American Association's St. Louis Browns, had tried out a tarpaulin because he was fed up with losing games, and revenue, to postponements due to wet grounds.

On the gambling and gaming front, American League President Ban Johnson urged a crackdown against betting on baseball in Detroit. In a rare move, between thirty and forty persons were arrested at Pittsburgh's Exposition Park for gambling in the stands during a series with St. Louis. These token actions bolstered organized baseball's antigambling image but created more smoke than fire. Betting on games and gambling in the stands would remain a popular diversion while viewing the national pastime, despite edicts from league offices and sporadic arrests by local authorities.

Beginning in the month of May in the American League cellar, the defending league champion Detroit Tigers and manager Hughie Jennings had some explaining to do. Jennings's reply to critics was simple: Detroit put together the best record in the majors during May (17–7), mostly against inferior eastern teams climbing to a tie for first with the fading Highlanders. In late April Jennings told *Sporting Life*, "Just wait until our pitchers get going right. . . . You cannot keep a good club down and Detroit has a good club. We will be up there before the season is very far advanced and the club that wins the pennant will have to beat us out."[3] His team's May performance lived up to his predictions and was a slap at those who succumbed to the "what have you done for us lately" syndrome.

On other American League diamonds, Cleveland, Philadelphia, and New York all occupied first place for at least a day during the month. The Highlanders increasingly looked like strong contenders, and Athletics manager Connie Mack called New York's 1908 edition the best Highlander team ever, adding, "[it] looks as if nothing will stop them from being factors for the pennant all season."[4]

But the seeds of New York's collapse had been planted and were beginning to sprout. On May 1, Jack Chesbro pitched the Highlanders to a 9–4 win over Washington. But the win came at high price. Shortstop Kid Elberfeld's playing season ended when he was severely spiked by Bob Ganley on a tag play in the fifth inning. Elberfeld was carried from the field, his left shin cut to the bone and his calf muscle badly gashed. The fiery Elberfeld, who had provided strong leadership of the infield, missed a good part of the rest of the year. At the close of the day New York was still in first, but the loss of Elberfeld would be costly. His replacement, Neal Ball, was error prone, at a critical defensive position. Elberfeld did little better when he assumed the manager's job a month later.

While Detroit was surging, Cleveland and St. Louis were holding their own as off-field problems began making as much news as the box scores. Both clubs hovered at or just below the .500 mark, while they coped with personnel problems. The Naps were still hoping that Elmer Flick and his bat would return to the lineup. Club officials initially blamed Flick's ailment on overeating. But as the year wore on, it became clear that Cleveland would have to make their run without their star outfielder, a consistent .300 hitter and a Hall of Famer. Flick's career was all but over. He saw limited action in 1908. It would be hard to believe that Cleveland would not have won at least one or two more games and perhaps the pennant with Flick's bat in the lineup.

While Cleveland's batting order may have been easier to face without Flick, pitcher Addie Joss was as close to a sure thing as there was in May. Joss went 6–0 for the month with one shutout and two three-hitters, giving notice to the rest of the league that his three previous twenty-win campaigns had not been flukes. Joss allowed four walks in his first nine starts, but his efforts were negated by inconsistent play. Cleveland dropped a three-game series to Washington and three out of four to St. Louis to close out the month. Despite the losses, the Naps were only a game and a half off the pace at month's end.

St. Louis's primary concern was their new acquisition, eccentric left-hander Rube Waddell. Waddell went 1–3 for the month and was the recipient of warnings about his drinking and other off-field behavior. In May Waddell was evicted and moved to another boarding house while becoming the target of criticism from his teammates. *Sporting Life* reported that several Browns believed Waddell's skills to be "retrograded," and that he had been seen "on divers occasions" tending bar at Barry's Baseball Headquarters near the Browns park.[5]

TABLE 3. *American League Standings — May 31, 1908*

	W	L	Pct.	GB	May Record
New York	19	15	.559	—	11–10
Detroit	20	16	.556	—	17–7
St. Louis	21	18	.538	$\frac{1}{2}$	12–12
Cleveland	20	18	.514	$1\frac{1}{2}$	11–13
Philadelphia	19	18	.514	$1\frac{1}{2}$	12–11
Chicago	17	19	.472	3	10–12
Washington	17	20	.459	$3\frac{1}{2}$	12–11
Boston	15	24	.385	$6\frac{1}{2}$	8–17

Waddell was winless for the month when he arrived in Philadelphia to face his old mates for the first time since being sold to St. Louis. On May 19 more than twenty thousand fans, the largest midweek crowd in Philadelphia history, paid to see Waddell's return. He gave up five hits in the first three innings and it looked bad for St. Louis until Athletics starter Chief Bender weakened in the seventh. In that frame the Browns bunched five hits and scored four times, to seal a 5–2 victory. Despite the win, Waddell left the team the next day. He did not return to the club until the May 28, missing at least two starts. Little was noted about Connie Mack's reaction to Waddell's return to Philadelphia, except that the decision to get rid of him looked good, despite the loss to Waddell.

One of the other dominant pitchers in the American League, Big Ed Walsh, was already in midseason form. His two shutouts for the month came at the expense of Detroit and Cleveland, while the White Sox spitballer notched a 7–1 record. The problem with the White Sox was the supporting cast. Without Walsh, Chicago's record for the month was a below-par 3–11.

As the Boston Red Sox settled into the cellar with an appalling 8–17 mark for May, their pitching star Cy Young remained a wonder to fans and press alike. By the end of the month, the nineteen-year veteran was 6–4 with two shutouts. Three of his losses were by one-run margins. In sharp contrast to the behavior of Waddell, the forty-one-year-old Young took good care of himself and dispensed some advice in a third-person article in *Sporting Life* about the growing habit of cigarette smoking: "Cigars in moderation are not harmful, declares Young, but cigarettes are deadly to the physical qualities most necessary to success in the strenuous base ball game."[6]

Another the interesting aspect of the sports journalism of the Dead Ball Era was what players and managers talked about. Most modern players and managers in an information- and media-intensive era are careful not to say anything that can inspire an opponent. Providing reading material for an opponent's locker room bulletin board has been the downfall of many a team.

Newspapers of 1908 often sought predictions from baseball officials, who willingly gave them. The reasoning for this behavior must have involved promotion of the game, a version of hype combined with healthy respect, or disrespect, for the opposition.

For instance, Cubs manager Frank Chance was asked about the Pirates, a team the Cubs had faced often early in the season. Chance said he wasn't afraid of Pittsburgh because — possibly referring to problems at first base and center field — "they have three minor league men in the line-up, and they are pretty sure to blow before the season is half over."[7]

Former Baltimore Orioles manager and John McGraw teammate Ned Hanlon weighed in about the Cubs, while picking his friend's Giants to win it all: "Cubs are not going to find it so easy getting clear of their rivals from the start this year. The race is a pretty one thus far."[8]

McGraw himself even got in on the act, with a prediction filled with irony. Noting that Cubs pitching was not as sharp as it had been in the past, McGraw said, "The Cubs have never been in a real fight. They have had walkovers, and it will be interesting to see what effect a close race has on them."[9] The Cubs were indeed part of a most interesting pennant chase, and the impact of the close race on the Cubs was eventually to be of painful interest to the Giants.

No quote can be matched for its expression of eternal optimism about a ball club that spent the entire season in the second division. Brooklyn Superbas owner Charles Ebbets saw nothing wrong with his club's 13–22 start. Perhaps with an eye on the turnstile, Ebbets noted that the 1908 club was stronger than that of the preceding year: "Lumley and Jordan will get to hitting, that is sure, and then Brooklyn will begin to crawl up."[10] Brooklyn indeed crawled up, inching their way all the way from eighth to seventh place by season's end.

The Cubs threatened to make a mockery of the National League race in May, as they had done the year before, putting a league best 15–10 record on the board. The big news for the Cubs was the 1908 debut of Three Finger Brown, who won five in May, including a one-hitter against Brooklyn. Despite five postponements, the Cubs took six of seven from St. Louis, four of six from Pittsburgh, two of three from Brooklyn and three out of four from Boston. Bad weather kept Chicago from avenging a 6–2 loss to Hugh McQuillan and the Phillies on May 12. That loss was significant. It marked the end of Cubs right-hander Orval Overall's fourteen-game winning streak, which had be-gun August 11, 1907, against the Phillies. Overall was a twenty-game winner in 1907 but was hampered by arm trouble for most of the regular season.

The only blemish on the month's work for Chicago involved the first on-field meeting between the Cubs and Giants in 1908. Brown won his matchup with Mathewson for the only Chicago victory in the four-game set, which featured hard hitting by the Giants in two games and a 1–0 three-hit whitewash job from Hooks Wiltse in a third. The near sweep of the Cubs on New York's first western trip rejuvenated the Giants, who were hovering near mediocrity. The Giants' problem was simple: Christy Mathewson was slumping badly, going 3–3 for the month. In the single loss to the Cubs, he was knocked out of the box.

An element of the unfair blame placed on Fred Merkle for losing the pennant in 1908 is ignorance of the fact there were many games during the year New York that should have won. McGraw knew this better than anyone. The Giants' first trip west, except for winning the series against the Cubs, was a disaster.

The western road trip started badly with New York losing two of three to Pittsburgh; and three of four to the Reds and Cardinals. Espe-cially galling was the doubleheader loss to lowly St. Louis on the eve of leaving for Chicago. The 6–9 western road trip did significant damage to the Giants' pennant drive, especially in light of winning only two games against second division–dwelling clubs Cincinnati and St. Louis.

Pittsburgh spent most of the month at home, which for most teams would assure a successful month. But not for the 1908 Pirates, who, as we have seen, played better on the road than at home. Despite Drey-fuss's tarp, a continuing problem affecting the Pirates was postpone-ments due to wet weather. It did not help the Pirates' cause to lose a three-game home set to lowly Brooklyn, nor to get shut out four times. The early-season problem for the Pirates was consistency, a trait diffi-

TABLE 4. *National League Standings — May 31, 1908*

	W	L	Pct.	GB	May Record
Chicago	23	13	.639	—	15–10
Philadelphia	17	14	.548	3½	10–7
Cincinnati	19	16	.543	3½	14–10
New York	19	16	.543	3½	11–10
Pittsburgh	18	16	.529	4	11–12
Boston	17	19	.472	6	10–12
St. Louis	15	25	.375	10	12–15
Brooklyn	13	22	.371	9½	7–14

cult to cultivate when the weather is not cooperating, whether or not your owner has purchased a tarp.

AFTERWORD: SPITBALL SYMPOSIUM

Any discussion of the Dead Ball Era has to include the spitball, a pitch banned in the major leagues since 1920. Mention the spitter to a modern batter and you become about as popular as garlic dip at a vampire convention. With the passage of time, its banishment has rendered it a subject of awe, the ultimate weapon against hitters. A limited number of spitball pitchers were allowed to continue their careers after the rules change in 1920. Few noticed that these pitchers were hardly any more effective than their colleagues who relied upon more conventional, and perhaps more sanitary, deliveries.

The spitter was far from the ultimate weapon, but concern over the lack of offensive production stimulated discussion on changing rules to restore balance to the game. The foul ball rule, adopted by the National League in 1901 and two years later by the American League, had more impact on offense that any rule change in the history of baseball. The pitcher had the clear advantage until the spitter was banned and offensive philosophies changed in the 1920s.

Adding to that advantage, the pitcher's mound was mandated to be no higher than fifteen inches above the base lines and home plate in 1903. This particular specification remained in effect until 1969, when the height of the mound was lowered to ten inches in an attempt to put more offense into the game and to remove an advantage pitchers had developed during the 1960s.

Discussion about the spitter was commonplace in 1908. In the 1909 *Spalding's Guide* there was detailed coverage of the issue, titled "Symposium upon the 'Spit Ball.' "[11] The symposium was a poll of twenty-nine sportswriters. Its introduction noted that the balance between pitchers and hitters is a delicate one and that pitchers make adjustments.

> The pitcher is an industrious and an ingenious player. No sooner is a penalty imposed upon him than he takes up the task of bearing it and eventually making the burden as light as possible. The editor of the GUIDE believes that the time is slowly approaching when the pitcher will again be the target of the rule-makers, who will make an effort to handicap his prowess, to the extent that the batter will have a better chance to cope with him successfully. It may not be this year, nor the year after, but the stars in the sky predict the coming of a new era.[12]

After briefly discussing proposals to reduce the number of balls for a walk to three and increasing strikes required for a strikeout to four, the *Guide* indicated in a roundabout fashion its support of a ban on the spitter: "Frankly it must be confessed that it is not a very elegant descriptive term, and the mere suggestion of it is not wholly pleasing to the vast army of those who are fond of Base Ball. It must be remembered that we got along without it once and possibly could again, and whether it would make such a decided difference with some pitchers as has been asserted is another question worthy of experiment."[13]

This ambivalent attitude about the spitter helps to explain why a ban on adding foreign substances to the ball did not come for more than another decade, despite almost universal opposition to the pitch. The poll of baseball writers revealed that seventeen of the twenty-nine responding strongly favored a ban, with six against and six others straddling the fence, expressing — for lack of a better term — deeply felt neutrality about the spitter. Most ban supporters seemed to believe it would clean up the game and help batters. Those neutral toward and opposing the ban expressed concern over enforcement of any ban and skepticism as to whether banning the spitter would improve offense. Consider the writers' opinions.

PRO—SPITBALL BAN

"It is an evil, and as such should be eliminated from an otherwise clean sport. The pitcher who cannot succeed without resorting to the spit ball should step aside."

C. B. Power, *Pittsburgh Dispatch*

"I have always regarded the spit ball as a sort of 'dog-faced boy' of Base Ball—one of the freaks that was not at all essential to the 'big show.' . . . As to its objectionable features, I've always had a horror for seeing even children put soiled fingers into their mouths, and that horror is not lessened by the increased size of the offender."

C. H. Zuber, *Cincinnati Times-Star*

"I do not think its value as a pitcher's asset approaches the many objectionable features in connection with its use."

Edward F. Bang, *Cleveland News*

"This disgusting practice has made effective pitchers of men who have neither brains nor skill, and I do not believe that outside of the spit ball pitchers a single person can be found who will countenance its use. More wild throws have followed its use and catchers are much more liable to be hurt."

Henry P. Edwards, *Cleveland Plain Dealer*

"There are plenty of good, orthodox pitchers to take care of the batsmen with the standard style of delivery. If a pitcher is allowed to spit on the ball, why should not his opponents have the right to apply to the sphere some sort of antidote, and where is the whole process going to legally stop?"

Paul H. Bruske, *Detroit Times*

"The spit ball, in my opinion, is not of such necessity to Base Ball that it could not be eliminated. In fact, I believe that by legislating against it batting would materially increase."

James C. Gilruth, *Chicago News*

"Bar the spit ball. To give the pitcher an artificial advantage over the batter does not smack of good sportsmanship."

Myron W. Townsend, *St. Louis Star-Chronicle*

"Into the cuspidor with the spit ball. It has hurt batting; frequently hurts fielding and more or less it is disgusting. Rules, such as bringing the catcher up behind the bat, the foul strike, and not permitting pitcher to soil the ball have livened up the game and improved it."

H. W. Lanigan, *St. Louis Times*

AGAINST AND/OR NEUTRAL TOWARD THE BAN
"If the spit ball were eliminated I believe the pennant races would not be so close, especially in the American League, and this fact must be considered, for close races stir the interest in Base Ball."

A. H. C. Mitchell, *Boston American*

"Opponents of the spit ball overlook the fact that it would be impossible to formulate a rule which would do away with it."

George M. Graham, *Philadelphia North American*

"The well-being of Base Ball does not hinge upon either the retention or elimination of the spit ball. Undoubtedly its abolition would work a special hardship on a large number of pitchers who have found the spit ball a life preserver, which has enabled them to remain in fast company longer than they could possibly have done had they not been aided by this mode of delivery."

Ren Mulford, Jr., Cincinnati correspondent, *Sporting Life*

"The spit ball is an evil, so far as batting averages are concerned, but its terrors are over-estimated. Scienced batters who will step into it and meet it before it breaks can slug it heavily, and should treat it just as they would any ordinary drop ball."

W. A. Phelon, *Chicago Journal*

"I do not believe the spit ball is a necessity in Base Ball, but do believe its elimination would be in the nature of class legislation which just now is so unpopular. In other words, it would work a special hardship to individuals instead of a general hardship to all. To my mind the elimination would be more difficult to accomplish than unjust."

I. E. Sanborn, *Chicago Tribune*

That it took twelve more seasons to ban the spitball was not only the result of ambivalence on the part of the baseball leadership about the delivery but also a matter of their conservatism, and a measure of self-interest on the part of clubs that had spitball pitchers. Opposition to the spitball was almost universal by nonpitchers and managers, which may surprise modern fans.

Cubs manager Frank Chance, a member of the rules committee, tried to mount a campaign against the pitch during the 1909 winter meetings.[14] National League President Harry Pulliam, prior to being fully occupied and totally overwhelmed by the Merkle case, indicated his opposition to the spitter in September 1908.[15]

Browns pitcher Handsome Harry Howell expressed doubt that the spitter would be abolished: "If they abolish it it will see the passing of many stars of the game, and will cause the players and umpires a lot of trouble."[16]

National League umpire Hank O'Day, a former pitcher himself, was not sympathetic with those wanting to ban the spitter. "The spit ball looks like nothing more than a straight drop ball when pitched overhand, and when pitched with a side arm movement will go out. It bothers the batsman a whole lot, but I find no trouble at all in gauging it as an umpire."[17]

In *Touching Second*, Johnny Evers summed up almost universal opposition to the spitter by nearly all parties involved on the field. Batters disliked it because it was hard to hit; pitchers risked arm injury throwing it; catchers found spitters hard to handle and throw; and the pitch was tough on fielders because it made the ball slippery, and when hit, the ball would take "doubly unnatural English, both from the bat and the ground, and darts in a weird manner."[18]

Hardly a month went by in 1908 without some anti-spitball statements in *Sporting Life* and other publications. Athletics manager Connie Mack indicated his dislike of the pitch because it was difficult to control. Mack also said the spitter was not commonly used in the late 1890s, as some believed:

[Eddie] Plank used to resort to this style of delivery occasionally. One day he started a high fast one up around the batter's neck and the ball came down and hit Schreck (catcher Ossie Schreckengost) in the pit of this stomach as he crouched low behind the bat. Then Plank dropped the spit ball and has not pitched it since. The old time pitchers — the Radbournes and Clarksons and Whitneys and all the rest of them — were all right. They had speed and curves but they never heard of the spit ball, and don't let anybody try to tell that they did."[19]

One of the enduring images of the Dead Ball Era is the spitter and other pitches that utilized foreign substances. Most casual fans believe the delivery was broadly accepted in the years leading up to its ban in 1920, but coverage of the issue in 1908 indicates otherwise.

7 June The Race Is On

The first indication that the 1908 pennant races were to be noteworthy emerged in June. By month's end the Highlanders, Tigers, and Cubs would not be leading their respective leagues as they did in May. During June the New York Highlanders were in the midst of one of the most dreadful swoons in baseball history. Detroit and Chicago played steady if not spectacular baseball, but they couldn't keep pace with opponents who played better ball during the month. June 1908 was full of significance for nearly every team in the American League.

For Washington, which had lost twenty of its last twenty-five games, the good news was the return of Walter Johnson on June 11. He lost his first start 6–3 to the Browns. But as he pitched himself into shape, the Nationals could no longer be taken for granted. Cleveland was discovering that Washington could be tougher than league standings justified, and the Naps' 8–14 season record against the Nats cost Cleveland the pennant.

The Philadelphia Athletics tasted the fruits of first place for the last time on June 6 on the force of Eddie Plank's three-hit shutout of St. Louis. The Athletics finished the month at .500, a mark the team would not reach again during the rest of the season.

The Red Sox were 14–8 for the month, but the red hot mark went unnoticed in the standings due to the team's horrific start. The bright spot for the Red Sox was Cy Young's no-hitter against the Highlanders on June 30. It was the first of six official no-hitters during this year of the pitcher. Young faced twenty-seven hitters in the 8–0 win. The only New Yorker to reach base, Harry Niles, was thrown out attempting to steal second. For Young, it was his third career no-hitter, and to cap the feat, he batted in four of Boston's runs. Young was the first major league pitcher to throw three no-hitters and, at the age of forty-one, was also the oldest to pitch a no-hitter. Young held this record until 1991, when on May 1 Nolan Ryan fanned sixteen Toronto Blue Jays on the way to his seventh no-hitter. Ryan was forty-four years old when he threw that masterpiece.

New York manager Clark Griffith resigned on June 24, his team's 24–32 mark good enough for seventh place. New York fell out of first for keeps on June 2 after losing a doubleheader to Boston. Griffith's replacement was Kid Elberfeld, elected by his teammates to be manager. Providing evidence that popular elections can never be considered an ultimate cure-all in any human endeavor, Elberfeld posted a dreadful 27–71 .276 mark for the year, his first and last as a big league manager.

Despite having the third best mark in the league for June, behind Cleveland and the White Sox, the St. Louis Browns found themselves in first at the end of June; one game ahead of Chicago, a game and a half ahead of Cleveland, and two and a half games up on Detroit. Browns manager Jimmy McAleer expressed confidence during the month that his team would be a contender, but he was concerned about his pitching staff.[1] He had good reason for his concern.

Rube Waddell was on and off according to his own schedule, exhibiting the kind of behavior that had put Mack and Waddell's teammates over the edge and had sent him out of Philadelphia. When he pitched, Waddell managed a 3–2 June mark, including a shutout of his former Athletics mates. Handsome Harry Howell matched Waddell's mark. The pitching stars of the month for the Browns were Jack Powell (6–1) and Big Bill Dinneen (3–0). The Browns' problem was getting a steady rotation and dealing with the disruption caused by Waddell's erratic behavior. The talented Waddell's unpredictability was planting the seeds of doom for the Browns' pennant hopes.

St. Louis wasn't the only club to be affected by a pitcher's mood swings. Frank Smith of the White Sox jumped the team in late June while the Sox were in Detroit for a four-game set. Smith was reportedly tired of early morning practices and being overworked by manager Fielder Jones. Sox owner Charles Comiskey initially said Smith would not be welcomed back, unless he reported for practice: "He did not make valid excuse for his absences . . . I consider that morning practice is absolutely essential for a team when it is at home."[2]

Smith's absence cost the Sox dearly and quite possibly cost the team the pennant. Reminiscent of the nineteen-game win streak that helped clinch the pennant for the '06 Hitless Wonders, the '08 edition of the Hitless Wonders staged a thirteen-game win streak with Smith still on the team. The streak was broken by a 5–2 loss to New York on June 17; subsequently the White Sox won another four in a row. Chicago was flying high on June 22 when the team arrived in Detroit for a two-game set without Frank Smith, who had gone home to engage in his trade of piano moving. Chicago lost both games and then four in a row to Cleveland before returning home to split a pair with the Tigers. The win streak of mid-June was the high-water mark for Chicago. The team reached first on June 8 and held the lead until June 25, when the Browns took the lead. The White Sox would come close but would never lead the league again in 1908.

Smith had been undefeated (2–0) in June when he left the team. He rejoined the team in late July and promptly won his start against Washington on July 31. Without Smith, White Sox pitching lost its depth, and the team was 16–20 from late June to the end of July.

Smith's absence became a source of dissension within the team. Manager Jones used him sparingly for the remainder of the year and passed him over in the rotation at times. Smith was a talented pitcher. Had he remained with the team all season and had he and Jones not quarreled so intensely, Chicago might have won the flag.

Napoleon Lajoie's club was doing well, despite injuries and batting slumps, which forced Cleveland to field a makeshift lineup virtually every day during the month. In play among the contenders, the Naps' 8–3 mark against Detroit, Chicago, and St. Louis was good enough for second place, just ahead of the White Sox. Glenn Liebhardt, who was 15–16 for the season, racked up six wins against one loss in June, giving the Naps a badly needed boost.

Superstar pitcher Addie Joss could normally be expected to match Liebhardt but managed only a 4–4 mark for the month. Joss's problems were twofold: lack of offensive support and the plain fact that he would face the best pitcher the opposition had available in almost every game he started. This was the kind of pressure almost guaranteed to trigger a slump eventually.

The defending American League champions, the Tigers, managed to stay in the hunt, despite hovering just above .500 in June. Detroit's problem was injuries to first baseman Claude Rossman and shortstop Charlie O'Leary. Their absence disrupted the infield, presenting manager Hughie Jennings with a problem he would not resolve until September. Jennings had another problem, over which he had only marginal control: the on- and off-field behavior of star outfielder Ty Cobb. Cobb, whose on-field performance was gaining him fans and enemies alike, was becoming increasingly unpopular with his teammates. Tension in the Detroit clubhouse was so high that the place resembled a powder keg with a short fuse in a room full of lit matches. The question was not whether Cobb would erupt but when and against whom.

Cobb's eventual target was not a teammate but a black construction laborer. The incident occurred on June 6 outside the Hotel Ponchartrain in Detroit. Cobb was crossing the street and stepped into freshly laid asphalt. The laborer, named Fred Collins, angrily told Cobb to leave the area. After a brief confrontation, Cobb slugged Collins and went on his way. Cobb was ordered into court on June 8 on an assault and battery charge brought by Collins. Cobb pleaded not guilty on the grounds that he had been "insulted and provoked" by a black person.[3] Judge Edward Jeffries found Cobb guilty but suspended the sentence. Cobb later paid Collins seventy-five dollars to avert a civil suit.[4]

If Ty Cobb was a walking powder keg, New York Governor Charles Evans Hughes provided the dry tinder that eventually fueled another controversy. Hughes's support of an anti–race track gambling bill was an attempt to stamp out gambling once and for all in New York. In keeping with the law of unexpected results, gambling merely changed venues. Bettors in New York turned their eyes toward baseball and the pennant races, which were attracting increased attention and rising attendance at the ballpark.

Sporting Life ran numerous stories on the gambling issue in June. In early July, the weekly reprinted a story from the *Philadelphia Record* in which gambling was called "a menace which must not be overlooked."[5] Noting that New York race track gamblers were seeking other outlets, the *Record* reported a noticeable increase in betting at the New York ball grounds. *Sporting Life* told its readers, "It has been said that it is unsafe to bet big money on anything that can talk or understand what is said.

TABLE 5. *American League Standings — June 30, 1908*

	W	L	Pct.	GB	June Record
St Louis	38	28	.538	—	17–10
Cleveland	37	26	.587	1½	18–8
Chicago	36	28	.563	1	19–9
Detroit	34	29	.540	2½	14–13
Philadelphia	28	28	.500	5	9–10
Boston	29	37	.439	10	14–8
New York	26	36	.419	12	7–21
Washington	22	40	.355	14½	5–20

Base ball players are no better and no worse than the average citizen and the managers and owners should see to it that they are not unduly tempted."[6]

Sporting Life's weekly competitor, *Sporting News*, also weighed in on the issue in early July: "There is little danger to base ball from parties who make individual wagers, but whose who post odds on games and conduct pool rooms are a menace to the people's pastime. . . . No owner, manager or player of a ball club can, with safety to the sport or himself associate with a gambler who wagers on the game by a straight wager or by offering odds to the public."[7]

Despite the talk about gambling, betting continued to bark at the heels of the national pastime throughout 1908 and would create a brief scandal. As it would turn out, baseball would talk the talk but would not walk the walk against gambling until a World Series was fixed in 1919.

While the American League race tightened, National League fans saw the Pirates make a 22–8 run in June. The Pittsburgh surge was aided in part by injuries to the Cubs, but when the month ended, New York, Chicago, and Pittsburgh were within three games of one another.

If the Cubs resembled a traveling sick bay, the Pirates were little better off. While pitchers Nick Maddox, Vic Willis, and Sam Leever were compiling a 17–3 record in June, staff ace Lefty Leifield came down with a sore arm and managed a dismal 1–1 mark. Leifield's arm woes cut into his effectiveness for all of 1908 and damaged the Pirates' pennant effort. Adding insult to injury, Leifield had just recovered from a case of sore ribs when he developed the arm problem.

Pittsburgh rounded out its fabulous month with its star Wagner getting his two thousandth hit, leading *Sporting Life* to remark, "Just think of it — two thousand hits in the National League!"[8] Nap Lajoie reached the milestone later in the summer with even less hoopla, in an age when individual records received little attention from the press and were generally scorned by many players. Players overly worried about their individual stats were often unpopular with teammates. The modesty of Wagner and Lajoie over their achievements contrasted sharply with Cobb's ambition and overriding interest in his individual numbers.

McGraw's Giants showed signs of life in June, despite injury to catcher Roger Bresnahan and the illness of pitcher Red Ames. The Giants' eighteen wins for the month were the second highest number in the league, but losing four in a row to the Pirates in midmonth was a bitter pill to swallow. Again, Mathewson led Giants pitchers, with two shutouts and a 6–2 record for the month.

Ironically, Iron Man McGinnity was placed on and cleared National League waivers in early June. During June, McGinnity turned in a 4–1 mark, which convinced McGraw to keep the star pitcher, whose better years were clearly behind him. The outcome of the 1908 National League race would have been vastly different had McGinnity switched teams or gone into forced retirement. His June performance proved that he still had a few wins in his arm.

As for the defending champion Cubs, June was a lackluster month as injuries, dissension, and plain old bad luck eroded the power of a starting lineup completely capable of dominating the league. Circus Solly Hofman and Del Howard earned their keep as reserves due to injuries to Heinie Zimmerman, Jimmy Sheckard, and Johnny Evers.

Sheckard's injury was particularly irksome. Shortly after establishing himself as a capable replacement for Sheckard, Howard was also sent home due to illness, leaving two spots to fill in the lineup. Initially, Sheckard's injury appeared to be a case of ill fortune, but months later it became clear the that injury was the result of serious dissension. Sheckard was nearly blinded when a bottle of ammonia exploded in his face on June 2 — at least, that was the story circulated in June.

In early August it was reported in *Sporting Life* that Sheckard's injury had hardly been an accident; instead, it had been the result of a disagreement and fistfight with Zimmerman. Chance had joined the scuffle, and it had taken the entire Cubs team to break up the fight. The writer said the story — headlined, "Chaotic 'Cubs': Report of Row in the

TABLE 6. *National League Standings — June 30, 1908*

	W	L	Pct.	GB	June Record
Pittsburgh	40	24	.625	—	22–8
Chicago	37	23	.617	1	14–10
New York	37	27	.578	3	18–11
Cincinnati	34	30	.531	6	15–14
Philadelphia	27	28	.491	8½	10–14
Boston	27	37	.422	13	10–18
St. Louis	24	40	.375	16	9–15
Brooklyn	22	39	.361	16½	9–17

Champion Team" — had been verified through several sources. The fight was described as follows:

> After a few hot words had been exchanged he [Zimmerman] went at Sheckard. During the melee Sheckard threw something at Zimmerman. Angered by this style of attack, Zimmerman picked up a bottle of ammonia and hurled it at Sheckard. The bottle struck Sheckard low in the forehead and between the eyes. The force of the throw broke the bottle and the fluid streamed down Sheckard's face. Manager Chance, thoroughly enraged, buckled into Zimmerman. Zimmerman stood his ground and was getting the best of Chance until the latter called on the other players to help him subdue Zimmerman."[9]

The report said Zimmerman was beaten by his teammates and taken to a hospital for "repairs." The Cubs tried to keep the story secret in the interests of team unity. The report predicted that Zimmerman would be traded soon to St. Louis for pitcher Bugs Raymond. Zimmerman remained a Cub for another eight years, winning a triple crown in 1912. He was traded to the Giants in 1916 and was eventually banned from baseball for fixing games in the wake of the Black Sox scandal.

As the month was winding down, the wounded Cubs headed east. Star pitcher Three Finger Brown remained at home in Indiana because of the illness of his mother. The unfortunate timing of Brown's absence was hard felt in New York, where the Cubs dropped three out of four, including a shutout at the hands of Mathewson.

As July's summer heat approached, the National League pennant race was shaping up to be every bit as close as that in the American League. For major league baseball, the tight pennant races meant growing fan interest and larger crowds. In June many game accounts were noting large, record, or near-record crowds. Owners who had promoted the game as the national pastime were now seeing their words become reality. That was a heady draft for them. Baseball was king in the summer of 1908, and the play on the field would justify those words as the dog days approached.

AFTERWORD: THE PLAYERS, THEIR ORIGINS, AND THEIR NICKNAMES

According to records in the *Baseball Encyclopedia* and the *1996 Edition of the Sports Encyclopedia — Baseball,* 431 men played in the major leagues in 1908. They came from forty of the forty-six states then in the union (as noted earlier, Arizona and New Mexico would become states only in 1912), five were from Canada and five from England, and there were two each from Ireland and Germany and one each from Norway and Switzerland. The majority, 258 (59.9 percent), came from states where major league ball was played.

That figure increases substantially when neighboring states in the northeastern quadrant of the United States are included. Almost three quarters of the players, 73.1 percent of major leaguers, were born east of the Mississippi and north of the Ohio River–Mason-Dixon Line. The top producers of major league talent were Pennsylvania (71), Ohio (56), New York (47), Illinois (32), Massachusetts (22), Missouri (15), Indiana and Wisconsin (14 each), Michigan (12), and Iowa, Kansas, and Kentucky (11 each). The sunbelt states of California, Texas, and Florida, which produced numbers of big leaguers during the post–World War II years, produced ten players, nine, and one, respectively, reflecting the location of the American population in 1908.

Another item of interest is the treatment of players from the Deep South, such as Shoeless Joe Jackson and Ty Cobb. Only thirty-two players came from the states of the old Confederacy. With such small numbers, the vast majority of players from the North, and the Civil War still a relatively recent memory, it is not difficult to understand why players from the South met hostility from their northern colleagues.

Ethnically, most players were of Irish, English, or German origins, reflecting the demographics of late-nineteenth-century immigration to the United States. There were few players whose ethnic origins lay outside northern Europe, but some significant groups in the American mosaic were beginning to be represented during the 1908 season. Pittsburgh's Ed "Batty" Abbaticchio was the first true Italian-American star, and Philadelphia's Harry "The Giant Killer" Coveleski was one of the first players of Polish origin to reach the big leagues. Hall of Famer Charles Albert "Chief" Bender was among the few Native American stars of the Dead Ball Era, many of whom were given the same nickname.

Players' nicknames were an earmark of the time, often reflecting an individual's ethnicity, name, physical stature or habits, professional status, background, or personality. Some players had multiple nicknames. John Peter Wagner of the Pirates was known as Honus, a derivative of his given German name Johannes. The great Wagner was also known as the Flying Dutchman. Cubs manager Frank Chance was called Peerless Leader by the press, but his Cubs charges and close friends called him Husk.

Where you were from could name you. Ty Cobb became the Georgia Peach. Ed Plank of Gettysburg College was Gettysburg Ed to teammates and writers alike. His fellow A's pitcher Jack Coombs was Colby Jack, not because he liked mild cheese but because he had played ball at Colby College. White Sox pitcher Frank Owen earned the nickname Yip because of his hometown of Ypsilanti, Michigan.

Your size or appearance could make your name as well. Big Eds Walsh and Reulbach of the Chicago teams were complemented by Wee Willie Keeler, Tubby Spencer, Little Joe Yeager, and Big Bill Chappelle. Cleveland's Charlie Hickman had big legs, so he was stuck with the moniker of Piano Legs. Red hair gave Ginger Beaumont his name, and Handsome Harry Howell's nickname spoke for itself. Good speed would earn you the name of Deerfoot, as in Needham or Milan.

Ethnic origin was fair game as well. If you were of German origin, you could expect to be called Heinie, as in Zimmerman or Berger or the other Wagner, or Dutch Knabe. Emerald islanders such as Highlanders outfielder Henry McIlveen could expect the nickname Irish, or Jiggs, as for John Donahue of the White Sox. Or personality or habits could mark you. Just ask Crab Evers, Bugs Raymond, Tabasco Kid Elberfeld, or Bad Bill Dahlen; or Noisy Kling, Silent Jake Volz, or Gabby Street; or — perhaps the best nickname of the Dead Ball Era — Slothful Bill Lattimore.

Nicknames could also arouse anger. Giants manager John McGraw was known as Little Napoleon, a reflection of his managerial style and

8 July Gain the Edge

In the last half of the ninth, with the score tied, two men out and a runner on third, the batter hits to left field and the runner scores. The batter, seeing the runner score, stops between home and first. The ball is thrown to first baseman, who touches his base before the runner reaches it. Can runner score on this?

— (signed) Joseph Rupp

No. Run cannot score when third out is made before reaching first base.

— "Inquisitive Fans," July 19, 1908

Each Sunday during 1908, the *Chicago Tribune* published a letter to the sports editor in a column titled "Inquisitive Fans." It was a forum for baseball enthusiasts, amateur umpires, and those merely curious about the rules of baseball. Many of the queries were mundane. But Joseph Rupp's letter may have started wheels turning that erupted into controversy a month and a half later.

G. H. Fleming, author of *Unforgettable Season*, linked this letter to the Merkle baserunning incident. The play depicted by Rupp is not exactly what occurred during the Merkle play, but it involves the same principle, which is that a run cannot score when the third out is a force-out. Technically, the batter-runner thrown out at first base is retired by force-out. In the Merkle play a Giants run was erased because Merkle, who was on first, failed to touch second base after a base hit and was forced out on appeal.

When you consider Johnny Evers's reputation for seeking an advantage, the relationship between Rupp's letter and the Merkle game is not far fetched. Evers was known to stay in his room studying newspapers and rule books, while munching on candy to maintain his weight. The Cubs were in the middle of an eight-game home stand when the letter was published in the *Tribune*. So it is not a stretch to believe that Evers may have read it, giving him an idea. By mid-July it was clear to National Leaguers that the pennant race was going down the wire. Up to the end of July, no third-place team had been further back than five games; at the end of the month Pittsburgh, New York, and Chicago were in a virtual tie for first place. The desire to find, and the motive for seeking, any kind of edge was clear the day Rupp's letter was published.

Nothing in the literature surrounding Evers mentions this letter or suggests that it gave him the idea of using the rule book to question the custom of base runners halting their advance once the winning run scored. It is uncertain whether Rupp's letter was the catalyst that unleashed one of the most troublesome controversies in the history of baseball. Nonetheless, Evers played a central role in the affair, whether he was influenced by the letter or not.

While Evers was recovering from a leg injury and reading the rule book, the defending American League champion Tigers regained their position atop the American League with a scorching 23–6 record during July. For manager Hughie Jennings, the mauling of American League opponents was a vindication of the confidence he had expressed in the spring, when little was going right and Tigers fans were hollering for his head. Remarking on Detroit's growing confidence in late July, Jennings predicted a strong run for his team into the dog days of summer: "It looks much easier than at this time last season for our boys. We have got the measure of the other cities, and all we ask is to escape serious accidents to our regular men."[1]

Sporting Life lightheartedly reported another possible factor in Detroit's run. The situation and circumstance would be a matter of justifiable outrage today, but in the sociocultural climate of 1908, the racist nature of the story was accepted without comment or criticism. "Detroit Tigers are carrying about as a mascot a little black boy who was picked up in Chicago. The youngster has been dubbed as Rastus [and] lies happy on the job."[2]

The month started with Cleveland on top of the league by a half game over St. Louis and with Detroit down three games. The Tigers began the month taking five of six from the White Sox and Cleveland at home. They left Detroit on an eastern road trip that put them in first place, a spot the Tigers would not relinquish despite ferocious challenges from contending teams.

The road trip saw the Tigers ring up a 15–4 record, the stars of the trip being Ed Willett and Ty Cobb. Willett went 7–1 for the month and contributed five wins on the road. Kickapoo Ed Summers was just off that pace with a 5–1 mark. But the big Tigers story was the offense, which was running on all cylinders. Timely hitting marked Detroit's month-long performance. In the 21–2 shellacking of Philadelphia on July 17, Tigers hitters rang out twenty-seven safeties, with Cobb going five for six and Sam Crawford and Germany Schaefer chipping in for five efforts. Cobb's July was one of the best months of his career. He hit .410 and slugged at an eye-popping .672 rate, with seven doubles, eight triples, and three homers.

Kicking off the eastern trip, the Tigers met the once high-flying Highlanders. Detroit went into second place on the first day of the road trip with a doubleheader sweep of New York by scores of 8–3 and 11–4 on July 7. George Mullin lead his mates to a 6–3 win on July 14, the day Detroit went into a tie for first, while New York completed its swan dive, settling into the American League basement. These teams retained those places for the rest of the season.

The St. Louis Browns nearly matched the Tigers win for win, but pitching and fielding weaknesses that would in due course fatally injure their stretch run began to emerge in July. The primary pitching problem was summed up in two words: Rube Waddell. Browns manager Jimmy McAleer knew he was taking a chance with the talented but troublesome lefty when St. Louis bought him from the Athletics in the preseason. McAleer gambled that new surroundings and leadership could change Waddell's behavior. Waddell's talent helped put the Browns in the middle of the race, but an early July slump was threatening to knock them out of the race. Compounding the team's slump were marital problems that kept Waddell from being with the team in Boston. The Browns split that four-game set. But the Boston series revealed another weakness, which would eventually sink their pennant hopes.

While Waddell was wrangling with his estranged wife, the Browns' pennant hopes took a big hit on July 21. The doubleheader loss to the Red Sox came with 2–1 and 3–2 scores. In both games, the team failed to get hits when needed, and catchers made errors that allowed winning runs to score.

Waddell rejoined the team in late July. He beat Washington 5–2 and victimized his former Philadelphia mates 5–4 and 4–2. In the first game against the Athletics on July 29, Waddell struck out sixteen A's to set an American League record. His off- and on-field performances in July starkly revealed the range of emotion those around him experienced. He was almost unmatched in talent for pitching as well as unmatched for causing off-field distractions.

July was not pleasant for Chicago, as the White Sox saw themselves slip from first place and begin to lose ground to Detroit. The absence of Frank Smith was keenly felt, despite Ed Walsh's 7–1 mark for the month. Without Smith in the rotation, Fielder Jones had to resort a three-man rotation of Walsh, Doc White, and a sore-armed Nick Altrock. Reserve pitcher Moxie Manuel started two contests and lost them both. One-time stalwart Yip Owen was ineffective with a 1–2 mark. Smith returned to the team in late July, breaking his vow never to return to the White Sox. His second debut came against Washington and he turned in a five-hitter and 4–1 victory.

July also marked another curiosity for the White Sox during this unusual season. Sox batters hit all three of the team's home runs in the 1908 season as Walsh, Frank Isbell, and Jones all homered to contribute to badly needed wins for Chicago.

Cleveland's 12–17 July record was better than that of only one other team, the Highlanders, whose 6–24 mark gave them exclusive possession of the American League cellar. Cleveland began the month in first and ended it eight games out in fourth place. Up to July the Naps' performance was almost too good to be true. But Cleveland had a perverse history of season-ruining slumps. At the end of July fans couldn't be blamed for saying, "Not again." The primary reason for the Naps' poor performance could be blamed on a slump so deep that staff ace Addie Joss was an uncharacteristic 1–4 for July. Manager Nap Lajoie, disconcerted by the pitching collapse, actually expressed interest in obtaining

TABLE 7. *American League Standings — July 31, 1908*

	W	L	Pct.	GB	July Record
Detroit	57	35	.620	—	23–6
St. Louis	56	38	.598	2	18–10
Chicago	52	41	.559	5½	16–13
Cleveland	49	43	.533	8	12–17
Philadelphia	44	46	.489	12	16–18
Boston	43	50	.462	14½	14–13
Washington	35	55	.389	16	13–15
New York	32	60	.448	25	6–24

Waddell from the Browns! While St. Louis might have been willing to unload their problem child, Waddell's behavior would no doubt have clashed with Lajoie's belief in discipline.

Cleveland's woes were not confined to the mound. Injuries had forced the Naps to use a series of different lineups, and it was only a matter of time before weaknesses were exploited by the opposition. The July 11 doubleheader loss to lowly New York stood as an example of the defensive problem. Both games were lost by 3–2 scores. In the first, reserve catcher Harry Bemis allowed the winning run to score in the ninth when he threw to first on a dropped third strike when no throw was needed. In the second game, New York executed a squeeze play to take the game.

On a personal front, Nap Lajoie achieved a career milestone by getting his two thousandth hit on July 31. The feat hardly received any notice, unlike when Wagner reached the milestone earlier in the summer. For manager Lajoie, the hit was just one of those things; he and the Naps had a pennant to win.

Off the field, Cleveland President John F. Kilfoyle was lobbying for better officiating. In a front-page story in the July 18 edition of *Sporting Life*, Kilfoyle said a two-man umpire system needed to be implemented at once in the major leagues. "Good umpires are scarce, scarcer probably than good ball players," said Kilfoyle, revealing the dilemma facing baseball.[3] The two-umpire system was a noble ideal to strive for, but manpower was thin.

July 1908 also marked an interesting footnote for the Boston Red

Sox. On July 6, Smokey Joe Wood was signed, and he joined the team full-time in 1909. Wood became a dominant pitcher in the American League for the great Boston teams during the next decade.

In the National League, off-field events were just as momentous as those on the field. Giants rookie Fred Merkle became gravely ill in late June. A spike wound had become infected and blood poisoning in the foot was so severe that amputation was considered. The infection was blamed on the dye used in socks at the time; the matter had led some teams to require players to use sanitary hose to prevent infection. Merkle, of course, eventually recovered to make history.[4]

The second off-field event was related to injury as well. The Cubs were doing all they could to avoid doubleheaders because of their injury-depleted roster. The National League required all games to be played, but both leagues were governed by Rule 43, which stated: "Each club shall play as many championship games with every other club as may be decided upon by the schedule adopted, but a tie or drawn game, or a game prevented by rain, shall be played off on the same ground on a succeeding open date with[in] the same scheduled series. An open date succeeding any series of games between two clubs shall be considered as belonging to and with the dates of the preceding series, provided such day is not absolutely required by either club to meet its next scheduled appointment."

The doubleheader in question involved a makeup game between the Cubs and Pirates on July 5. The single game was played and the Pirates won 10–5 to go into first place. When Chicago refused to play a second game, umpire Jim Johnstone ordered a forfeit. The subsequent Cubs protest was upheld by league president Pulliam. Pulliam overturned the forfeit on a technicality. The league had not been formally notified that a doubleheader was to be played. Needless to say, the outcome of the pennant race would have been significantly altered had the protest been allowed.[5]

Schedule manipulation was not limited to the Cubs. John McGraw and the Giants postponed a game with St. Louis on July 22 so that the team could get an early start for Pittsburgh for that all-important series with the tough Pirates. The Cubs vainly protested that maneuver. While the National League did nothing, McGraw's move was not universally well received, even among the keenly partisan New York press. *The*

Evening Mail thundered its unhappiness: "Unless checked sharply, such practices can evolve into great injury to the game. From postponing a game to help a club, it is only a short step to laying down for the same purpose."[6]

The series of protests about who should play who and when was setting a disturbing precedent, namely that an executive decision could overturn results on the field. Schedule manipulation such as that by Chicago and New York was raising a serious question. Eventually a baserunning error, and not dodging doubleheaders, forced a board-room decision that helped determine the outcome of the National League pennant race.

Frank Chance's Cubs, when they weren't trying to duck a double-header, were involved in what military historians call a holding action. The Cubs sick bay in July included Johnny Evers, Circus Solly Hofman, Heinie Zimmerman, Del Howard, and Jimmy Sheckard; sore arms afflicted pitchers Three Finger Brown and Chick Fraser; and on July 2 catcher Johnny Kling was added to the list. The injury list was so long that it wasn't until July 20 that all Cubs first string players were in the same lineup. The absence of Kling may have hurt most. Sportswriter W. A. Phelon observed, "With John in, the team plays like a unit — with John gone, they play a disjointed game, brilliant in spots, and falling short in other places."[7]

Despite injuries, the Cubs played gamely even against the Giants and Pirates in July, because their pitching gave them the chance to win nearly every game. Big Ed Reulbach and Three Finger Brown were almost invincible. Reulbach overcame a tendency toward occasional wildness and turned in a 9–0 mark. Brown overcame personal crises that kept him off the team most of the summer and went 6–2. Brown had left the team in June to be with his sick mother, missing a critical eastern road trip. In July his sister died. When Reulbach and Brown weren't on the mound, the Cubs' record was a below-par 3–11.

Shortstop Joe Tinker always stepped up his game in clutch situations, and 1908 was Tinker's year for key hits. His inside-the-park homer on July 17 helped Brown defeat Christy Mathewson 1–0. The round-tripper kept New York out of first, but there was a tragic footnote. A fan named William Hudson was watching the game from the top of a four-story building. Tinker's hit excited him so that he fell from his perch and died of a broken neck. Apparently unfazed by the tragedy, the next day Tinker hit a two-run triple that provided the winning runs in a 5–4 win over New York. Tinker's bat was also instrumental in a 2–1 win over Brooklyn on July 24 and a 6–0 pounding of Boston five days later.

Kling's return to the lineup in late July also provided more than inspirational leadership. Kling's home runs against Brooklyn on July 28 and Boston on July 31 helped Orval Overall win tight games. With the starters back at the end of July, the Cubs believed the holding action was successful. Though the team was lower in position and winning percentage than it had been in more than two years, the defending World Champions were only a half game off the pace.

McGraw's Giants, who had started slowly, were now playing the best ball in the league, causing many observers to register surprise when noting the team's strong showing. Christy Mathewson put up a 7–2 mark for the month, but the gem of July belonged to Hooks Wiltse.

Wiltse threw a no-hitter at the Phillies in the first game of a Fourth of July doubleheader. He missed perfection by one pitch when he hit Philadelphia pitcher George McQuillan with a pitch in the ninth inning. Some observers claimed that a pitch before the one that nailed McQuillan was strike three but was missed by umpire Cy Rigler.[8] Wiltse kept the no-hitter intact through the tenth inning and won the game on Art Devlin's run. The Giants' third baseman had singled and scored as the result of two Phillies errors. Iron Man McGinnity won the night-cap for the New York sweep.

Two days later Mathewson defeated Cincinnati 2–1. McGraw was not at the game. He and Giants owner John T. Brush were in Columbus, Ohio, scouting a young left-handed pitching prospect named Rube Marquard. The sixth of July also marked a key roster change for the Giants: outfielder Moose McCormick joined the team and replaced Spike Shannon in the lineup. Shannon was waived by New York and hooked up with the Pirates later in the month. McCormick's bat played a major role in the Giants' stretch drive. Marquard's big league debut was a horrible flop.

When the dust of July had settled, the Giants felt pretty good about themselves. They were in first by a half game over Pittsburgh and Chicago, to the surprise of those who had written them off in the pre-season. The Giants were also becoming a huge box office draw. The New York Giants were the premium franchise in baseball with a history of strong attendance. In 1908 the crowds were getting larger and larger. On July 25, thirty-four thousand fans, the largest crowd in Polo

TABLE 8. *National League Standings — July 31, 1908*

	W	L	Pct.	GB	July Record
New York	58	37	.590	—	21–10
Pittsburgh	56	36	.609	$\frac{1}{2}$	16–12
Chicago	55	36	.604	$\frac{1}{2}$	18–13
Philadelphia	47	40	.541	$6\frac{1}{2}$	20–12
Cincinnati	48	46	.511	9	14–16
Boston	40	52	.435	16	13–15
Brooklyn	33	56	.371	$21\frac{1}{2}$	11–17
St. Louis	31	60	.375	$24\frac{1}{2}$	7–20

Grounds history, saw Wagner go five for five as Pittsburgh beat the Giants 7–2. The loss was hard to take, as all losses were for McGraw, but the game marked the first of many record-breaking crowds at the Polo Grounds during this season.

Day in and day out, the great Wagner was earning his money carrying his Pirates teammates closer to a pennant. By mid-July Wagner led the league in home runs, stolen bases, and runs scored and was second in batting average. Eventual home run king Tim Jordan of Brooklyn made his presence known on July 22 when he hit the first homer to clear the fence in Pittsburgh in nine years, during a 2–1 losing effort. Pirates pitchers Nick Maddox, Vic Willis, Lefty Leifield, Irv Young, Howie Camnitz, and Sam Leever were effective as a unit, but none of them put up the gaudy individual won-lost marks of a Reulbach, Brown, or Mathewson.

Pittsburgh manager Fred Clarke, sensing a close race, sought his own edge for victory. Clarke did not employ any unusual tactics in seeking his edge. He decided that the best approach would be to keep all of his available players eligible and ordered his team to leave umpires alone. Clarke told *Sporting Life*, "There's nothing to be gained by paying attention to the umpires but it may mean a big loss when men get put out of the game."[9]

Abandoning the time-honored Dead Ball Era tactic of umpire baiting seemed like a radical departure, but the tight pennant races were giving everyone pause to think about how best to gain the advantage. The Pirates listened to their skipper; they had only three ejections for the year, all coming before Clarke issued his edict.

AFTERWORD: TINKER, EVERS, AND CHANCE
AND THE HALL OF FAME

Franklin Adams's doggerel titled "Tinker to Evers to Chance" gets a great deal of credit for the selection of the "trio of Bear Cubs fleeter than birds," as Adams would have it, to the Hall of Fame in 1946. As a unit, the Cubs infield of the early Dead Ball Era is one of the very few to have more than one or two Hall of Famers. It is known as a double play combination; Tinker to Evers to Chance don't come close to modern standards, or even to being outstanding among contemporaries.

But teams with many double plays often have pitchers who allow lots of base runners. Base runners mean trouble, and raw double play numbers are no true indication of a team's quality. Cubs pitching was dominant. Three Finger Brown or Big Ed Reulbach often mowed down hitters like so much alfalfa in a hay field. As a result, the Tinker–Evers– Chance unit did not have the double play opportunities others may have had.

In terms of comparison with other individual first and second basemen and shortstops in the history of baseball, the truth is that this Cubs trio does not fare very well. Partly this is a reflection of offensive and defensive statistics of the Dead Ball Era. Not one of these men ranks high in any category of individual performance, unless you want to note that Chance ranks sixth in winning percentage among managers. In light of all this, some declare that Tinker, Evers, and Chance do not belong in Cooperstown.

But baseball is a team sport, and selection to the Hall of Fame isn't always strictly a numbers game. Other factors must be considered, such as how did they rank among their contemporaries, were they among the best at their respective positions at the time, what was their impact on the game, and were they winners? Tinker, Evers, and Chance rank above the average, although not outstanding, in most of these categories.

Above average, however, should not equal immortality. Wagner was a better shortstop than Tinker and than most others, too. At second, Evers was overshadowed by Lajoie and later Eddie Collins, but those two players were in the American League. Chance was a dominant first baseman for a brief period, until injuries hurt his effectiveness and shortened his career. Among his contemporaries, Chance was one of the best, if not the best. Some might say Hal Chase was better, but

Chase's poor moral character and ultimate banishment from the baseball for fixing games effectively eliminate him from the running.

On paper it is easy to conclude that Tinker, Evers, and Chance should not have been enshrined. Poem or no poem, on the field they played well as a unit on a dominant team; they were clutch performers and winners. Perhaps those intangibles rather than hard numbers justify their Hall of Fame status.

Bill James has written extensively about the Hall of Fame, its selections, the politics involved, and related issues. His well-researched opinions are guaranteed to get a discussion going. As with other baseball historians, he has blown hot and cold about the Cubs trio. There are good arguments to be made on both sides of the issue, and James made both. Having once passionately defended the trio's Hall of Fame status, in *Whatever Happened to the Hall of Fame?* James places Tinker, Evers, and Chance on the All Why-Did-They-Elect-Him Team: "The 1946 group induction of Tinker, Evers and Chance is the Hall of Fame's most ridiculed selection. . . . I defended this group of selections, arguing that their qualifications weren't as weak as people will say. In retrospect, having developed now a few methods to study the issue, I have to say that I was wrong on that issue; they were as bad as people say. They stand out as being among the least qualified players in the Hall of Fame."[10]

James's passionate defense of their Hall status is found in the *Bill James Historical Baseball Abstract*. In that volume, he wrote: "Tinker, Evers and Chance were the guts of a great team, maybe the greatest team ever. Between 1906 and 1910 they won 530 games and lost only 235, the best five-year won-lost record of this century. In 1906 they had the best one-year won-lost record of this century. They went into the Hall of Fame together; they were a team. What's wrong with that?"[11]

Indeed, what is wrong with that? On balance, the Hall of Fame would be poorer if key members of one of baseball's great teams were excluded because they do not stack up with players of other eras. There were better players at their positions during their playing days, but Tinker, Evers, and Chance were key representatives of a dominant team. That ought to count for something. The debate will continue about whether they deserve the Hall or if the Hall deserves them. They are in and no one is going to throw them out. The fact is there are others in the Hall whose election is also debatable.

While the 1908 Cubs are well represented in Cooperstown, there is one member of the team whose statistics and contributions have been totally overlooked. That player is catcher Johnny Kling. His achievements have been forgotten, partially due to the attention paid to Tinker, Evers, and Chance. Also, and this is no small factor, universally accepted opinion was that his contemporary Roger Bresnahan was a better catcher during this era. A comparison between the two reveals a slightly different picture.

Bresnahan was a fine player and an outstanding hitter during the Dead Ball Era. Elected to the Hall of Fame in 1945, the Duke of Tralee benefited from playing in New York under McGraw, as did a number of New York Giants' Hall of Fame members. Compared to Kling, Bresnahan was the more versatile player. Besides catching, Bresnahan was a competent outfielder and first baseman. Kling was primarily a catcher; almost 93 percent of his games were spent behind the plate, while Bresnahan caught in only 68 percent of his games.

If Hall of Fame status is conferred upon the best player at his position during his playing days, Kling's defensive numbers support the argument that he was the dominant defensive catcher of the Dead Ball Era. From 1902 to 1910, Kling led the National League in putouts five times, in assists and double plays once, and in fielding percentage during three seasons. As a catcher, Bresnahan led the National League in defensive categories twice, in chances per game in 1905, and in putouts in 1906.

Offensively, both Bresnahan and Kling were key members of their teams and were evenly matched. Both were dangerous clutch hitters. Bresnahan usually batted third with the Giants, a power and RBI spot. Kling provided punch in the eighth slot, a difficult position to hit consistently because batting in front of a light-hitting pitcher usually meant a steady diet of bad pitches or intentional walks. Noteworthy in this comparison is that Kling drove in more runs than Bresnahan, despite their respective positions in the batting order and Kling's sitting out of the 1909 season. Bresnahan, however, hit for a better average and slugged more homers (see appendix H).

Bresnahan had better lifetime numbers mainly because his career was four years longer than Kling's. By 1909 Bresnahan's attention was devoted to his managerial career in St. Louis, where he served in a utility role as a playing manager. In 1909 Kling pursued a billiards career. He returned to the diamond in 1910, the last year during which both players can be compared fairly.

During the Cubs dynasty from 1906 to 1910, it is significant their only nonpennant year was the one Kling sat out. Looking at the numbers, it is not clear that Bresnahan can claim clear title as the best catcher during the first decade of the twentieth century. No doubt Johnny Kling's billiards sabbatical hurt his case. But opinions about the credentials of Tinker, Evers, and Chance should not block consideration of John Gradwohl "Noisy" Kling as deserving a serious look by the Veterans Committee for admission into Cooperstown.

9 **August** The Storm Clouds Gather

As August came around, Giants manager John McGraw was feeling unusually charitable. His charges were competing for the pennant, an undreamed of status during spring training. The players obtained in the trade with the Boston Doves had exceeded reasonable expectations, and none of his opponents had been able to run away and hide. His thoughts turned to former Orioles teammate Hughie Jennings and the American League race. McGraw's Orioles blood line ran stronger than his hatred for the American League. "I think the Detroit Tigers will play us for the world's pennant," said McGraw, "I would like to see Hugh Jennings win again, as we played together ten years ago in Baltimore." In a *Sporting Life* story McGraw admitted that he'd like to see St. Louis win the American League flag, though he believed they lacked the talent. He gave Chicago no chance to win due to a lack of offense and Cleveland a slight chance if injured players could return to the lineup.[1]

Detroit seemed poised to run away from the rest of the league in August. The July streak shows the Tigers' potential and Jennings's players were 100 percent behind him. First baseman Claude Rossman was a true believer. He told everyone who would listen, "It's the college spirit instilled by Hugh Jennings that makes the Tigers play and win."[2]

There was one Tiger who marched to a different drummer, Ty Cobb. Cobb had a key role in Detroit's dominant play in July. The twenty-one-year-old Cobb left the team to get married in early August, temporarily giving up his passion for hitting a baseball to taste wedded bliss and giving Jennings another problem to cope with in the midst of a red hot pennant race.

The blessed union of Cobb and Charlotte Lombard was scheduled for August 6 at the Lombard estate near Waycross, Georgia. Jennings and the Tigers were given no advance notice and had virtually no choice but to okay Cobb's leave of absence. Cobb was gone from August 3 to August 8. The moral of the story was clear to all: Cobb did what he wanted, when and where he wanted to do it, on or off the diamond. Cobb's wedding was a major distraction and an unnecessary obstacle for Detroit to overcome on the way to the pennant. The discord over his special treatment added to Cobb's unpopularity among his teammates and nearly cost Detroit the pennant.

With or without Cobb, the Tigers spent an awful August against the weaker eastern teams both at home and on the road. Winning 11 of 24 was not a pennant-winning formula, and had it not been for rookie pitcher Ed Summers's 6–1 August mark, the Tigers would have made a date with oblivion in October and not with the National League champion in the World Series.

There were two bright spots in the month for the Tigers, though neither was apparent at the time. First, Detroit played only two games with a pennant contender. The Tigers lost both of them. The Naps were the recipients of the largesse, but Lajoie's charges needed more than just two wins to recover from their July swoon. In a pennant race, it is best not to play poorly at all, but if you do play poorly, it is better to do it against also-rans than against the nearest competition. The two losses to the Naps hurt, but they weren't fatal to Detroit.

The second silver lining actually occurred in late July but became public in August. Infielder Donie Bush of Indianapolis was signed as Detroit outbid seven other teams, including the New York Giants. The addition of Bush stabilized the Tigers' infield during the stretch run. Bush played a significant role in the outcome of the pennant race.

The St. Louis Browns finished the month in second, but their 11–12 August mark indicated to the Browns faithful the July fade was for real. The mercurial Rube Waddell finally focused on baseball and turned in a 5–1 mark for the month. For once, Waddell's behavior could not be blamed for the Browns' woes.

In late July, Waddell's colleagues were telling sportswriters that

Rube's left arm was worth a two-thousand-dollar World Series share. Perhaps that message was soaking in. But just when you thought Waddell's pranks were over with, in late August he volunteered to umpire a game between St. Louis College and the Boston Bloomer Girls.[3] His umpire service was harmless enough, but it showed that Waddell, like Cobb, danced to his own tune, a song only he heard and on a schedule only he knew. Stability would never be Waddell's strong suit. For the Browns to win the flag, they needed Waddell's presence both in body and in spirit.

Of all the contenders, Cleveland looked the best in August, but only for half the month. The Naps' 5–4 win over New York on the fifteenth of August gave them an 11–2 mark. Not a team to tolerate prosperity, Cleveland closed out the month with a 6–8 record. Consecutive doubleheader losses to Washington on August 28 and 29 capped the month and determined the season's outcome for the Naps. In those four games, Cleveland was beaten by scores of 2–0, 8–0, 4–2, and 3–0 at the hands of the league's seventh-place team. Cleveland's inability to handle Washington in late August and throughout the season contributed to the Naps' coming up short in October.

Especially disturbing about the twin double dip was that Washington was a team that was playing out the string. The Nats were good enough to be a spoiler, especially when Walter Johnson or Long Tom Hughes was on the mound, but had a penchant for self-destruction. In early August, pitcher Sleepy Bill Burns and outfielder Bob Ganley got into a fight on the bench. Reports indicated that Ganley hit Burns with a bat and broke his ribs. The rookie Burns was done for the year with a 6–11 won-lost record and an ERA of 1.69. Like most of the rest of his career, Burns's exit in 1908 was little noticed; he is remembered for his role in the 1919 Black Sox scandal.

Cleveland and Washington were also involved in one of the more notorious umpire baiting incidents of the year. On August 4, Silk O'Loughlin was working the game alone. He became the target of verbal abuse by outfielder Otis Clymer and second baseman Jim Delahanty. O'Loughlin ejected both players. Accounts of the day noted that Delahanty's language was "particularly vile."[4]

Because of the incident, American League President Ban Johnson fined Delahanty fifty dollars, suspended him for ten days without pay, and in a unique move, banned Delahanty for one year from playing at the Cleveland grounds. Delahanty was a Cleveland native, and the ban kept him from playing in his home town. Johnson made an example of Delahanty to make his point about foul language directed at umpires and about rowdyism on the field. The punishment received acceptance from the partisan Cleveland press, which universally regarded the incident as "the most flagrant ever witnessed at the Cleveland Ball Park."[5]

Just a few days before playing Cleveland for the first time in the month, catcher Gabby Street engaged in an off-field stunt, which served as further evidence the Nats were pulling the pin on another mediocre season. On August 21 Street caught a ball dropped from the top of the Washington Monument. The catch was made after a number of attempts, which must have endangered the participant and witnesses alike. As we have seen, it had been done before. Such stunts are a thing of the past. We can only imagine present-day reaction to the deed. In today's legal climate, it would not be allowed by National Park Service out of fear of violating the sensibilities of our modern age and running up against the trial lawyer's bar.

Street's achievement spanned the Cleveland series and an August 12 upset doubleheader sweep of Chicago by the Nats. In the opener Walter Johnson blazed a two-hitter to ice a 1–0 victory, as The Big Train began to establish himself as a premier pitcher in the majors. Long Tom Hughes won game two to put the Sox in fourth place and, in retrospect, dealt a body blow to Chicago's pennant hopes.

Big Ed Walsh turned in seven wins during the month, accounting for half his team's wins. By late August the baseball world was taking note that Walsh was having a special year. As of the week of August 24, Walsh was responsible for almost two-thirds of the sixty-one Sox victories. *Sporting Life* also noted that by then, Chicago had been involved in twenty shutouts, or one third of the entire American League total for the year.

The White Sox's 14–11 mark for August allowed them to gain ground on Detroit and St. Louis and remain just ahead of Cleveland. The problem for Fielder Jones's charges was getting down to a usual team strength, pitching. Without Walsh, the Sox were noncontenders.

The White Sox question marks were two. How far and how long could Big Ed carry the team without help? Would Smith, Altrock, White, or Owen find their skills of previous years and give the South Siders a badly needed boost? Answers to those questions were: Big Ed Walsh carried the White Sox as far as he was able, and Smith and White contributed, but Sox pitching was wearing thin because Altrock and Owen were not the pitchers they had been.

TABLE 9. *American League Standings — August 31, 1908*

	W	L	Pct.	GB	August Record
Detroit	68	48	.586	—	11–13
St. Louis	67	50	.573	1½	11–12
Chicago	66	52	.559	3	14–11
Cleveland	66	53	.555	3½	17–10
Philadelphia	58	57	.489	9½	14–11
Boston	56	62	.475	13	13–12
Washington	48	66	.421	19	13–11
New York	38	79	.325	30½	6–19

Mid-August featured one of those events common during baseball's early days, a day honoring a star ball player. On August 13, Cy Young was honored in Boston. He was presented with six thousand dollars, given three silver loving cups by teammates and opposing players, and presented with a traveling bag from the umpires. An exhibition game was played involving players from around the league, and for one day Boston was the center of attention of the baseball world. The American League All Stars included White Sox manager Fielder Jones; Wee Willie Keeler, Jack Chesbro, and Hal Chase of the Highlanders; Detroit's George Mullin, who played outfield rather than pitch; and Athletics pitcher Colby Jack Coombs. The Stars defeated the Red Sox 3–2 on a triple by Jimmy Collins and a single by Coombs in the tenth inning.[6] This game was remarkable in that teams involved in a tight pennant race furnished star players to participate in an otherwise meaningless contest to honor an opposing pitcher. It was an indication of the measure of respect the league had for Cy Young.

The Boston franchise made news two weeks later when Red Sox manager James "Deacon" McGuire was dismissed as skipper, being replaced by Fred Lake. The managerial change came a few days after Boston President John I. Taylor had expressed satisfaction with the team's progress and confidence that the Red Sox would contend seriously for the pennant in 1909.

While McGuire's firing shows that little has changed in the dynamics between owners and managers where votes of confidence are concerned, Ban Johnson again unfurled the antigambling filibuster in mid-August. Johnson asked owners to enforce the ban on gambling in the stands at all American League ballparks. In the National League, Harry Pulliam sang a different tune, telling the press there was no need for the senior circuit to issue a similar edict. The announcements again gave editorialists a chance to mount the soapbox on the issue, but as in previous clean up campaigns, much was said and little done.

While the newspapers were thundering against gambling and covering the tight pennant races, Cincinnati owner Garry Herrmann stood the baseball world on its ear by announcing his intent to use the Cincinnati Park as the site of an experiment with night baseball. The headline lent an air of disbelief with this weighty phrase: "A Possible Upheaval of the National Game Owing to Invention Which Makes Playing at Night Practical."

In the story, which commanded the entire front page of *Sporting Life*, Herrmann expressed confidence that the experiment would be successful in that it would open baseball to an entirely new group of fans: "If the innovation works as well as we expect it to, base ball will be revolutionized, for it will be possible for us then to cater to a large mass of people during the week who heretofore have had their opportunities for seeing games restricted to Sunday exhibitions."[7]

George P. Cahill of Holyoke, Massachusetts, owned the firm conducting the experiment, the Night Baseball Development Company. The experiment went ahead with some success on June 24, 1909, at the Cincinnati ballpark. But night baseball did not catch on immediately in the major leagues. The sporting press was critical of baseball under the lights mainly because it was not a natural setting for the game.[8] Calling night baseball unnatural was a convenient excuse not to pursue the idea. In reality, the owners were doing well enough not to feel the pressure to add night games and expand the market base until the Great Depression forced the issue. The bottom line was that many owners, already spending large sums to build ballparks, were unwilling to spend more to provide night games.

On the playing field, the National League race was close and getting closer. Unlike in the American League race, where contenders were playing noncontending teams, the National League contenders played a total of twelve games against one another. When the month of August ended, not one of the three — not Giants, Cubs, or Pirates — had been able to gain a decisive advantage. The clubs were separated by a half game and .007 points in won-lost percentage. New York hung on to first just .003 points ahead of Chicago, while Pittsburgh was a half game off the pace.

The Chicago Cubs had a month that tested the mettle of players and fans alike as they went from being left for dead in mid-August to being a revitalized contender at month's end. August began with stories of dissension and fighting within the club. Stories surrounding the fight among Jimmy Sheckard, Heinie Zimmerman, and Frank Chance back in June surfaced in late July and early August. The fight was a distraction that had been overcome, but publicity surrounding the matter may have affected the team's play early in the month.

The Cubs began August losing 14–0 to Boston and ended the month with a nine-game winning streak. August served as a metaphor for the Cubs' season, as the team responded to adversity by winning. Winning can cure many ills, even fighting and dissension. August 1908 gave the Cubs a critical boost in their bid for greatness.

As of August 15, Chicago was 3–8 for the month and five and a half games out of first. The month's dismal start was one of those funks any team suffers. After the loss to Boston, Three Finger Brown beat the Phillies. But his mates lost the next three to Philadelphia and two more to the Giants. Jack Pfiester's 4–0 two-hit win over the Giants on August 11 broke the losing skid but failed to pull the team out of the dumps. The near disastrous eastern trip for the Cubs ended with a split with Pittsburgh.

Upon returning home, the Cubs split eight games with Philadelphia and Boston before getting on track and closing the month without a loss. The turning point was a doubleheader with Brooklyn on August 23. Both games were settled by 2–0 scores, with Orval Overall pitching a two-hitter and Ed Reulbach tossing a four-hitter at the Superbas. That twin bill performance ignited Frank Chance's charges, as over the next three days, the Cubs victimized Brooklyn by 4–2, 10–2, and 6–4 scores. Those victories set out the welcome mat for the Giants, and a three-game series established a Cubs legend.

The scene was set for the three-game series by the earlier three-game series in New York, during which the Giants took two of three. The sole Cubs win came from the left arm of Jack Pfiester. The Cubs-Giants games in early August continued the attendance pace for the rest of the season. Sixty-five thousand fans witnessed the three-game set. From then on, record crowds spun the turnstiles at ballparks in New York, Chicago, and Pittsburgh as fan interest reached fever pitch. The Polo

Grounds were remodeled to handle expected overflow crowds during the August Pittsburgh series.

The first-place Giants checked into Chicago on the evening of August 26 three and a half games up, fresh from a four-game sweep of Pittsburgh that put New York in first place. During that series, Giants fans who could not get to the Polo Grounds viewed a doubleheader at Madison Square Garden and at Gotham Theatre on 125th Street with the help of an electric diamond. This innovation before the days of commercial radio allowed spectators to view action with the help of small lights, which showed the players' positions on the board. This form of electronic baseball was used in other cities across the country as the 1908 pennant race progressed.

The four-game sweep of Pittsburgh on August 24–26 was the high-water mark for the Giants in 1908. Christy Mathewson and Hooks Wiltse got things going with a doubleheader sweep of the Pirates. Giants hitters did damage when it counted, and poor defense hurt Pittsburgh as the Pirates fell out of first place for the first time since late July. Doc Crandall beat Nick Maddox in the third game by a 5–3 margin. During that game the great Wagner was thrown out at home twice. Iron Man McGinnity capped the series with a 4–3 win as the Giants scored twice in the ninth to win.

While the Giants were flying high on August 27, the Cubs were riding a five-game win streak but still three and a half games behind New York. The next three games at the West Side Grounds put the Cubs back in the running.

Game one of the August 27 doubleheader pitted Pfiester against Wiltse, and the Cubs won easily, 5–1. Errors by Mike Donlin and the usually sure-handed Wiltse contributed two runs. Harry Steinfeldt iced the game in the fifth with a two-run single. It was Pfiester's second win in a month against New York. The second game saw another duel between Hall of Famers Three Finger Brown and Mathewson, with Brown emerging victorious, 3–2.

Base-running errors by Donlin and Larry Doyle kept New York from scoring more than they did, while Chicago scored all three runs in the fourth. Circus Solly Hofman, one of the heroes of the first game, led off with a double and got to third on a sacrifice. He scored on Chance's single. Johnny Evers, Steinfeldt, and Del Howard followed with base hits. The four consecutive singles were enough to give the Cubs their seventh win in a row.

TABLE 10. *National League Standings — August 31, 1908*

	W	L	Pct.	GB	August Record
New York	69	45	.605	—	11–8
Chicago	71	47	.602	—	16–11
Pittsburgh	70	47	.598	½	14–11
Philadelphia	60	52	.536	8	13–12
Cincinnati	58	60	.492	13	10–14
Boston	50	67	.427	15½	10–15
Brooklyn	43	71	.377	26	10–15
St. Louis	42	74	.362	28	11–14

Game three was another tight, one-run contest, with Pfiester and Doc Crandall matching five hitters as the Cubs prevailed 2–1. Hofman was again the key man in this victory, scoring after his leadoff walk in the first and driving Joe Tinker home with the winning run in the fifth with a single. Hofman went 5 for 11 and scored three times in the series, which was witnessed by almost seventy-two thousand fans. Circus Solly's stellar performance was overshadowed by Pfiester. His win in the third game gave him one of the colorful nicknames of the era. Upon witnessing Pfiester's third victory over McGraw's charges, *Chicago Tribune* sportswriter I. E. Sanborn dubbed him "Jack the Giant Killer," a nickname Pfiester carried for the rest of his fine career.

When the dust settled in August, you could throw a hand towel over the top three contenders. The home stretch run in September favored New York, as the Giants would play their last twenty games at home. McGraw was predicting victory. The Giants manager was superstitious. During the western trip, McGraw acquired a good luck charm of sorts, in another one of those actions that by today's standards can only be called an outrageous case of racism and gross insensitivity. While in Springfield, Illinois, for an exhibition game, John McGraw was taken to the site of a lynching. He was given a piece of the rope that had been used to hang a black man. McGraw claimed that the rope would "take the place of a rabbit's foot for the Giants."[9]

August featured a no-hitter, not officially recognized because it was not a nine-inning performance. St. Louis hurler Johnny Lush no-hit Brooklyn on August 6. The 2–0 game was halted after the sixth inning because of a severe thunderstorm. The rain deprived the Cardinals of one of their few bright spots during 1908, unless you include the August 4 game against Brooklyn during that same series: during that game one ball was used throughout the contest. For both of these mediocre teams it was an achievement nonetheless and a comment on playing conditions of the day.[10]

AFTERWORD: THE GILL PLAY

Had just a few of the circumstances had changed, Pirates rookie Doc Gill, and not fellow rookie Fred Merkle, would have been branded the goat of the 1908 season. As described earlier, Gill did the identical thing Merkle did — that is, not touch second base and hightail it to the clubhouse after an apparent game-winning hit. The crucial difference was that Gill's deed did not cost Pittsburgh a victory, while Merkle's oversight cost the Giants a game and, arguably, the 1908 National League pennant.

Warren "Doc" Gill was one of four players used at first base for the Pirates during the 1908 season. None of the them made much of an impression, and the weakness at first base was a prime reason Pittsburgh's 1908 pennant hopes fell short. When Gill got his shot at the majors, the Ladoga, Indiana, native was twenty-nine years old. He appeared in twenty-five games at first, pinch hit in two others, and batted .224 (17 for 76). Gill's only year in the majors was 1908.

Called the "one of the most crucial games in the history of baseball" by G. H. Fleming in *Unforgettable Season*, the Cubs-Pirates game on September 4 in Pittsburgh was a classic pitcher's duel between Hall of Famers Vic Willis and Three Finger Brown. At game time both teams were in a virtual tie for second place, a game behind New York. For nine innings both pitchers had their way. Brown was steadier, while Willis had to overcome early wildness. Willis settled and held the Cubs to four hits, retiring them in order in the top of the tenth.

In the home half of the extra inning, Fred Clarke led off with a single and went to second on Tommy Leach's sacrifice. Honus Wagner singled, and accounts say Clarke could have scored but was held up by the coach. It is tantalizing to think how baseball history would have been changed had Clarke scored and had the subsequent action not happened. With men on first and third, Gill came to bat and was hit by a pitch to load the bases. Ed Abbaticchio struck out for out number two. Rookie outfielder Chief Wilson stepped up to bat. Wilson wasted no time and lined Brown's first pitch into center for a hit, bringing Clarke home. Gill, upon seeing the hit, took off for the clubhouse without touching second base.

Cubs second baseman Johnny Evers, seeing Gill not touch the base, called for the ball, tagged the base, and asked umpire Hank O'Day to declare Gill out, thus nullifying the winning run. One account notes that all of the Cubs were expecting the play and had not left the field after the base hit. Whether Evers had read about it or not, he and the rest of the Cubs team were applying the same principle outlined in the "Inquisitive Fan" letter published in the *Chicago Tribune* in July.

Evers was applying to the situation what was then Rule 59, which states: "One run shall be scored every time a baserunner, after having legally touched the first three bases, shall legally touch the home base before three men are put out; provided, however, that if he reach home on or during a play in which the third man be forced out or be put out before reaching first base, a run shall not count. A force-out can be made only when a baserunner legally loses the right to the base he occupies and is thereby obliged to advance as the result of a fair hit ball not caught on the fly."[11]

Accounts differ on what happened next. Some say O'Day refused to allow the out because the winning run had already scored. Other accounts say O'Day did not see whether or not Gill touched second and applied the ancient and worthy umpiring principle, "don't call what you don't see."

The modern version of the rule is Rule 4.09 (a), How a Team Scores, states: "One run shall be scored each time a runner legally advances to and touches first, second, third and home base before three men are put out to end the inning. EXCEPTION: A run is not scored if the runner advances to home base during a play in which the third out is made (1) by the batter-runner before he touches first base; (2) by any runner being forced out; or (3) by a preceding runner who is declared out because he failed to touch one of the bases."[12]

As noted, Gill was following a traditional practice that had grown up largely out of self defense—leaving the field as quickly as possible as soon as the game was over. We have seen that postgame security was not a high priority among the owners, and once a game ended, often it was every man for himself. The problem was this traditional practice was that it was in direct violation of the rules. In their biography of Wagner, Dennis and Jeanne Burke DeValeria aptly describe the practice, which would end in 1908. "Gill's action on the controversial play was like that of many others in similar game winning situations over the years. Despite the 'letter of the law,' it was commonly assumed that, regardless of the movement of the other baserunners, the game was over when no play was made on the runner crossing the plate with the winning run."[13]

Bill James notes in his *Historical Baseball Abstract* that many of the controversies in baseball stem from traditional practice clashing with sudden enforcement of a rule already on the books. He is critical of O'Day's decision in the Merkle play, stating that a rule not enforced is not enforceable.

That is hard to dispute, but the National League could have done something about the matter before putting O'Day into the situation of having to make a similar call nineteen days *after* the Gill game. James's position on the matter is succinct: "It is in principle most dangerous to have rules on the books which are not enforced, or have one set of rules written down and another acted out."[14] Lack of clarification of the rules after the Gill play compounded the problem, especially when there was an opportunity to clarify the rule while the Cubs' protest was under consideration.

The protest cited witnesses who saw Gill head for the clubhouse and not touch second base. At the same time the Cubs argued for a two-umpire system to help make calls of this nature easier. The protest was noted in some sectors of the baseball press, but in most quarters the rejection of the protest, rather than its substance, was more important.

In a commentary in *Sporting Life*, Francis Richter noted that because O'Day did not see the play, there was no way a call could be made. In the editorial, Richter made a prophetic statement: "The attention of O'Day was called to the play, but he said he did not see it. Technically, Gill would have been out, but it is believed that Pulliam will rule otherwise, because of precedent. If he should not, however, this decision might have a great effect on the result of the league race."[15]

The competing *Sporting News* disdained the protest, calling it ill-advised. It argued that the protest was based on a technicality and that making the protest "served only to afford a carping class of patrons an opportunity to question the integrity of the game."[16]

Baseball historians have examined how widely the details of the protest were reported in the press? In *The Rules of Baseball*, David Nemec says it was widely reported.[17] G. H. Fleming in *Unforgettable Season* says the New York press covered the game routinely; only the *Globe* noted the protest, giving no reason why the Cubs protested. The incident, of course, was widely reported in the Chicago and Pittsburgh papers. The *Pittsburgh Press* noted: "That final play of Friday's game between the Cubs and Pirates is one that does not come often, but next time it happens it is safe to predict that none who took part in the game will overlook the importance of touching the next base."[18]

The *Press's* statement was uncannily prescient. The next time it happened, Evers and O'Day would be involved again. The result would shake the baseball world and decide the outcome of the National League pennant race.

Pulliam received the protest and quickly ruled that an umpire's call was not subject to being overruled by others, eyewitnesses or not. It was much like other rulings he made upholding his umpires' decisions. Pulliam's formula response to the protest was issued September 9, two weeks before the Merkle game. He ruled that the question of the force play could not be established by evidence of players or spectators and that the question rested "solely with the umpire. The umpire in this case, by allowing the winning run, ruled that there was no force at second, because if there had been the run could not have been scored. The protest is denied."[19]

Pulliam believed he had done the right thing in upholding O'Day's call. The problem lay in what he did not do. While he alluded to the impact a third out on a force play would have, he did not comment on either the substance of the protest or the application of Rule 59. That stance contrasted starkly with what Ban Johnson had done in the previously noted incident (in chapter 4) involving an attempted squeeze play in a Detroit-Chicago game. In retrospect, Pulliam's inaction regarding the Gill play was the equivalent of lighting the fuse to a bomb. The subsequent explosion cost the Giants a pennant and contributed to Pulliam's nervous breakdown and eventual suicide. Had Pulliam taken the lead of the *Pittsburgh Press* and directed his umpires to be aware of the Gill play, there probably would have been no Merkle boner.

O'Day himself is not altogether an innocent party in this instance. Many accounts note that he had thought about the play, decided that Evers was right, and told him so, though there is no written record or clear reference as regards his thinking. O'Day was a notorious loner and may well have kept his thoughts to himself; he preferred to work alone and may not have aired his views to anyone, let alone discussed the matter with a partner. Under the rules of the day, there was no requirement for O'Day to submit any statement to the league office other than his simple account of the play. Under today's rules — 9.05 (a) — umpires are required to report to the league president within twelve hours "all violations of rules and other incidents worthy of comment."[20] How baseball history would have changed had O'Day been required to make such a report.

10 **September** All Hell Breaks Loose

If baseball fans believed August play was exciting, they had not seen anything yet. September 1908 was one of the most exciting, tumultuous, and controversial months in the history of major league baseball. The season was coming down to a situation where every game was life and death. The same pressure was on the contenders' front offices as they urgently sought help on the diamond.

For the Giants and Cubs, off-field maneuvering had profound impact on the eventual outcome of the pennant races. Desperate to shore up pitching staffs depleted by injury and by the rigors of a long season, both clubs were seeking help. In mid-August, *Sporting Life* reported that the Giants were close to acquiring Andy Coakley from the Reds, but a planned trade fell through. This was more significant than it seemed at the time.

Coakley was acquired by the Cubs on September 2 and won two crucial games during the stretch drive. The Giants settled for signing and bringing up rookie pitcher Rube Marquard. His contract was bought August 3 for eleven thousand dollars after scouts saw him pitch a perfect game in Indianapolis. Marquard started only one game in 1908. In that game the future Hall of Famer was bombed in one of the most horrific debuts any Hall member endured.

In the American League there was off-field news as well. Citing Ban

Johnson's suspension of Jim Delahanty, Boston owner John I. Taylor demanded that Ty Cobb be banned in Boston for using "vile and abusive language."[1] In tacit admission that the demand for suspension was ultimately self-serving, Taylor said he was making the request to save Cobb's life because the Detroit outfielder had become the target of death threats.

In another off-field event of note, Hal Chase jumped the Highlanders on September 3 to play for an outlaw California team. Accurately rumored to be bitter over not getting the manager's job when Clark Griffith was released, Chase used newspaper accusations of his questionable character, honesty, and integrity as his rationale for jumping the team and claiming he was the wronged party.[2] Chase was allowed to return to New York in 1909 despite his behavior. He replaced George Stallings as manager in 1910 and ran the team in 1911. In 1912 he was replaced as skipper by Harry Wolverton. Chase was eventually banned from baseball in the wake of the Black Sox scandal. His presence in the game from 1909 until his expulsion was symbolic of the gap between rhetoric and action on the part of the game's leadership when it came to gambling and its potential influence in baseball.

Many of his contemporaries considered Chase the best first baseman of his day, which explains why so many baseball people tolerated his obvious moral flaws. Chase spent fifteen years in the majors. A lifetime .291 hitter, he played for five teams, the Giants and Highlanders, White Sox, Reds, and for Buffalo of the Federal League. He led the Federal League in home runs with seventeen in 1915. There is no question Hal Chase was a talented player, but his greed and selfishness eclipsed that talent.

On the field, September was marked by contests in which nearly every at-bat, pitch, out, hit, and error mattered. During those thirty days, American League fans were treated to pitching feats that would become baseball legend. The most impressive of these achievements was performed by Washington right-hander Walter Johnson, who chose the first week of September in 1908 to serve notice that he had arrived.

In one of the most dominant feats of pitching ever, Johnson threw consecutive shutouts against New York on September 4, 5, and 7 with scores of 3–0, 6–0, and 4–0. During those games Johnson struck out twelve, surrendered twelve hits, and walked only one hitter. In going 6–4 for the month, Johnson lost three games by a run, including losses to fellow Hall of Famers Ed Walsh and Rube Waddell, and won three games by the same margin. Despite this second year of his career being curtailed by illness, Johnson had pitched himself into shape and took his place among the top pitchers in the game. During his string against New York, Philadelphia, and St. Louis, Johnson went 5–1 and allowed only eight runs in fifty-eight innings. Johnson's iron man performance was not only the result of his talent; it was an open admission that he was the only healthy and available pitcher on the Washington staff. From that point on, Johnson was starting with little rest but making an impact.[3] Just over a week later, Johnson's teammate Burt Keeley started both ends of a doubleheader because of a shortage of available pitchers. He won the first game and lost the second.

For the American League contenders, September was marked by head-to-head competition, which left Detroit, Cleveland, and Chicago within a game and a half of each other. As they had threatened to do all summer, the St. Louis Browns finally faded and dropped off the pace. Managing only a 6–11 mark against their fellow contenders, the Browns split the thirty games they played in September and finished the month four and a half games back, with five games left to play.

Disaster for the Browns came in the form of losing seven of eight games between September 6 and 12; the slump was double trouble because the opposition was Detroit and Cleveland, the teams they had to beat. The man upon whom St. Louis pinned their pennant hopes, Rube Waddell, was ineffective. The Browns could not gain on the league as long as staff ace Rube Waddell was winning only as often as he lost.

A nine-game win streak in September fueled the Cleveland Naps' stretch run, which extended to a 15–1 mark. Addie Joss started the month with a one-hit, 1–0 win over Detroit and responded like a champion every time Nap Lajoie started him. Against Boston on September 17, Joss and Cy Young locked up in a classic duel. Cleveland won it in the home half of the ninth on singles by Bill Hinchman, Lajoie, and George Stovall.

If the Cleveland faithful weren't excited by Joss's heroics, Bob "Dusty" Rhoades did Joss one better on September 18. Rhoades pitched the season's fourth no-hitter against the Red Sox. Boston led the game 1–0 until the fourth, when Lajoie tripled and scored the tying run. The Naps scored the winning run in the eighth on a single by Wilbur Good, who got into scoring position on an error and scored on a wild pitch. After nearly an entire season of poor attendance, fans began spinning the turnstiles in Cleveland, and for six glorious days from September 21 through 27, the Naps were in first place. They would have remained in first had Detroit not risen from the dead.

While the Browns were falling off the pace and Cleveland was tearing up the league, the Tigers were going about the business of defending their league title by winning close games and hanging on for dear life. Seventeen of Detroit's thirty-two September contests involved the contenders, and Hughie Jennings's charges managed to post a 9–8 mark in those games. Nine of those contests were decided by one run, and in an amazing four-game set with Chicago in midmonth, each game went extra innings. The Tigers came from behind to win two of those games, overcoming inconsistency, which plagued the Detroit offense for most of the month.

One of the key reasons the Tigers' offense was sputtering was Ty Cobb. The hero of July and August newlywed was precariously close to being September's bum. Cobb's production had fallen so much that Jennings vowed never to allow any midseason wedding on any team he managed in the future.[4] Third baseman Bill Coughlin, a key part of the Tigers' infield, was feeling the strain. Telling anyone who would listen, Coughlin vowed that 1908 would be his last year as a player. It was.[5]

As the Tigers were entertaining the eastern teams, a roster change was made that contributed mightily to their winning the pennant. During a 5–1 loss to New York on the September 18, Donie Bush made his debut at shortstop for the Bengals. His presence in the lineup immediately stabilized the Detroit infield, which had been a makeshift affair due to injuries and batting slumps. Appearing in twenty games, the Indianapolis native hit .294 and scored thirteen runs.

While Bush shored up the team, Detroit struggled and fell out of first on September 21 by virtue of a 4–3 loss to Boston. That defeat launched a three-game tailspin and marked a low point for the Tigers. On September 23 a three-run error by catcher Boss Schmidt gave the Red Sox a 4–1 victory and put Detroit two and a half games behind Cleveland.

Philadelphia came to town the next day. The Tigers, in danger of falling too far off a pennant-winning pace, came from behind to tie the game, which was called by darkness. The turning point for the Tigers came on September 25.

Detroit was short of pitching and facing a doubleheader. Jennings gave the ball to Kickapoo Ed Summers, who took matters in hand. The rookie knuckleballer started and won both games, 7–2 and a thrilling 1–0, ten-inning two-hitter. First baseman Claude Rossman's home run was the clincher in the second game. Summers's feat ignited a home stretch nine-game win streak, which put the Tigers into position to win the pennant on the last day of the season. Summers's twin wins were matched a couple of days later by the Big Eds of Chicago, Walsh and Reulbach.

Chicago's White Sox spent the month bouncing between second and third place, playing well enough to stay in the hunt but not quite well enough to break into the lead. Part of the reason for this situation was their inability to beat Cleveland, losing five of nine games to Lajoie's charges. One of the primary reasons for this state of affairs was a shortage of pitching, a fatal weakness for a team with a weak offense. A shoulder injury shelved Nick Altrock for the year. Ed Walsh, Doc White, and Frank Smith were carrying the team.

The September 16 Cleveland game gave evidence of the extent of the White Sox pitching shortage. Having already lost three of four to the Naps, Fielder Jones sent Lou "Big Finn" Fiene into the breech. Fiene's only start in 1908 was a disaster. He was shelled 7–1 as Heinie Berger threw a three-hitter. Why Fiene with his lifetime record of 3–8 was brought out is not clear. Frank Smith, who was in Jones's doghouse for deserting the team in June, had last pitched on September 12, winning 2–1 over Detroit. Four days' rest was more than enough for most Dead Ball Era pitchers. The well-rested Smith made history on his next start, but why Fiene and not Smith got the ball against Cleveland on September 16 remains a mystery.

Another mystery is what led Sox owner Chuck Comiskey to discuss gambling and baseball with *Sporting Life* writer Charles Zuber. Appearing in the September 19 number of the weekly, Comiskey's interview carried the banner headline: "Races Are Not Fixed!" Responding to the question of whether the pennant races were on the level, the owner of a team that would throw a World Series eleven years later was royally dismissive: "Such questions are ridiculous," thundered the Old Roman. "Fix a baseball race? Pshaw!"[6] One wonders what he thought of the decision to start Fiene. The story stands in stark irony when viewed in the context of the 1919 World Series fix.

The Fiene debacle seemed to act as a tonic for the Sox, who streaked to end the month winning nine of the last ten games. The game of greatest note occurred on September 20, when Frank Smith no-hit the

TABLE 11. *American League Standings — September 30, 1908*

	W	L	Pct.	GB	September Record
Detroit	87	61	.588	—	19–13
Cleveland	87	62	.584	$\frac{1}{2}$	21–9
Chicago	85	62	.559	$1\frac{1}{2}$	19–10
St. Louis	82	65	.558	$4\frac{1}{2}$	15–15
Boston	70	76	.479	16	14–14
Philadelphia	65	80	.448	$20\frac{1}{2}$	7–23
Washington	61	82	.427	$25\frac{1}{2}$	13–16
New York	48	97	.331	$30\frac{1}{2}$	10–18

Athletics 1–0. Eddie Plank of Philadelphia lost the game in the bottom of the ninth as Frank Isbell singled and advanced to second and third on a passed ball and wild pitch. Isbell scored on a fielder's choice, beating the throw to the plate.

If Smith's no-hitter were not enough, Walsh capped his best season on September 29. Walsh took matters into his own hands and pitched a doubleheader sweep over Boston with scores of 5–1 and 2–0. Big Ed allowed seven hits in the contests, striking out fifteen and walking only one. In that first game, Smokey Joe Wood put in two and two-thirds innings of relief, in one of the first appearances of his illustrious career.

The Sox capped the month with an incident that ignited a scandal in the Windy City. On September 28, Boston and Chicago played to a 2–2 tie in a game called by darkness after the tenth inning. As umpires John Sheridan and John Kerin were leaving the field, Kerin was knocked out cold by a punch delivered from behind by prominent Chicago attorney Robert E. Cantwell. Kerin suffered a broken nose and was done umpiring for the season.

Cantwell was the kind of defense attorney you would hire if you were in really big trouble. He was also one of the organizers of the White Sox Rooters Association, a fact that embarrassed Comiskey. Comiskey's discomfort over the incident was compounded because it happened while league president Ban Johnson was in attendance.

Kerin filed charges, Cantwell was fined, and organized rooting in Chicago was given a figurative black eye. Cantwell's reputation as an attorney was unharmed, and perhaps enhanced, even after the following assertion during coverage of the incident: "The crafty attorney has admitted since that he went into base ball fanning as a business and organized the Association for the purpose of commending himself to such base ball fans as he might find on juries before which he tried cases."[7]

Reading accounts of the 1908 pennant races, you get the impression that the leagues were trying to outdo each other. In terms of historic attention and closeness of the race during September, the National League outdid the American. At month's end the Giants, Pirates, and Cubs were within .006 points and a half game of one another, and one of the great controversies in baseball history was still brewing.

The defending World Champion Cubs were at the center of the National League universe in September 1908. This team was involved in all of the controversies of the month and, despite distractions born of controversy, won when they had to. Of the contending teams, the Cubs lacked tangibles that New York and Pittsburgh had. The Giants had McGraw coaching from third base and a home field advantage going into the stretch drive. The Pirates had the incomparable Wagner and a nine-game winning streak by pitcher Nick Maddox. All the Cubs had was an intangible. They knew how to win. This ability to win despite adversity and pressure was the decisive edge, especially when you take into account September's record for the three contenders: New York 24–8, Pittsburgh 25–8, and Chicago 23–8.

In the head-to-head competition of the month, the Cubs were 4–3-1 against the teams they had to beat. This record included a loss and a tie in games that were historically significant. We have already reviewed the circumstances surrounding the Gill game, the 1–0 Pirates win over Chicago on September 4. Nineteen days after the Gill game came the Merkle game, the contest that would eventually determine the outcome of the National League race. All eyes in the baseball world were on the late September four-game set between the Cubs and Giants in New York. Both teams were playing excellent baseball.

The Cubs had compiled a 17–6 record before arriving in New York late on September 21. Prior to the New York series, the Cubs were down five games in the loss column, despite their steady play and the contribution of two wins by newly added pitcher Andy Coakley. Coakley threw a four-hitter against his old Reds teammates in the second game of a September 7 doubleheader. On the eve of the big Giants series on September 21, Coakley won a close 3–2 game over the Phillies to ice a doubleheader sweep. The game-winning run was scored by Frank Chance, the result of a mishandled pickoff throw.

The Giants were playing like a house on fire. They had put up an 18–3 mark prior to the Cubs series. Mathewson was 5–1 during the streak, putting him at thirty-three wins for the year. Matty's only loss was at the hands of Pittsburgh by a 2–1 score the day before the Cubs came to town. Just three days before that game, the Giants had thrown a monkey wrench into Pirates hopes with a doubleheader sweep, courtesy of pitching by Mathewson and Hooks Wiltse. Playing before an overflow crowd of thirty-five thousand at the Polo Grounds, Turkey Mike Donlin was the hero of game one and contributed a double in game two. Donlin's presence in the lineup was probably the result of being at home. During game one, Donlin became upset with a fan and socked him in the eye. Police broke up the fight and Donlin was allowed to remain in the game. The unfortunate fan, whose name has been lost to history, left the field with a cut over his eye and probably a shiner from Donlin, who was as handy with his fists as with his bat.

The stage was now set for the long-awaited final Cubs-Giants series of the year. Interest in the pennant races had promoted the use of electronic boards, or automatic scoreboards, across the land. In Chicago this series was seen by fans who paid to watch, with proceeds going to the Chicago Tribune Hospital Fund. Even in an era before mass media and television, it seemed that all eyes were on the Polo Grounds. Games between Frank Chance's Cubs and John McGraw's Giants were often described as war. Nothing happened during the next four games to dispel that notion.

The Giants opened the series with a disadvantage of sorts. Mathewson had been used against Pittsburgh the day before and McGraw was forced to start Red Ames and Doc Crandall against Orval Overall and Three Finger Brown. Umpires for the series were Hank O'Day and Bob Emslie, significant in that O'Day had been sole umpire in the Gill game.

September 22 was a disaster for New York. Ames and Crandall were no match for Overall and Brown. In game one the Cubs hung on to win 4–3, with Brown coming in to relieve Overall in the seventh inning. It was fairly common practice to use ace starters in critical relief situations. What was uncommon was that Brown got the start in the second game. The Hall of Fame righty dueled Crandall for five innings. The

Cubs broke it wide open in the sixth. Johnny Evers and Frank Chance walked and Harry Steinfeldt doubled to score Evers. Circus Solly Hofman, a key performer in August, drove in Chance with a sacrifice fly. The final score was Cubs 3, Giants 1.

New York was faced with having to take the remaining two games to salvage a split. McGraw sent Mathewson to the mound, while Jack the Giant Killer Pfiester started for the Cubs, setting the stage for one of the most written about games in baseball history.

A larger than normal Wednesday crowd, twenty thousand, watched the game in person, with countless others viewing the proceedings on automatic scoreboards. Attendance and interest in the game served as proof to any skeptics that baseball as a viable mass entertainment had arrived. Unlike some big games in professional sports, this particular contest lived up to all advance billing.

Mathewson and Pfiester locked themselves into a classic pitchers' duel. The Cubs drew first blood on Joe Tinker's home run. The Cubs shortstop had hit Matty all year long. For a while, it looked as if Tinker's homer would be enough. But in the sixth, Buck Herzog reached base on Steinfeldt's error and scored on a single by Mike Donlin.

The Cubs were retired quietly in the ninth. With one out, the Giants' Art Devlin singled but was forced out on Moose McCormick's grounder. Fred Merkle, fatefully starting at first because regular Fred Tenney was ill, singled to right. Some accounts claim Merkle could have reached second on the hit, but with two out the risk was not worth it, and Merkle stayed at first. Al Bridwell ripped a single to center, scoring McCormick and sending Giants fans into seventh heaven.

The hit also sent Merkle straight to the Giants clubhouse. In a carbon copy of the Gill game, Merkle had neglected to touch second. The deed had not gone unnoticed by Johnny Evers, who screamed for the ball. The throw from Circus Solly Hofman was wide of the mark and the game ball was lost in a mass of celebrating Giants fans. A ball — whether or not it was the game ball is subject to debate — was recovered despite the energetic efforts of Giants pitcher Iron Man McGinnity to keep the game ball from getting into the hands of Cubs players. Evers tagged second in an appeal to base umpire Bob Emslie.

Emslie did not see the play and refused to make the call. Emslie asked his partner, Hank O'Day. O'Day said he had seen the play, granted Evers's appeal, and called Merkle out on a force. Because the crowd had taken over the field and the Giants had left the diamond celebrating a win, O'Day declared a tie game.

One can only imagine the fury of McGraw's reaction. New York management had declared a 2–1 win and had already sent the result to the National League office and the Associated Press wire service when O'Day's decision became known. The Cubs initially argued that the September 23 game should be a forfeit but then demanded it be made up the next day. The Giants maintained that they should not be penalized for Merkle's act, a deed the like of which had gone unpunished by umpires in the past. National League President Harry C. Pulliam, as he had done all year long, supported the umpire's call. His decision was appealed by the Giants. Eventually the New York team was told that the game would be replayed on October 8 if necessary to decide the pennant.

The next day Frank Chance and the Cubs appeared at the Polo Grounds early in order to press their demand for a doubleheader or a forfeit. That ploy did not work. The Giants won the game the day after the Merkle game 5–4. New York had been ahead 5–0 as late as the fifth inning. The Cubs staged a furious comeback against Hooks Wiltse, but with the score at 5–4, Mathewson came in to put out the fire and preserve first place for the Giants.

John McGraw never blamed Merkle or anyone else for the blunder that cost a win. Perhaps he realized that the error was as much his fault as anyone else's. After all, a crucial common link between the Gill and Merkle games was umpire Hank O'Day. Despite his well-known contempt for umpires, McGraw was a stickler for detail in analyzing baseball strategy, and it is hard to believe that McGraw would have said nothing about the Gill contest. In an editorial titled "A Regrettable Incident," *Sporting Life* editor Francis Richter noted that "the Gill incident should have been so well discussed in every player's dressing room as to render its repetition so soon and in such an important game, by even an inexperienced player, impossible."[8]

McGraw always maintained that there were other games the Giants could have and should have won and that blaming Merkle for losing the pennant was unfair. Two of those games came on September 25, just two days after the Merkle affair. The fifth-place Reds came to town and the Giants promptly dropped a doubleheader. Iron Man McGinnity lost the second game. The opener was lost by eleven-thousand-dollar rookie Rube Marquard. In one of the most embarrassing debuts ever by a Hall of Famer, Marquard was ko'ed in the fifth and lost the game 7–1. Marquard gave Mathewson an account of his thoughts that day: "When I saw that crowd, Matty, I didn't know where I was. It looked so big to me, and they were all wondering what I was going to do, and all thinking that McGraw had paid $11,000 for me, and now they were to find out whether he had gotten stuck, whether he had picked up a gold brick with plating on it very thin. I was wondering myself, whether I would make good."[9]

The next day the Giants swept the Reds in partial atonement for the previous double loss. In the final four games of the month against the Phillies, the Giants won three and lost one. The sole loss came at the hands of Harry Coveleski of Shamokin, Pennsylvania. Unknown at the time, Coveleski became the second pitcher of 1908 to earn the nickname "Giant Killer." His name would be burned into the collective memory of Giants fans everywhere.

As for the Cubs, the final five games after the Giants series saw them record four wins. On September 26, Big Ed Reulbach started and won both ends of a doubleheader against Brooklyn. It was the fourth time in the month that a pitcher had started both ends of a doubleheader. Of all the performances by Keeley, Summers, Walsh, and Reulbach in pitching two full games in a day, Reulbach's feat was the most impressive. He completely dominated the Superbas. Both games were shutouts, a 5–0 five-hitter and a 3–0 three-hitter. Of particular note was that no Brooklyn runner got past second base in either game. Reulbach's feat gave the Cubs a big lift in morale and, more important, from the standpoint of giving other pitchers an additional day's rest.

Three Finger Brown won 6–2 over the Reds on September 29. The next day, Overall lost a close one 6–5. On that last day of September, the defending World Champion Chicago Cubs lost the last regular season game they would lose in 1908.

The Cubs ended the month with a severely depleted pitching staff. Overlooked in accounts of the Merkle game was the effort of Pfiester. Apparently Jack the Giant Killer had started the game severely injured. Communications of the day being what they were, the public was not made fully aware of the situation until two and a half weeks after the fact.

Charles Dryden of the *Chicago Tribune* and *Sporting Life* wrote that Pfiester started the Merkle game with what he described as a dislocated elbow. Immediately after the Merkle game, Pfiester set sail for Youngs-town, Ohio, for an encounter with one of the more colorful characters of the Dead Ball Era, John "Bonesetter" Reese. Dryden described the encounter between the ailing pitcher and the healer with a mixture of awe and matter of factness and a dash of hyperbole: "Reese felt around, located the dislocated tendon, and snapped it back in place with his powerful fingers. The entire diagnosis and cure occupied less than ten minutes. Think of it, constant readers, Mr Pfeister [sic] pitched nine full innings with a dislocated arm and held the Giants to five hits! Had Jack's neck been broken he would have shut them out."[10] Pfiester re-joined the Cubs after the session.

Bonesetter Reese served as an unofficial physician for major league baseball players well into the 1920s, treating dozens of them, including stars such as Young, Walsh, Speaker, Sisler, and Hornsby. A former Welsh iron worker, Reese was one of those unique originals who foot-note the history of small town America. He had no formal medical training but was expert in the art of skeletal manipulation. The self-taught Reese was so skilled that the Ohio Legislature granted him special medical licensing.[11] A man of many talents and interests, in 1926 Reese became a Druid.

Johnny Evers in *Touching Second* confirms that Pfiester pitched the Merkle game hurt, but Evers describes the injury as a "strained liga-ment" in Pfiester's pitching arm, adding that "a lump had formed on his forearm, the muscle bunching. He could not bend his arm, and to pitch a curve brought agony." Evers noted in his account that Pfiester threw only three curve balls the entire game, all to Turkey Mike Donlin in clutch situations. Describing Pfiester's pain, Evers said the pitcher had to be helped to the bench after throwing each curve.[12] The true nature of Pfiester's injury cannot be known, but describing it as a "dis-located elbow" was probably a journalistic embellishment of the kind common for the times. Jack the Giant Killer Pfiester's injury likely involved muscle and ligament more than bone and joint.

Overlooked in the furious battle between Chicago and New York were the Pirates. Their brush with controversy in the Gill game came without the bitterness of the Merkle incident, simply because the Pi-rates did not have their run nullified and won the contest. While the Cubs and Giants were at one another's throats, Pittsburgh was com-petently disposing of its foes with timely hitting and bulldog-tough pitching.

TABLE 12. *National League Standings — September 30, 1908*

	W	L	Pct.	GB	September Record
New York	93	53	.637	—	24–8
Pittsburgh	95	55	.633	—	25–8
Chicago	94	55	.631	$\frac{1}{2}$	23–8
Philadelphia	78	68	.534	15	18–16
Cincinnati	72	77	.484	$22\frac{1}{2}$	14–17
Boston	63	85	.426	31	13–24
Brooklyn	49	98	.333	$44\frac{1}{2}$	6–27
St. Louis	49	101	.327	46	7–27

Nick Maddox was 5–2 for the month; he won thirteen in a row before losing to the Giants 7–0 in that fateful double loss to New York on September 18. Like the Giants and Cubs, the Pirates sought additional pitching. Pittsburgh received a boost from rookie Chick Brandom, who beat Cincinnati 3–1 on September 3 and St. Louis 9–7 on September 7. Brandom won one other game for Pittsburgh in 1909 and was 1–1 for Newark of the Federal League in 1915. The five-foot, eight-inch Brandom's accomplishment in 1908 has been forgotten, but of all the stopgap starters of contenders in this season, his 2–0 mark matches that of Coakley and stands well above the losses notched by Fiene of the White Sox and Marquard of the Giants.

The doubleheader loss to New York was a tough blow for Pittsburgh to withstand, but Fred Clarke's charges bounced back. They won the remaining two games in the Giants series and nine of the next ten. In one of the most exciting doubleheaders of the year on September 29, Howie Camnitz threw a one-hitter at St. Louis and Vic Willis won the wild second game 6–5 for a Pirates sweep. In that second game, no runs were scored until the seventh, when Pittsburgh put three on the board. In the eighth inning, the Cardinals scored four times, and Pittsburgh responded with two scores to take the lead. In the visitors' ninth, St. Louis tied the score. Pittsburgh won the game in the home half of the inning in a game in which the last three innings were as tightly played as in any game during the entire season.

The furious pennant race overshadowed a performance by a pitcher whose Hall of Fame ability was clearly neutralized by his team's decidedly lackluster performance. On September 5 Brooklyn's Nap Rucker threw the season's third no-hitter. Rucker struck out fourteen Doves in his 6–0 win. He had to overcome three errors on his way to the win. Rucker spent his entire career with some of the worst teams Brooklyn ever fielded. Many National League observers believed that Rucker was among the game's elite pitchers but suffered from a profound lack of support, which effectively took attention from his considerable skills.

AFTERWORD: PULLIAM, MCGRAW, O'DAY, AND THE MERKLE PLAY

No game in all of baseball history has had more written about it than the September 23 Cubs-Giants game or, as it is called here, the Merkle game. Any treatment of the 1908 season must cope with this pivotal contest. While there is no argument against its importance, this game overshadowed an entire season, which as we have seen was full of thrills and controversy. Yet in terms of the people involved, no single game had an impact comparable to that of the Merkle game on the lives of its participants.

The chief victim of the game was rookie first baseman Fred Merkle, who was guilty of following a precedent that had been ignored by umpires until 1908. Merkle's above average career was stained by his baserunning mistake, which many journalists of the day called stupid; they gave Merkle the nickname "Bonehead." As already indicated, Giants manager John McGraw never blamed Merkle and even raised his salary after the 1908 season. Following his retirement, Merkle refused all contact with major league baseball until 1950, when he returned to the Polo Grounds at the urging of Giants owner Horace Stoneham. Merkle attended the old-timers' ceremonies on his own terms: he would not wear a uniform. According to accounts, Merkle had the time of his life, and the burden of his mistake seemed to disappear from his shoulders.[13] It was indeed sad that Merkle bore the burden for such a long time.

John McGraw's role in this mess deserves mention. McGraw managed in an era during which managers were not held accountable as they are today. Contemporary accounts blame only Merkle, not McGraw. This is patently unfair. In his memoirs, McGraw fumes about the 1908 season, but significantly, he never mentions the Gill game in the context of how the season turned out. Those seeking to put the monkey on McGraw's back must consider how widely the Gill incident was reported. It was covered in *Sporting Life* and *Sporting News*, but only the

New York Globe bothered to give the incident much attention in New York City.

David Nemec in his *Rules of Baseball* asserts that McGraw must bear some blame: "Since the Gill incident was widely reported, it should have been incumbent upon McGraw to remind his players of what Evers had tried to do against the Pirates, particularly when a repeat attempt was imminent with two out in the ninth and Giants runners at the corners."[14]

Nemec neglects to mention O'Day's presence at both games. It is indeed puzzling that a manager who would dictate what his players ate for breakfast, as McGraw did, should have overlooked the situation. While Merkle's reputation as a player was besmirched by the game, McGraw's image as one of the smartest baseball minds ever was barely shaken by the so-called Merkle Boner. McGraw must bear some of the burden for the oversight. Arguably, the Merkle game should rank as a major failure by McGraw. He never explained why he overlooked the Gill play and did not brief his players about it. And considering O'Day's presence on the diamond that fateful day, the oversight was particularly egregious.

If the game cost Merkle his reputation as a ball player, it can be argued that the events of September 1908 cost the life of National League President Harry C. Pulliam. Pulliam had served as secretary for the Pittsburgh Pirates and had spent one term in the Kentucky Legislature. In late 1902 he was named National League president in a compromise move, after attempts to get the job by John Montgomery Ward and William Temple fell short of the required votes.

Pulliam's relationship with the Giants franchise was always poor, or worse. Giants owner John T. Brush, who eventually would not even allow a free pass for Pulliam at the Polo Grounds, had to be convinced that Pulliam's appointment was not a move to favor Pittsburgh over New York. This initial enmity only intensified as Pulliam repeatedly clashed with Giants management over on-field behavior.

Pulliam's term in office was controversial, marked by constant conflict with Giants' management over support of umpires and other issues. In 1908, as in previous years, Pulliam did whatever he could to support umpires in the field. This carte blanche blanket policy served him adequately until September 1908. During this month full of controversy, he departed briefly from total support of umpires in the field when he fired John Rudderham. Rudderham had been at the center of a fierce controversy involving Charles Ebbets and Brooklyn; his dismissal came only days before the Gill game.

The decision involving the Gill game stands as an instance of what can happen when a policy fails to take into account unique situations and circumstances. The Gill game presented Pulliam with a golden opportunity to clarify the force-out rule, but he failed to recognize the peril of allowing tradition to stand in the way of enforcement of a rule already on the books. His blanket policy of supporting umpires and their judgment decisions in the field betrayed him.

As we have seen, Pulliam noted that Gill would have been forced out, had O'Day called it, but since the force was not called, the run was allowed. Pulliam offered no further clarification, and by not issuing an interpretation or point of emphasis of the rule, he created an opening for the Merkle controversy.

Pulliam should also be criticized for indecision immediately after the Merkle game. A lid could have been put on the affair by allowing a doubleheader on the day after. Playing two games could have kept the controversy from simmering for days and ultimately festering. Instead, the National Commission got involved because of protests lodged by the Cubs and Giants. It took ten days for the governing body of baseball to straighten things out and to order that the game be replayed. Deferring the decision hurt Pulliam's credibility and may have contributed to his subsequent breakdown. When the National Commission released its findings, it echoed Pulliam's belief that on questions of fact on the diamond, the umpire's call must be upheld.

Pulliam took leave of absence in early 1909, having been pilloried unmercifully in the New York press. He told close friends he blamed McGraw for the situation, and he obviously felt the press criticism because National League offices were based in New York. He returned to work in the early summer and committed suicide with a gunshot wound to the head on July 28, 1909, at the New York Athletic Club. Pulliam was thirty-nine years old. He left no suicide note.

The only major league team not represented at Pulliam's funeral was the New York Giants. McGraw's reported response to the suicide revealed the depth of his hatred of Pulliam. McGraw commented, "I didn't think a bullet to the head could hurt him."[15]

Pulliam was a tragic figure. He was a gentleman, ill-equipped to deal with people who always sought advantage in every situation and confrontation.

The final figure in the Merkle controversy was the man who made the call, umpire Hank O'Day. A native of Chicago, O'Day was one of the few men to play, manage, and umpire major league baseball. He was also one of the most taciturn men ever involved in American sport. In a career that spanned over five decades, he left behind little in the way of written record. Instead, we have to rely upon the impressions of others about this complex man.

In his 1951 interview with *Collier's Magazine*, Bill Klem described O'Day as a "misanthropic Irishman . . . [who] would not speak a civil word to any body he had not known 20 years."[16] Klem, who was critical of O'Day's call in the Merkle game, revealed Silk O'Loughlin's impression of O'Day: "Look at O'Day. One of the best umpires. Maybe the best today. But he's sour. Umpiring does something to you. The abuse you get from the players; the insults from the crowds, and the awful things they write about you in the newspapers."[17]

O'Day died in 1935, so Klem's words about the Merkle play go without response. The remarks are fascinating, in that they reveal a measure of respect for but also a strong dose of criticism of a fellow umpire whose term of service was second only to that of Klem. They could also have come from the mouth of Klem's friend and adversary, John McGraw. An interesting aspect of the series of interviews in *Collier's* was Klem's revelation that he and McGraw developed a "strange off-the-field relationship."[18] This relationship included postgame dinners during spring training and those rare seasons when the Giants were not in contention.

In reviewing the Merkle game, Klem told *Collier's* that Johnny Evers "talked a great and good umpire into making the rottenest decision in the history of baseball."[19] During the interview Klem blamed gutless thinking at the league level and then launched into using the force play rule to make the call. Klem maintained that a player had the right to leave the field when there was no reasonable doubt that the game was over. He added, "The intent in this rule applied to infield grounders and such. It does not apply to cleanly hit drives to the outfield that make a force-out impossible unless the runner on first drops dead."[20]

The logic behind this assertion does not stand up. A runner on first can be forced out at second on a fly to the outfield, if the ball is dropped. In the case of Gill and Merkle, what you have is an appeal play, a call no umpire makes until a side requests it. This explains partially why the rule had not been invoked earlier.

In words mixing admiration with criticism, Klem delivered the final blast against O'Day: "He was accepting a technicality and ignoring perhaps a half a century of custom, usage, tradition and the intent of the rule. He was, to repeat, making the worst decision in the history of baseball. There can be no question of O'Day's physical courage because, had he been short on guts, he would not have favored the visiting team against the home team."[21]

These words from Klem represent more than O'Day ever said in one place about the Merkle play. Indeed, O'Day's comparative silence about the Gill and Merkle plays has contributed to the controversy. While many sources indicate that O'Day realized Evers and the Cubs were correct in the Gill game and promised to make the correct call if it happened again, there is no direct statement from O'Day indicating his thinking; there are only his actions.

In defense of O'Day, there was no rule at the time requiring umpires to report unusual rule violations to the league. Yet it seems indefensible that he did not report his impressions about the Gill play to the league or discuss the matter with his colleagues. If you frequent any meeting among umpires, you know that it is not long before there is discussion of strange plays and how rules apply; in O'Day's case in the Gill and Merkle calls, there does not appear to have been any such discussion.

In analyzing the Merkle incident, O'Day's classic silence does the historian few favors. McGraw, in his memoir *My Thirty Years in Baseball*, says O'Day called Merkle out because he did not touch second base.[22] Baseball historian Harold Seymour comes up with a different twist to the matter.

In his official report to the president after the game, O'Day stated that he did not order play resumed because it was too dark to continue. Furthermore, in the report he indicated only that Merkle had not touched second and that McGinnity had interfered with the play; he did not say precisely why Merkle was called out. It could have been for several reasons: because Evers actually touched the base with the ball in his possession, because of McGinnity's interference, or even because Merkle ran out of the base line. Six years later O'Day was quoted as saying that it was because of interference.[23]

While O'Day can be criticized for his silence, his ability as an umpire remained unassailable. In the wake of the Gill and Merkle controversies, some questioned O'Day's integrity, but he was ably defended by sportswriter Sam Crane. In a column noted in *Unforgettable Season,* Crane wrote: "O'Day makes mistakes, of course, but when one thinks of all that an umpire must go through during a baseball season one feels like giving a medal to good old Hank O'Day. . . . I would be the first to 'produce' for a medal for Hank. I have played ball with him and against him, and I can say that no squarer man ever lived."[24]

As an umpire, O'Day was known as a stickler for the rules. Ironically, while serving as a member of the rules committee, he opposed a 1920 rule change that credited a player with a home run if it was hit in the bottom of an inning and resulted in scoring more than just the winning run. Prior to the change, a batter was given the number of bases necessary to score the winning run. O'Day believed that when the winning run scored, the game was over and that was that. This was an interesting position to take in light of the Merkle call, where the run that had scored was erased by a force play.

Finally, O'Day was known to be stubborn, tough, and unafraid. Christy Mathewson charged that O'Day would sometimes make calls against teams who protested too much. But had O'Day been overt about that practice, his umpiring career would have been quite short; besides, Mathewson could not be expected to be too kind to the man who made the Merkle call. Mathewson's final words about O'Day paint a vivid picture of the man and the umpire: "It is as dangerous to argue with him as it is to try to ascertain how much gasoline is in the tank of an automobile by sticking down the lighted end of a cigar or cigarette."[25]

O'Day was a complex and sometimes controversial man. Human history is a blend of circumstance, coincidence, and fate. No one could have known that scheduling O'Day to be in Pittsburgh and New York for those two days in September would have such a profound impact on baseball history and the lives of Merkle and Pulliam.

There is an interesting footnote to this controversial chapter in baseball history. In the October 17, 1908, edition of *Sporting Life* in a column across from the account of the replay of the Merkle game, there was a story about a Merkle-like play in the National League in the 1890s.

The account began: "Ex-Umpire W. L. Wilson recalls a game a la Merkle and Gill. Was at Chicago about fourteen years ago. Pfeffer, batting against the Louisville team, hit safely when last man up in the ninth, scoring a runner from third base. The batter started for first bag, but suddenly ducked out of the base path and ran in the club house. Umpire called men back and, after a row, Louisville won by forfeit."[26]

The above verbatim account contains tantalizing information but does not stand up to scrutiny. In trying to reconstruct the situation, we must consider three key pieces of information. First, four umpires named Wilson officiated in the National League in the 1890s, but none bore the initials W. L. There was a William C. Wilson, but he umpired in 1890 and 1892–93. According to the account, the incident occurred "about fourteen years ago," which would place the year as 1894, when Parke A. Wilson and no other Wilson umpired.

Second, assuming that the incident occurred between 1890 and 1894, there is the matter of Fred Pfeffer. He played for Chicago of the Players League in 1890, a league that had no Louisville entry. Pfeffer then went to Chicago of the National League in 1891 and to Louisville in 1892 through 1895. For the *Sporting Life* account to be accurate, either the storyteller or the reporter got the teams mixed up. And finally, the account gives no evidence that it was an eyewitness or second-hand account.

Chalk it up as another of those baseball stories that are almost too good to be true. The editors of *Sporting Life* made little of it. You could argue that the National League likewise made little of it. Perhaps the *Sporting Life* people were humoring an old man. But if the story were true, the mistakes made by Gill and Merkle were worse than anyone could have imagined.

11 **October** Down to the Wire

For baseball fans, October is the cruelest of all months. The hopes of April, if not shattered during the oppressive heat of summer, are laid to rest by the cold reality of the standings or the outcome of the World Series. For fans in Chicago, Cleveland, Detroit, Pittsburgh, and New York, hopes were alive in this roller-coaster season. The American and National League pennants would be won on the last day of the season by visiting teams before hostile crowds.

The American League race ended furiously, with the four contenders playing one another exclusively in the stretch drive. Each of the teams played five games. The Tigers, Naps, and White Sox all recorded 3–2 marks, while the fading Browns won only one of their five contests. That controversial St. Louis victory kept Cleveland from winning the pennant. Here is how the last five days of the season went.

AMERICAN LEAGUE

OCTOBER 2

The Tigers defeated the Browns 7–6 in a thriller. Detroit hammered Browns starter Rube Waddell early with a three-run first inning. The visiting Browns stormed back to make it close, thanks to four Detroit fielding errors and poor decisions on the base paths. Sam Crawford and Claude Rossman were the hitting heroes for the defending league champions, doubling home the tying and winning runs in the ninth inning. The victory kept Detroit up a half game over Cleveland and two and a half over Chicago.

At Cleveland's League Park, 10,598 fans witnessed one of the greatest baseball games ever played. Cleveland defeated Chicago 1–0. Big Ed Walsh of the White Sox struck out fifteen and threw a four-hitter. In any other game Walsh's effort would have been an easy victory. But Naps hurler Addie Joss was better. He pitched a perfect game and placed his team within a half game of the Tigers. During his masterpiece game, Joss delivered only seventy-four pitches to the plate.[1]

The six-foot, three-inch Joss was a sinker baller with a wicked curve and an above average fastball. One of the finest pitchers ever, he was a threat to win any game he started. Joss tragically died in his prime at the age of thirty-one in 1911. He won 160 games in a nine-year career.

Joss was typically modest in describing his feat: "I never could have done it without Larry's [Lajoie's] and Stovall's fielding and Birmingham's base running."[2] Walsh noted in the oral history *My Greatest Day in Baseball* that the game "was a surprise to both of us for we were sitting on a tarpaulin talking about having some singing in the hotel that night when Lajoie, who managed Cleveland, and Fielder Jones told us to warm up. A pitcher never knew when he'd work in those days."[3]

Cleveland outfielder Joe "Dode" Birmingham stole fifteen bases in 1908 and saw his playing time cut by an arm injury. But he was well enough to be a hero in this game. Birmingham's brush with immortality occurred in the third inning when he led off with a single. When Walsh spotted Birmingham getting a huge leadoff from first, he tried to pick him off. Birmingham, instead of diving back to first, set sail for second. The throw to second hit him on the shoulder and caromed into the outfield. When the dust settled, Dode Birmingham was on third with no one out.

Walsh bore down and retired the next two hitters. He had two strikes on Wilbur Good when he threw a wild pitch. The wild pitch was a case of living and dying with the spitball. Walsh's regular catcher, Billy Sullivan, was hurt. Ossie Schreckengost, recently acquired from the Athletics, was unable to receive the fateful pitch. Birmingham scored what turned out to be the winning run.

Meanwhile, Joss had several close calls during the perfect game.

Manager Nap Lajoie had eight assists and two putouts at second, and first baseman George Stovall accounted for sixteen putouts. Joss himself preserved his gem in the seventh when, behind 3–0 to Sox player-manager Fielder Jones, he delivered three consecutive strikes.

In the ninth, the Sox sent up three pinch hitters. Doc White grounded out. Jiggs Donahue struck out. The last batter was Honest John Anderson, arguably the toughest hitter on the Sox roster. He lined the first pitch foul down the left field line. The second pitch was a sharply hit grounder to third. Bill Bradley described the final play of the game: "[Anderson] was a pull hitter, and so when he came up in Addie's big game, I moved closer to the base. John hit his grounder rather sharply over the bag. I was playing deep and I took the ball in back of the cushion. I threw to Stovall, but I threw low. George made a fine pickup of the ball out of the dirt."[4] Joss's perfect game was the sixth and final no-hitter of the season.

OCTOBER 3

Detroit retained their narrow lead with an easy 6–0 win over the sagging Browns. Wild Bill Donovan scattered seven hits and was never threatened. As they had the day before, Detroit jumped off to an early 3–0 lead in the first inning to ice the contest. The loss eliminated St. Louis from the pennant race.

Cleveland fans, who had not exactly mobbed League Park earlier in the year, finally turned out in record numbers for the game after Joss's gem — 20,729 paid to watch the Sox come back and win 3–2. The White Sox scored twice in the second on singles by George Davis and Billy Sullivan, who executed a double steal and scored on Lee Tannehill's single. Cleveland answered with a run in the second and were down 3–1 in the eighth when Stovall doubled, advanced on a fielder's choice, and scored on a bad throw to the plate. Big Ed Walsh, who came in in relief of Smith in the seventh, allowed the second Naps run. In the ninth Walsh had the bases loaded with one out, but he escaped when Piano Legs Hickman's grounder forced George Perring at the plate and Lajoie fanned to end the game.

The Tigers were now a game and a half up on Cleveland and two and a half ahead of Chicago. Detroit and Chicago swapped opponents for the final games of the season with the American League pennant in the balance.

The 3–3 tie in St. Louis between the Naps and Browns remains one of the most controversial games in Cleveland's long and often star-crossed history in major league baseball. Fans along Lake Erie will always claim they were jobbed out of the pennant by a bad call, or that Bill Hinchman did not hustle, or that other forces were involved. The fans were clearly unhappy with the work of umpire Jack Egan that day, a day that saw him arrive late to the game because his train was late.

The controversial play occurred in the ninth, when with two out Hinchman hit a sharp grounder up the middle, which was snagged by shortstop Bobby Wallace, who threw to first. Egan called Hinchman out. Some accounts indicate that Browns first baseman Tom Jones was pulled off the bag by Wallace's throw and Hinchman beat it out. If he had, Addie Joss would have scored the fourth and possibly game-winning run. Accounts in *Sporting Life* make no mention of the play. In his biography of Lajoie, J. M. Murphy says Egan accused Hinchman of loafing, and Lajoie recalled that "even the St. Louis fans were yelling 'Robber.' "[5]

Cleveland newspapers unanimously panned Egan's call. A Cleveland Press description indicated that Egan made the call late and without emphasis. We cannot know from admittedly biased accounts whether the call was correct or not, but if Egan "nonchalanted" a close call, his failure to sell the call created as much controversy as did the call itself. It does not help Egan's case to consider that the Browns made a play on the trailing runner before Egan issued his belated decision. Such an action implies a belief that Hinchman was thought to be safe by the defense, quite apart from what the umpire thought.

While Cleveland fans may have felt betrayed by the call, the game did not end there. Play continued for two more innings before the game was called due to darkness. Some may want to blame the umpire, but the fact remains that Cleveland still had a chance to win the contest after the call, including one inning with a runner on third with none out.[6] In fairness to Egan it must be noted that during the season the Cleveland press had been critical of Naps players for not running hard on ground balls, but no players were named. Nonpartisan accounts of the game indicate that accusations against Hinchman for loafing may have contained more than a grain of truth.[7]

Egan's reputation as an umpire was roundly questioned in all of Cleveland's papers. Many of the stories questioned why Egan had umpired so many Cleveland games and blamed him for the loss of the pennant by a half game. Egan umpired sixty-two Naps games in 1908. Two of the games were ties. Out of the sixty remaining contests, Cleveland went 34–26 for a .566 percentage or .017 points under the team's season record. Those Cleveland fans who expressed umbrage over Egan's presence on the field were reacting to an event of the day and not to the overall record. In Cleveland Egan umpired thirty games and the Naps won twenty-one of them. On the road the Naps' record with Egan on the field was 14–16, a mark including the disastrous double doubleheader loss to Washington in late August (two doubleheaders in two days). If Egan had anything personal against the Naps, evidence of a grudge is not found in the won-lost records of 1908.[8]

Meanwhile in Chicago, spirits were high as the Tigers came to town for a decisive three-game series. The White Sox had to win all three to take the pennant, while Detroit needed just one victory to win their second straight flag. Walsh was unavailable for the opener and the ball was handed to Doc White. Twilight Ed Killian was the Tigers' starter.

The Sox jumped all over Killian in the first inning, scoring three times. Eddie Hahn's leadoff walk set the stage for the early game-winning rally. Patsy Dougherty and Fielder Jones also scored in the decisive frame, providing a 3–1 margin. White allowed one meaningless run in the Tigers' ninth and surrendered four hits. In typical Hitless Wonder fashion, the Sox managed only two hits against Killian. The White Sox were now a game and a half out of first.

OCTOBER 5

October 5, 1908, is a day of infamy for the Cleveland franchise. A doubleheader with the Browns was scheduled due to the previous day's tie. In the first game Bill Dinneen got the start for the Browns, while Lajoie tapped Glenn Liebhardt.

Both hurlers were knotted in a 1–1 pitchers' duel after five and a half innings. Disaster struck Cleveland in the Browns' sixth. Danny Hoffman's leadoff grounder to Lajoie turned into a two-base error and Dode Criss doubled him home. Criss was safe at third when he advanced on the cutoff throw. Some accounts say it was a perfect throw and the umpires missed another one. Criss scored on a single by Jimmy

Williams, but his run was not decisive. The 3–1 loss eliminated Cleveland from the pennant race. Lajoie's charges won the relatively meaningless second game 5–3.

While the Naps' hopes died, the White Sox forced the entire race to an all-or-nothing final game with their 6–1 victory over Detroit. For Big Ed Walsh, his four-hitter was his fortieth win of the year. For the White Sox, the eleven-hit attack gave them all the confidence in the world for the decisive game on their home ground. For the Tigers, nothing short of an all-out effort was required for the next day's game.

OCTOBER 6

The Naps won their last game of the year against St. Louis by a 5–1 margin and clinched second place. Jack Ryan was the winning pitcher, evening his record at 1–1. His career mark was 4–5 and the win on October 6 was the only one he would notch in a Cleveland uniform. The season of 1908 had been a successful one for Cleveland, but to lose the pennant by the narrow margin of a half game rendered the entire effort a season of what-ifs and led to changes in American League rules requiring contending teams to play all games on their schedules.

Twenty-seven thousand fans, including members of the Chicago Cubs, were on hand at the South Side Grounds for the last regular season game of the American League pennant race. The Cubs would soon be catching a train for New York. They were taking time to scout their World Series opponent and to cheer on their fellow Chicagoans. The stakes were high and the outcome simple. The winner goes to the World Series, while the loser finishes a close, but distant, third. A Tigers victory meant a half-game edge over Cleveland; a White Sox win would give the Pale Hose the flag by .002 points.

The Tigers had been beaten convincingly and easily during the first two games. Things did not look all that bright for Detroit. Sox manager Fielder Jones had a well-rested Frank Smith available. But while Smith was fresh, Jones and Smith had been at odds since June when Smith jumped the team. Apparently placing personal feelings ahead of other considerations, Jones chose Doc White to start, with just a day's rest. White was dog tired. His performance cost the Sox the pennant and led to Jones's departure as manager. The hard feelings and resentment engendered by Smith's jumping the team in June had finally taken their toll.

TABLE 13. *Final American League Standings*

	W	L	Pct.	GB	October Record
Detroit	90	63	.588	—	3–2
Cleveland	90	64	.584	$\frac{1}{2}$	3–2
Chicago	88	64	.579	$1\frac{1}{2}$	3–2
St. Louis	83	69	.547	$6\frac{1}{2}$	1–4
Boston	75	79	.487	$15\frac{1}{2}$	5–3
Philadelphia	68	85	.444	22	3–5
Washington	67	85	.441	$22\frac{1}{2}$	6–3
New York	51	103	.331	$39\frac{1}{2}$	3–6

The inexplicable choice of White became a source of second-guessing after the first four Detroit hitters came to bat and won a pennant. Matty McIntyre singled. Donie Bush struck out, but Sam Crawford hit a ground-rule double. Ty Cobb tripled to drive in two runs. Jones brought in Big Ed Walsh, but after 450 innings pitched, his arm was all but spent. Walsh finally retired the Tigers, but only after two more runs had scored. As they had done earlier in the month against the Browns, Detroit struck hard and early, playing what Tigers players called wild ball to overwhelm an opponent early in a game.

Tigers starter Wild Bill Donovan had a 4–0 lead and the pennant within reach for Detroit and practically out of the reach of the White Sox. The offensive efficiency of the previous two days was now but a distant memory as Donovan shut out the Sox on two hits. Jones's charges never threatened as Detroit won their second straight American League crown.

The slow start of April and the struggles of summer had been forgotten. Hughie Jennings had cheered, cajoled, and challenged his team to win. The American League champions returned to Detroit to await the outcome of the National League race, which would also go down to the last day of the season.

Meanwhile the Cubs boarded a train and headed for New York, or if circumstances dictated, Detroit. The day the American League race was decided was also the day the Merkle game was declared a tie, and a one game "play-off" or replay of the Merkle game was scheduled for October 8, provided that the Giants won their remaining games against Boston.

NATIONAL LEAGUE

The final days of the National League race were every bit as thrilling as those in the American League, despite featuring only two games between the contenders. The Cubs won both must-win games against the Pirates and the Giants. The final week of the season witnessed the birth of another Giant-killing legend and saw the regular season end under a shadow.

OCTOBER 1

The Chicago Cubs knew their next five games would be decisive. The October 1 game against the Reds was critical. A well-rested Ed Reulbach, fresh from the doubleheader win over Brooklyn on September 26, had no trouble with Cincinnati. His two-hitter was his fourth straight shutout. The performance set the tone for the rest of the Cubs team, who went undefeated through the rest of the regular season. Reulbach's streak also showed how great teams create their luck. But it must be added that there was no better time than late-season 1908 for a pitcher like Reulbach to get hot.

Meanwhile, the Giants were locked in mortal combat with the pesky Phillies. The day's work was another doubleheader, the fourth within a week for the Giants. The workload was stretching a thin Giants pitching staff, and no one was feeling the strain more than Christy Mathewson.

Making his fifth appearance in nine days, Mathewson was shellacked by the light-hitting Phillies. Matty surrendered ten hits—but stubbornly did not allow the Phils to take the lead. The Giants won game one 4–3.

The second contest was a decidedly different story. Harry Coveleski threw a four-hitter and beat New York for the second time in a week. This win loosed a flurry of derision from New York newspapers, including this screed from the *Press*: "The only way in which McGraw can beat that gentleman with the Russian suffix to his name, which is pronounced like an automobile with its muffler off, running on three cylinders, is to dress the team in kimonos and disguise them as Japs. Then, if the same disguised ballplayers make a noise like the Mikado's army, Covaleskie [sic] might dig for the tall timber."[9]

The reporter was referring to Japan's recent success against Russia in the Russo-Japanese War. The reference was a stretch. But it was a reflection of the frustration felt by the Giants and their fans, and an indication of the racial and ethnic sensitivities of the day.

OCTOBER 2

Idle on the first of the month due to travel, the Pittsburgh Pirates announced their claim to the 1908 National League pennant with a doubleheader sweep against the lowly Cardinals in St. Louis. The 7–4 and 2–1 wins put the Pirates in first place by a half game over New York and a full game ahead of Chicago. Lefty Leifield and Howie Camnitz were the winning pitchers. In the first game, thirteen Pittsburgh hits made it easy. Honus Wagner provided the heroics in game two with a come-from-behind, game-winning home run in the ninth.

Stung by the previous day's loss to Coveleski, the Giants jumped on George McQuillan early and coasted to a 7–1 victory. Red Ames was the winning pitcher, benefiting from a seven-run first by the Giants offense.

The Cubs kept pace in Cincinnati with 5–0 win over the Reds. Frank Chance went three for three to lead Chicago. Three Finger Brown allowed no runner past second base, while allowing only four hits.

OCTOBER 3

While war was raging on the diamonds in the American and National leagues, senior circuit officials began hearing evidence on the Merkle game. League president Harry C. Pulliam started the review process on October 3. He recommended that the Cubs-Giants game of September 23 be declared a tie and that a play-off game be scheduled for October 8, if needed. As he had throughout the year, he upheld the on-field decision of the umpires.

As Pulliam was arguing for reaffirmation of his earlier decision to the National League board of directors, the Pirates kept their lead with a 3–2 win over St. Louis. Nick Maddox was tough on the mound, and Wagner's two-for-four hitting combined with his fielding and that of Ed Abbaticchio gave Pittsburgh the contest. Unfortunately for Pittsburgh, the victory allowed the Pirates only to keep pace with the league and not to break away.

The score of the Giants-Phillies game was also 3–2, with McGraw's charges on the short end of the score again. Harry Coveleski continued his bedevilment of New York, defeating Christy Mathewson, who was called to start with just one day of rest. The Giants started off fine, scoring once in the first. Philadelphia took the lead in the fifth on Fred Osborne's triple. The Phils went up 3–1 in the sixth thanks to Otto Knabe's double and a sacrifice fly by Sherry Magee. Knabe scored from third on an error by Mathewson.

In the home ninth, the Giants rallied. With one run in and men on second and third and with none out, Coveleski earned the nickname "Giant Killer" forever. Turkey Mike Donlin, a fearsome clutch hitter and second only to Wagner in batting average in 1908, was retired on a pop fly. Cy Seymour grounded to Knabe, who was able to retire Moose McCormick in a rundown. Art Devlin struck out to end the game.

Again the New York press was beside itself, this passage appearing on the pages of the *Herald:* "If the Giants lose the pennant, Coveleski deserves the credit for defeating them. He seems to have the Indian sign on the stickers, big and little from Coogan's Bluff. He hails from Shamokin, Pennsylvania, in the coal field, and is a Polak."[10]

While Coveleski was beating New York for the third time in five days, the Cubs destroyed Cincinnati 16–2. Ed Reulbach started and pitched five shutout innings before being relieved by Chick Fraser, who surrendered two runs in a mop-up role. The Cubs' win meant that all National League teams were tied in the loss column with fifty-five defeats. The Pirates' lead was a half game over Chicago and one and a half over New York. The next day's action would prove decisive for one of the contenders, either the Cubs or the Pirates.

OCTOBER 4

The Giants were idle on this day, giving them a chance to lick their Coveleski-inflicted wounds and to rest before a three-game set with the Boston Doves, a team stocked with former Giants. For the Cubs it was one last game with Pittsburgh, a team who had beaten them in twelve out of twenty-one games. For each team a win meant a chance to clinch at least a tie for the pennant. Defeat would bring mathematical elimination from the pennant race due to the deadlock in the loss column.

Looking back at this Cubs-Pirates game produces an odd sense of symmetry and déjà vu. It was played a month to the day after the controversial Gill game, which had been a Cubs loss. As in the Gill game, the outcome of this contest would be determined by a crucial decision by umpire Hank O'Day. Completing the circle was the fact that Pittsburgh could be considered a favorite, due to their outstanding road mark of 56–20. But the Pirates would lose their last road game of the year, and this road loss was fatal to Pittsburgh's pennant hopes in 1908.

Fans numbering 30,247 jammed into West Side Park to witness the last regular season home game for the Cubs. At the time it was the largest crowd ever to witness a game in a western National League city.

The game had other witnesses. About five thousand fans and players from the Giants and Boston Doves put down a quarter each to see the game on an electronic board at the Polo Grounds.

The *New York Times* account noted that it was the same board as had been used in Madison Square Garden during a recent Giants road trip. Because of circumstances surrounding the Merkle game, which could still be declared a Giants victory, the crowd found itself in the unusual position of rooting for the hated Cubs. A Pirates win would mean no better than a tie for New York, provided that the next three games and the Merkle contest wound up in the win column. A Pirates loss would mean at least a tie with the Cubs and perhaps the pennant for the Giants. The New York pennant scenario depended upon an unlikely combination of events — the Merkle game being declared a Giants victory and New York sweeping over the Doves.

A tie depended on the sweep and a ruling the Merkle game was indeed a tie game. Noting the interest in the pennant race as expressed by attendance at the site of the electronic board, the *Times* reported: "No greater tribute was ever paid to the National game, and the extent to which enthusiasm can be carried was never better illustrated."[11]

The game's starting pitchers had also started the Gill game. Mordecai Brown for the Cubs and Vic Willis for Pittsburgh. Chicago drew first blood in the opening frame on Wildfire Schulte's single, scoring Jimmy Sheckard. The Cubs went up 2–0 in the fifth. Johnny Evers singled and reached second on an error by Honus Wagner. He scored on another single by Schulte.

Pittsburgh rallied to tie in the sixth. Roy Thomas led off with a single and reached third thanks to an error and a fielder's choice. With two strikes on him, Wagner doubled to score Thomas. The Dutchman reached third on a wild pitch by Brown and scored on Eddie Abbaticchio's single. Johnny Kling's throw to second on an attempted steal retired Abbaticchio for the third out.

As they had done all year, the Cubs found a way to win. In the home sixth with two out, Brown helped his own cause with a tie-breaking single to score Joe Tinker, who had doubled with two out. In the seventh the Cubs went up 4–2. Sheckard reached base on an error by Wagner. With the bases loaded and one out, Del Howard hit a sacrifice fly to Thomas, scoring Sheckard. Chicago went up 5–2 in the eighth inning. Brown hit a two-out single, went to second on Sheckard's base hit, and scored the insurance run on Johnny Evers's double.

It all came down to Pittsburgh's turn in the ninth, and the Pirates would not go down without a struggle. Fitting for this peculiar year, the Pirates' loss was marked by controversy. Wagner led off with a single. Abbaticchio scorched a shot down the right field line. To the Pittsburgh faithful it looked like a fair ball, but plate umpire Hank O'Day ruled it foul. The Pirates bitterly protested the call, which threatened to cut off a potential rally. The *Chicago Tribune* account of the game noted that the protest was so loud and long that O'Day asked his base partner Cy Rigler for help. The rhubarb subsided when Rigler backed his partner's ruling.[12]

This sort of appeal is unusual because in the two-man mechanics of the day, the base umpire was stationed in the middle of the infield, hardly the position to call any drive down either line fair or foul. The play was O'Day's to call. That O'Day allowed an appeal without ejecting anyone was an indication of the importance of the call and his trust in his partner.

In *Honus Wagner: A Biography*, the DeValerias note the play and describe it differently. Contradicting the *Tribune* account, their sources say Rigler called Abbaticchio's hit fair and O'Day overruled him.[13] As noted, such a call by Rigler would have been contrary to a key principle of umpiring: that the umpire who has the best position to see the play makes the call. O'Day's call may still be considered controversial by some, especially those looking for blown calls exercising undue influence on a pennant race. The difference in the accounts of the game can be partially attributed to the partisanship of local newspapers in this heated year.

In *The Ballplayers: Baseball's Ultimate Biographical Reference*, the entry under the name of Abbaticchio notes that the Pirates "had lost the pennant when Abbaticchio's apparent grand slam against the Cubs was called foul. Later, a woman who was struck by the ball sued for damages and swore in court that the ball had been fair."[14] While there is little doubt as to how a Cook County, Illinois, jury would rule on such a claim, it is clear that Abbaticchio's drive was not a grand slam homer, and the call itself did not cost the Pirates the pennant. If Abbaticchio's liner had been ruled fair and Wagner had scored, Pittsburgh would still have been down two runs, a huge obstacle to scale with Three Finger Brown pitching and with Reulbach, Overall, and others lurking in the bullpen.

A final footnote to the call and the play comes from none other than

Barney Dreyfuss, president of the Pirates. In his postgame statement, he did not refer to the call but did not hide his disappointment. "Somebody had to lose. It was Pittsburgh. We lost to a good team. We hope for better luck next time."[15]

After the controversy subsided, Abbaticchio returned to the batter's box and struck out. Wagner was forced at second for the second out of the frame. Owen Wilson set up the final out of Pittsburgh's season with a grounder to Tinker, who flipped to Evers to force Alan Storke. That out meant Chicago led New York by a game and a half. Pittsburgh's only hope was for the National League to rule the Merkle game a Giants win and for the Giants to lose at least one game to the Doves. Such a scenario would create a three-way tie.

For the Cubs, the next three days would be spent practicing and watching and rooting for the White Sox against Detroit. Manager Frank Chance wanted a rematch with the Sox, but he also appreciated the value of being able to scout his squad's prospective World Series opponent, provided all went the Cubs' way.

In a season filled with unlikely controversy and coincidence, the Fates now played one more trick. During the Cubs-Pirates game and at about the time Brown singled to break the tie in the sixth, an unidentified woman gave birth in the grandstands. The *Chicago Tribune* was unable to get any more information than a brief account of the event: "The mother fell forward in her seat and the crowd, thinking she had fainted, fell back to give her air. To a woman who raised her head she told what was happening and immediately mother and child were carried to the club house, where medical attention was summoned."[16]

The account noted that all west side hospitals denied having had any maternity case come to them from the ballpark. Ironically, the site of the Cubs' West Side Grounds is now occupied by Cook County Hospital; the hospital purchased the stadium site years later. The Cubs moved to present day Wrigley Field when the Federal League folded after the 1915 season. The West Side Grounds, site of many of Dead Ball Era Cubs dynasty achievements, was just another parcel of land in a hospital expansion project.

OCTOBER 5

As the Giants were preparing to play the first of three games against Boston, the National League board of directors — Garry Herrmann of Cincinnati, Charles Ebbets of Brooklyn, and George B. Dovey of

Boston—were concluding the hearing on the Merkle game and starting two days of deliberations. Thus the board was still determining the outcome of that game when the Giants and Doves met at the Polo Grounds for the first of three crucial games.

Like many other important games and series during this season, the conclusive Giants-Doves series had subtle and not so subtle overtones. The teams had been involved in a seven-player trade during the preseason, and New York clearly got the better of it. Fred Tenney and Al Bridwell had become key members of the Giants' infield, while Tom Needham was an able substitute behind the plate for Roger Bresnahan. The Doves received aging stars Bill Dahlen, Dan McGann, and Frank Bowerman. All three were starters but were well beyond their prime. Pitcher George Ferguson was also involved in the trade and was the only regular Boston pitcher to finish with a winning record.

The opener pitted Red Ames for the Giants against Tom Tuckey for Boston. Before a large Monday crowd of twelve thousand, Ames allowed only one hit through the first seven innings, and New York coasted to an easy 8–1 win to come within a game of the Cubs.

OCTOBER 6

As the Doves and Giants prepared for game two, the decision of the National League board of directors was made public, and the news was not good for the Giants. The board voted that the Merkle game was a tie and that the Cubs and Giants would have to replay the controversial contest the day after the regular season ended on October 8.

The board decision was not popular in either New York or Chicago. Giants fans believed the Merkle game should have been a victory and nothing less. The Cubs and their followers just as fervently believed the Merkle game should have been a forfeit, a Giants loss and nothing less. The decision for a one-game play-off at the Polo Grounds was drawn down the middle and pleased no one. The angry and disappointed Cubs boarded the Twentieth Century Limited for the fateful meeting with McGraw's Giants.

The board's decision uncomfortably set up the possibility of a three-way tie for the pennant, if New York lost one game to Boston and beat Chicago in the so-called play-off game. This scenario would bring the Pirates back from the dead, a troublesome question, since team members had returned home after the October 4 loss to the Cubs in Chicago, and gathering them back together would be difficult. Two Giants losses to the Doves and a victory over Chicago in the play-off would place the Cubs and Pirates in a tie. Fortunately for the National League board, none of these messy scenarios became reality.

As word of the board decision spread among New York fans, the Doves and Giants loaded it up again. Former Giant George Ferguson started for the Doves and McGraw sent Hooks Wiltse to the hill for New York. Typical of a year that featured pitching, Ferguson and Wiltse dueled evenly until the sixth, when the Giants scored once. New York iced the contest in the seventh with a three-run outburst. Wiltse lost his shutout when Cy Seymour muffed a fly ball in the eighth.

The next game with Boston was crucial. A Giants win would mean that the play-off game was for all the marbles and the privilege to meet Detroit in the World Series. A New York victory against Boston would also eliminate the Pirates once and for all. The Tigers, as we have seen, won the American League pennant on October 6, defeating the White Sox in Chicago, and were heading home for the October 10 World Series opener.

OCTOBER 7

In a year when fans broke attendance records on an almost daily basis, only five thousand of the Giants faithful came to the Polo Grounds to witness the final contest between New York and Boston. With an eye on the play-off game with the Cubs, McGraw gave Mathewson another day of rest and started Red Ames again. The Doves' starter was Patsy Flaherty, a game veteran who led the team in wins with twelve, matching the win figures of Ferguson and Vive Lindaman.

Unlike in the previous games, Boston jumped out into the lead early. Dan McGann scalded his former mates with a two-run triple in the first inning, marking the first time the Doves had led during the series. Unfortunately for Boston, Flaherty was unable to stand the prosperity of a two-run lead. In the second, Mike Donlin reached on an error and scored on Moose McCormick's single. New York took the lead in the third. Ames singled and went to third on Fred Tenney's double. Buck Herzog's sacrifice bunt scored Ames. Tenney scored on Roger Bresnahan's grounder to shortstop. The issue was settled in the fourth frame, when the Giants put four runs on the board.

The victory was welcome. But the celebration was dampened by the harsh fact that the Cubs were in town to replay the Merkle game, and the three-game sweep of the Doves did not come without controversy.

In his biography of McGraw, Charles C. Alexander notes rumors and ultimately unproven accusations that the Doves threw the series to the Giants.[17] In light of subsequent disclosures of attempted bribes late in the season involving Giants games, those accusations might have had some credibility. After all, Boston manager Joe Kelley and McGraw were old Orioles teammates, and stories of teams "laying" down to help another team became common when the Black Sox scandal broke years later.

It can never be proven that Boston threw this series. Accusations were not backed with evidence other than speculation. Despite the former Giants on the Doves' squad, there is no credible evidence of a fix from accounts of the three games. On the face of it, a fix was possible. If the series was fixed, the conspirators worked well together and kept silent. But a surface analysis would seem to lean away from a fix. First, Boston started the best pitchers they had available. No unproven rookies or inexperienced hurlers took the mound for the Doves. Second, traded players often take perverse pride in beating the team that dumped them. That was the common theme of stories in early-season Boston–New York matchups. Revenge is a powerful motive, especially when the standings of the two teams are in stark contrast. Third, the Giants had dominated the Doves all season long. Going into the series, New York held a 13–6 edge, and they built it to 16–6.

Admittedly, the Doves were out of the running; only the most committed conspiracy theorist would positively assert that a fix was on. The idea of a fix remains plausible, but unlike in other incidents late during the 1908 season, there was no proof, just the circumstance and coincidence of the sweep.

OCTOBER 8

The final game of the 1908 regular season was special. As must by now be more than clear, games pitting Chance's Cubs and McGraw's Giants often resembled open warfare, and this so-called play-off game was no different. More than thirty-five thousand fans jammed into the Polo Grounds to watch the high-stakes replay of the Merkle game.

A well-rested Christy Mathewson was the expected Giants starter. After all, Matty's strong right arm had carried New York all year long. The Cubs were better rested, and Chance gave Jack the Giant Killer Pfiester the start over Ed Reulbach and Three Finger Brown. Brown had started or relieved in eleven of the Cubs' last fourteen games. He had a winning record against the Giants ace but was weary. Reulbach was rested but he could be wild; besides, Pfiester's track record against New York was better. Fresh from his visit to Bonesetter Reese, Pfiester was presumably ready to pitch.

The decisive game of the 1908 National League pennant race lived up to expectations, though fan behavior left much to be desired. The overflow crowd provided the appropriate championship atmosphere and triggered the need for special ground rules. The Cubs and Giants provided the entertainment and drama. A tense atmosphere prevailed over pregame activities.

Brown provided a graphic description of the game setting in an interview in *My Greatest Day in Baseball*. He said Cubs players had been targets of death threats before the game, and at the ballpark they were recipients of insults and worse: "I never heard anybody or any set of men called as many foul names as the Giant fans called us that day from the time we showed up till it was over."[18] Brown noted that McGraw added to the tension by instructing his players to try to pick fights with Cubs players before the game started. Chance, no angel himself when it came down to the basics of self-defense, instructed his players to pick out one Giant and "call 'em everything in the book."[19] The Cubs' pregame practice concluded without incident, despite taunts and challenges. Chance had ordered his men not to respond physically to any provocations.

Ten minutes before the game was to begin, Christy Mathewson emerged from the clubhouse wearing a white linen duster, a common pregame ritual for the great hurler. In what Brown called a "lordly" entrance, Mathewson's every step was greeted by increasing applause and cheers.

Mathewson's grand entrance ratcheted up the pregame tension. The cheers and the open antagonism between the teams drowned out a situation that could have cast a pall over the contest, and perhaps the entire season. There was a very poorly kept rumor circulating among the sporting crowd: that the game was fixed. In his memoir *Touching Second*, Johnny Evers observes that "the rumor ran all over New York that the game was fixed for New York to win. Tinker was called from the Chicago bench an hour before the game and advised to save himself by betting on New York because the umpires were fixed, and offers to bet large sums were made at all saloons and in the Polo Grounds itself on the strength of the rumor. When the Kreamer [sic] case was exposed months later, the probable origin of the rumor was revealed."[20]

This is all Evers says about the matter, which is fully examined in the next chapter. He neither commented on the origin of the rumor nor named anyone he thought responsible. The mere existence of the rumor, open betting in the stands, and an attempt to bribe game umpires Bill Klem and Jimmy Johnstone revealed the total ineffectiveness of all the antigambling talk the baseball establishment had put out throughout the season.

Despite all of the distractions, the game was well played and called honestly and ably by Johnstone and Klem, who had worked together in forty-five games, including twenty-nine Giants contests. In those games New York enjoyed a 22–7 mark in 1908. The seventh loss would occur on this day.

Mathewson retired the Cubs in the first. Pfiester did not match Matty's performance. The Giant Killer was neutralized by wildness and clutch hitting. New York leadoff man Fred Tenney was hit by a pitch and Buck Herzog walked. Roger Bresnahan struck out, reacting to Johnny Kling dropping the pitch; Herzog was tossed out trying to make second. Mike Donlin doubled home Tenney. When Pfiester walked Cy Seymour, Frank Chance had seen enough and brought in Mordecai Brown. Art Devlin was no match for Three Finger's curve and struck out. The stage was now set for another classic Mathewson-Brown pitching duel.

In the Cubs' second, Chance singled but was picked off by Mathewson, to the great delight of the partisan crowd. Klem's call was protested loudly by the Cubs, and starting center fielder Circus Solly Hofman was ejected. The inning ended with strikeouts of Harry Steinfeldt and Hofman's replacement, Del Howard.

While Mathewson was indicating that he was having an "on" day, Brown matched him out for out. Giants fans greeted the third inning loudly, cheering as if they could will their beloved team to the pennant. The Cubs' third on October 8 would be a complete disaster for the Giants. Matty's nemesis, Joe Tinker, led off with a triple over the head of Seymour, who had apparently ignored orders to play deeper. Kling's single tied the score. Brown bunted him to second. Jimmy Sheckard flied out and it appeared that the threat from the Cubs was passing.

Mathewson was a great control pitcher. In 1908 he issued only forty-two walks. But a base on balls to Evers set the table for Wildfire Schulte, who had been having a terrible year at bat, hitting only .236. Usually Mathewson would easily take care of a slumping hitter, but Schulte lined a double to left, scoring Kling and leaving Evers at third.

Up came the hated Chance. The Giants partisans had spared nothing in their scorn and hatred of the Cubs' leader. The first-inning pickoff gave them the opportunity to ridicule Chance. The third-inning situation gave him the opportunity to shut them up. He applied the silencer with a booming double to the right field fence, scoring Evers and Schulte and putting Chicago up 4–1.

Those were all the runs the Cubs would need. For the next three innings, Brown and Mathewson silenced the bats and settled into the kind of duel expected of these immortals. In the seventh, Brown faltered and the Giants were ready to pounce. Back-to-back singles by Devlin and Moose McCormick shook Brown. Al Bridwell walked to load the bases.

With none out and the tying run at first, McGraw lifted Matty for pinch hitter Larry Doyle, who had hit .308 in his second year in the majors. Doyle hit a foul pop-up. Kling caught it despite Giants fans throwing paper, hats, and bottles in a vain attempt to distract him. Fred Tenney made the score 4–2 with a sacrifice fly. The inning ended on Herzog's sharp grounder to Tinker.

That ended the scoring and the Giants' hopes for the pennant. Before the Giants could bat in the ninth, a huge fight broke out in the crowded stands and fans broke over the lines. The game was delayed while police took care of the mob.

The Giants' ninth was anticlimactic. Brown described what transpired: "As the ninth ended with the Giants going out, one-two-three, we all ran for our lives, straight for the clubhouse with the pack at our heels. Some of our boys got caught by the mob and beaten up some. Tinker, Howard and Sheckard were struck. Chance was hurt most of all. A Giant fan hit him in the throat and Husk's voice was gone for a day or two in the World Series that followed. Pfiester got slashed on the shoulder by a knife."[21]

Chicago's ordeal in New York was far from over. The Cubs were trapped in the clubhouse, protected by a thin blue line of policemen. Fortunately for the Cubs, the policemen's sense of duty overrode any partisan feelings for the Giants. Again, Brown described the scene: "We made it to the dressing room and barricaded the door. Outside wild men were yelling for our blood — really. As the mob got bigger, the

TABLE 14. *Final National League Standings*

	W	L	Pct.	GB	October Record
Chicago	99	55	.643	—	5–0
New York	98	56	.636	1	5–3
Pittsburgh	98	56	.636	1	3–1
Philadelphia	83	71	.539	16	5–3
Cincinnati	73	81	.474	26	1–4
Boston	63	91	.409	36	0–6
Brooklyn	53	101	.344	46	4–3
St. Louis	49	105	.318	50	0–4

police came up and formed a line across the door. We read the next day that the cops had to pull their revolvers to hold them back. I couldn't say as to that. We weren't sticking our heads out to see."[22]

The Cubs had to celebrate their unprecedented third straight pennant on the train for Detroit. They left town with a police escort.

AFTERWORD: WORLD SERIES ANTICLIMAX

If Hollywood had been making baseball movies in 1908, the World Series in this tumultuous year would have ended in seven games, with a heroic rally with two out in the ninth before a hostile crowd. Fitting as such an ending might have been, it was not to be.

The World Series opened on October 10 at Detroit. The Tigers were well rested, having spent almost a week at home after winning the pennant in Chicago. The Cubs had just one day of rest before facing a battle-tested Tigers club. The casual observer might have been tempted to favor Detroit purely on the basis of battle fatigue on the part of the Cubs. But as the Pirates and Giants had found out, a beat-up Cubs team was more dangerous than a well-rested one. The 1907 World Series was a 4–0 Cubs sweep. The 1908 Cubs-Tigers series rematch was just like their first meeting — no contest.

Fans numbering 10,812 braved a heavy rainfall to witness the first game of the 1908 World Series. As in the early season, the weather affected the quality of play. Loads of sawdust were used to give pitchers and hitters a foothold during the storm, which did not let up until the sixth inning. The starting pitchers were Big Ed Reulbach for the Cubs and Twilight Ed Killian of the Tigers.

Detroit drew first blood as Matty McIntyre scored on Ty Cobb's single in the first inning. The Cubs roared back in the third with four runs. Jimmy Sheckard led off with a double and Evers hit a bunt single. Schulte scored Sheckard with a base hit. Chance's bunt wound up forcing Evers, but Steinfeldt's hit scored Schulte and Chance. He reached third on McIntyre's wild throw. A walk issued to Circus Solly Hofman sent Killian to the showers. Ed Summers came in in relief of Killian. Summers was effective, but Chicago scored a fourth run on an error by Germany Schaefer.

The Cubs scored once in the seventh on a double steal by Evers and Chance. In the Detroit half of the inning the Tigers erupted for three runs, the key hit being a double by Red Downs. In the eighth, Detroit added two more runs to take a 6–5 lead. Sam Crawford scored on Claude Rossman's single and Cobb scored on an error by Evers.

Down in the ninth inning, the Cubs did what they had done throughout 1908 — come back and win. Chicago scored five times to ice the opener on the force of consecutive singles by Schulte, Chance, Steinfeldt, Hofman, Tinker, and Kling. Up 10–6, Brown snuffed an attempted Detroit rally to end the contest and take the series to Chicago for game two.

Orval Overall and Wild Bill Donovan were the starters for Chicago and Detroit in the Windy City. Donovan was one of the Tigers' aces, while injury made Overall more of a member of the supporting cast. Despite the difference in status and performance, Overall was the eventual winner thanks to better offensive support. No runs were scored until the eighth, when Chicago scored six times, the key blows being a two-run homer by Tinker and a bases-loaded double by Kling. There were echoes of another Cubs sweep, as the demoralized Tigers had lost two games in a row due to late-inning rallies.

Game three was played on Monday, October 12, in Chicago. Up to then the Tigers had amassed a dismal 0–6–1 record against Chance's Cubs in World Series play. George Mullin took the mound for Detroit. Jack Pfiester, recovered from his wounds at the hands of New York fans, was the Chicago starter. Detroit drew first blood in the opening frame when Charley O'Leary reached base on Steinfeldt's error and scored on Cobb's single.

Mullin was strong until the fourth, when Chicago put three runs on the board, thanks to errors by Coughlin and Rossman. What was particularly painful for Tigers fans was that the errors occurred after two outs. Up 3–1 after four innings with Jack the Giant Killer on the hill, the Cubs faithful began to smell another world title.

As if the pressures of the National League pennant race and fighting a sore arm finally got to him, Pfiester blew up in the sixth. He walked Mullin; McIntyre singled; then Pfiester tried to force Mullin at third on O'Leary's bunt. The throw was late and the bags were loaded, with Crawford and Cobb coming up.

The Detroit power hitters managed back-to-back infield singles to tie the score. Rossman redeemed himself with a two-run single. The always aggressive Cobb was retired at home on Schaefer's fly to Hofman. The scoring ended on Ira Thomas's single, which drove home Rossman.

Up 6–3, Mullin pitched as though he was ridding the Tigers of all the frustration growing from the seven previous matches with the Cubs. Chicago never seriously threatened for the rest of the game, and the Tigers added two insurance runs in the eighth to win easily at 8–3. It was the first Cubs loss in October 1908, and the last one too.

Almost thirteen thousand Tigers fans came to see game four the next day in Detroit. It was clearly one of the best crowds of the year in this growing future automotive capital and was the result of the previous day's victory. The pitching matchup held promise as young Kickapoo Ed Summers faced the battle-hardened Mordecai Brown. Summers had won twenty-four games in his rookie year, while Brown had cashed in twenty-nine times. Both hurlers turned in great performances, but Brown and his supporting cast went up in the series three games to one with a 3–0, four-hit shutout.

Playing errorless ball, the Cubs were as good on defense in the field as Brown was on the mound. The Cubs infield played outstanding defense, ending Tigers threats time and again. In the sixth inning, Detroit had Crawford and O'Leary on first and second with none out. Cobb attempted a sacrifice bunt. Brown fielded the ball and without pause threw to Steinfeldt, who stayed at third to force O'Leary. Crawford was picked off second by Kling's strong throw to Tinker, and the Detroit threat was squelched.

Two Cubs runs in the third were enough for the win. After two outs, Summers walked Schulte and Chance. Back-to-back singles by Steinfeldt and Hofman chased home the runs. An insurance run was added in the ninth, when Evers scored on Cobb's error.

Wednesday, October 14 marked the end of play in 1908. As on other days in Detroit, the gate was small—only 6,210 fans witnessed the game — and as in other decisive games in this tumultuous year, the visitors won. The Tigers sent Wild Bill Donovan to the mound to face Orval Overall, who had been the Cubs' ace in 1907. His regular season effectiveness in 1908 had been blunted by a nagging hand injury. But Overall was his old self during the World Series, winning games two and five.

In this contest Overall limited Detroit to three hits, winning his second World Series game 2–0. The Cubs scored once in the first on successive hits by Evers, Schulte, and Chance. The second run scored in the fifth when Kling came home on Evers's double. Detroit threatened in their half of the first, but Schaefer struck out with the bases loaded. In the fifth, the Tigers had men on second and third with one out, but Matty McIntyre flied weakly to Hofman, and Crawford struck out.

Overall retired the last nine hitters he faced, to give the Cubs the world title and a thirteen-hundred-dollar winner's share paycheck. Like that of the previous year, the win over the Tigers was easy and as one-sided on paper as it was on the field. Cubs pitchers were stifling in 1907, holding Detroit to a .209 team batting average. Results in 1908 were even better. The hard-hitting Tigers were held to a paltry .203 team average. Cubs hitters, paced by Chance's .421 mark, posted a .293 team average. In the field Chicago committed five errors, while the Tigers defense committed ten.

The 1908 championship put the Cubs on a short list of immortals, teams who have won two straight World Series. Other teams have won three or more pennants in a row, but none of those teams won a pennant by a closer margin than the Chicago Cubs. This Cubs team finished second to the Pirates in 1909 and won another pennant in 1910. As of this writing, the 1908 World Championship has been the last for the Cubs franchise.

As for the Tigers, Hughie Jennings's charges also had one more pennant in them. The 1909 Tigers won by three games over the next American League dynasty, the Philadelphia Athletics. However, the World Series result was no different. This time Detroit lost to Honus Wagner's Pittsburgh Pirates in what would be the last postseason play for Ty Cobb.

In tribute to this final World Championship by the Cubs dynasty, *Cincinnati Post Inquirer* writer W. Ross Tenney wrote a poem honoring the Cubs. It also provides a note of lightness to the end of play in this roller-coaster ride of a season. Further events associated with the 1908 season would not be so joyous.

(With Apologies to Paul Revere and Henry W. Longfellow)
by W. Ross Tenney

Listen, my children, and you shall hear,
Why the Cubs are champs of this whole blamed sphere.
    On October 14, in nineteen eight,
    Detroit and its Tigers met their fate,
And the bugs in Chicago madly cheer.

Chance said to big Jeff: "You go to the box
    With curves and shoots, and this town tonight
No lanterns aloft will hang, old fox,
    To tell that the Cubs got the worst of the fight.
One game is ours, and two, also three —
Make it four, and I at first will be;
So take the slab with your good right arm,
So limber and sturdy, to work the charm,
And we'll lick that bunch, I'll bet the farm."

Said the umps, "Play Ball," and the game began.
Sheckard was first to step to the pan.
A swipe, and the ball sailed up in the air
But with swinging stride Dutch Schaefer got there
Just barely in time to make the catch;
John Evers next proved more than a match
For Donovan's wiles his hit was no scratch.
But a solid swat, for which Crawford tried,
And failed to reach by a single stride.

Meanwhile, Fred Schulte had stepped to the plate
With eager bat, to swipe or to wait —
    Did a little of both, for 'twas two and three
With that hefty stick of second growth ash.
The bat met the ball with ringing crash,
    And a corking single to the left had he.

Then forth from the bench came the husky Chance;
    He didn't wait, but swung right out
    At the first ball pitched — 'twas a nifty clout —
And Evers sailed home with never a glance

Afield to see where the ball would strike,
For he knew 'twas no time to look, but to hike.
The speedy Cub got home O.K.:
That run was enough to win the day.
But eight more innings were still to play.
And no one could tell what they'd be like.

No more in the first Chicago made;
Around the stands the fans still stayed.
For Wahoo Sam and the Slugging Cobb,
Big Rossman and Schaefer, who is no slob.
The bugs felt sure would get on the job.

Meanwhile Big Jeff, so cool of nerve,
Was a perfect master of the shoot and curve;
So you'd never have known 'twas the same Overall
Whose balloon ascensions lost many a game
When knocking Red fans would jeer and call —
But really and truly it was the same.
No "rattles" for him since he's been a Cub.
He's proved that the knocker's the one that's the dub.
And never once on this day did he flinch,
He showed at his best when in a pinch.

When hits meant runs the Tigers fanned —
Somehow or other they couldn't land.
The mighty Cobb and Big Wahoo,
Schaefer, the German, and others too,
Were on the list of those who whiffed
When it might have been diff'rent if they had biffed.
Bigger and bigger grew the list
'Till eleven total had struck and missed;
And the Cubs meanwhile weren't satisfied,
And just to get their title clinched
They added a tally on their side
And felt that they had the vict'ry clinched.

'Twas thus they pounded the horsehide sphere,
While Overall worked that good right arm,
And kept the Tigers from doing harm —
And he never once got out of gear.

The series is over, the pennant is won,
The Cubs are the champs, the Tigers are done,
And in the future fights for the base ball flag,
    When the umpire cries aloud "Play Ball,"
The fans will remember the time that rag
Was won by the Cubs and Overall.[23]

As the daylight dimmed on October 14, the Cubs celebrated another championship in a visiting locker room, without police protection as in New York. Baseball owners also celebrated a successful season
and planned for the future of the sport. A great deal had been accom-
plished, but before plans for future seasons could become reality, baseball's leadership had to deal with a bribery scandal that threatened to
ruin all that had been established on the playing fields of 1908.

12 **Scandals of 1908** Delayed Reckoning

The 1919 World Series will always be associated with the gambling scandal that finally forced major league baseball to come to grips with the issue. Details of the Black Sox Scandal need not be repeated here. The draconian official response by newly named baseball commissioner Judge Kenesaw Mountain Landis to the 1919 World Series fix and other gambling incidents was, in part, due to the lip service paid to the issue during previous years. Baseball's zero tolerance policy toward gambling, unique in professional sports, was a result of the ineffectiveness of antigambling rhetoric and unofficial tolerance of betting on games during the first two decades of the twentieth century. Judge Landis's harsh policy saved the integrity of baseball and the future of the sport.

Viewed in a modern context, the investigation of the attempted bribe of umpires in 1908 to fix the Cubs-Giants play-off game was a farce. It was a successful cover-up. The 1908 bribery scandal and the investigation sent a clear message that preserving the status quo was more important than getting to the truth or confronting the gambling issue.

The 1908 season was a success both on and off the field. Baseball officialdom had been campaigning for years to boost the sport as the national pastime, and the 1908 results showed that the effort was working. The owners' campaign against rowdyism and their attempts to attract a better class of people to the ballparks were bearing fruit. The success of the 1908 season spurred the baseball establishment to build larger, permanent ballparks. Any hint of scandal could burst the bubble and jeopardize what had been already invested and built and, of course, any plans for the future.

As a result, owners were extremely reluctant to air dirty laundry that would cast a shadow over a season that had helped establish the dominance of baseball on the American sports scene. The owners' motive for keeping things as they were is clear. Protection and preservation of the status quo was also firmly grounded in a philosophy of not tolerating any outside scrutiny, governmental or journalistic. To put it in other terms, protecting the status quo was a high-stakes gamble, but the owners had to roll the dice. The owners were betting that those dice were loaded in their favor. They were.

As we have seen, a great deal had been said but little had been done about gambling during the 1908 season. When confronted with an incident with unimpeachable witnesses, the official response was clearly inadequate. The response likely involved protection of prominent people in baseball who were directly connected to the prestigious New York Giants franchise. A major reason 1908 wasn't seriously marred by scandal was the fundamental honesty of those who were targets of attempted bribes — umpires and players alike. The official investigation uncovered a perpetrator but little else, and it left behind troubling questions.

Despite credible eyewitnesses in the shape of umpires Bill Klem and James Johnstone, the bribery investigation unfolded slowly. Baseball's leadership was first preoccupied with looking into a ticket scalping controversy involving the World Champion Cubs. This probe was conducted by the National Commission, members of which knew of the bribe attempts before the World Series started.

National League Secretary John Heydler had early knowledge of the bribe attempts. On the day before the contest, Klem and Johnstone told him of two separate attempts to give them money to throw the October 8 Cubs-Giants game to the Giants. This story was kept under wraps until the ticket scalping investigation was well under way. From a public relations perspective, taking on the scalping probe first made sense simply because there was undeniable public knowledge of the practice. News of the attempted bribe of umpires leaked out more slowly because it was insider, not public, knowledge.

Scalping of World Series tickets was not entirely the fault of Cubs President Charles Murphy. The National Commission itself had to shoulder much of the blame because of a World Series ticket policy forbidding customers from buying individual game tickets. Instead fans had to buy tickets for all games scheduled in a particular city. This policy was guaranteed to encourage ticket scalping. As Stephen Reiss notes in *Touching Base*, "If a fan wanted to attend just one game, he still had to buy tickets for all the games and then try to sell the rest. Or he could buy a single pasteboard from a broker or ticket scalper, in which case he would pay considerably more than the established price."[1]

There was convincing evidence that Murphy cooperated with scalpers and brokers, many of whom had clout in city hall and/or connections with the criminal underworld. During the 1908 World Series, fans seeking tickets were turned away while tickets were being distributed to speculators. Reiss writes that Chicago's Mayor Fred Busse threatened to stop the World Series because he did not get his share of tickets. As a result of the mayor's ire provoking a fan boycott, attendance was low for the two games in Chicago.[2]

Reiss's conclusions contain a large measure of truth, in that attendance figures for at the two World Series games in Chicago were 17,760 and 14,453. While those attendance numbers were significantly larger than those at Detroit and average home figures, they were far short of the more than thirty thousand who mobbed West Side Park for the final Cubs-Pirates game. Average Cubs home attendance in 1908 was just over eight thousand. World Series attendance at Chicago was well below the average gate for late-season games with the Giants as well as the Pirates.

The specific charge leveled by the National Commission stated that blocks of World Series tickets got into the hands of scalpers with the help of Cubs employees before sale to the public. The National Commission met in Chicago in November in the face of bitter opposition to the investigation by Murphy and other Cubs officials. The commission considered the evidence for more than a month and on December 18 mildly censured the Cubs for lax business methods in allowing series tickets to get into the hands of speculators. The commission found no evidence that any Cubs officials were directly connected to the matter.

While the scalping brushfire was being stomped out, the heat was building in the probe of the attempted bribe of umpires Klem and Johnstone. A week before the scalping verdict was released, National

League President Pulliam appointed a committee to investigate the attempted bribe. In making their announcement, Pulliam and the owners assured the public that the attempted bribe did not involve anyone associated with organized baseball. This was a statement that events proved to be an outright lie. For the unfortunate Pulliam, already thoroughly beaten up over the Merkle affair and on the verge of nervous breakdown, the statement may have reflected wishful thinking rather than any attempt to hide the facts.

The members of the investigating committee may have reflected that same wishful thinking or perhaps an attempt to appease Pulliam's main enemy, the New York Giants. The four-member committee was chaired by none other than Giants owner John T. Brush. Pulliam as National League president also sat on the panel, along with Brooklyn owner Charles Ebbets and Cincinnati owner and National Commission president Garry Herrmann. The appointment of Brush to head the committee drew harsh criticism from the Cubs and Murphy, who were still smarting from the ticket scalping probe.

Brush's appointment seemed strange at the time and was outrageous in view of the facts of the case. In light of later revelations, the appointment of Brush was a true case of the fox watching the chicken coop. For Pulliam, it may have been an early signal of his eventual breakdown. For the game itself, Brush's presence on the committee meant that full disclosure of all facts of the case was unlikely and questions resulting from it would be unanswered and unresolved.

To initiate the probe, National League owners issued a statement presenting the panel with an open and shut case. Referring to statements given the league by umpires Klem and Johnstone, the owners noted: "In one of the statements the name of the person who approached the umpire was given as well as the name of persons he claimed to represent. In the other statement the names of the persons who approached the umpire were not given, this umpire stating that they were strangers to him."[3]

What was not reported in the official statement was which umpire was which. Bill Klem's later account of the incident makes it clear that he was the first umpire referred to and Johnstone was the latter. Johnstone said and wrote little about the bribery incident. In fact, he resigned as an umpire in late October, just a couple of weeks after the World Series. He was eventually rehired for the 1909 season and remained on the National League umpire staff through the 1912 season.

Klem's account comes from his 1951 interview with *Collier's Magazine*. Curiously, Klem does not name the perpetrator, and in that respect what he does not say is as significant as what he says. The Klem article was published forty-three years after the incident. His account differs significantly from the affidavit he gave investigators in 1908. Klem told his interviewer that he quickly realized a man whom he had known for some time was trying to bribe him:

> Listen, there isn't enough money in the world to bribe me, I told him. "And I have no reason to believe I will umpire the playoff. Nor have you."
>
> I was stretching a bit there. I knew I was to umpire the game with Jim Johnstone. But it hadn't been announced publicly and I wasn't telling him.
>
> "Bill, you'll work the play-off and you'll be set for life if the Giants win. Tammany Hall has assured me of that."
>
> "Don't talk such damned nonsense. You're being silly."
>
> I wanted to duck this man and I wanted no approaches from anyone else before the important game that would decide the National League pennant. I tried to ditch him by leaving the train at Forty-second Street, making him believe I was going to my home.[4]

Klem told *Collier's* that he returned home and immediately went to his hotel, where he went straight to his room, leaving instructions not be bothered unless called by National League officials. Upon rising the next morning, Klem went directly to league offices, where he saw Johnstone with league secretary John Heydler. Klem told the magazine:

> "I told Heydler I had something for Pulliam's ear.
>
> Heydler said Pulliam was in Detroit. I wanted to talk only to Pulliam, but Heydler said, "Oh, what's on your mind, Bill?" I did not want to talk about it in front of Johnstone, but Heydler gave me no choice. So I said, "John, they're after me with money."
>
> "Oh," sighed Heydler.
>
> "They're after me too," said Johnstone. He [Johnstone] told a vague story about a couple of men telling him on a train that they would like to talk to him. I said nothing more.[5]

Klem's account indicates that all in the room were upset, but there seemed to be a conclusion that little could be done. Changing umpires was all but impossible since the game was set for that afternoon. Klem told his interviewer there was one more bribe attempt just before the game by the same man who had approached him the day before at the ballpark.

Klem's account is fascinating. Aside from the fact it comes from memory of an event of more than four decades before, Klem doesn't reveal much. What is interesting is that Klem apparently had a good night's sleep before reporting the attempted bribe. Also of note is his overriding, and perhaps understandable, desire to umpire the game. He had told *Collier's* that substituting umpires would be done over his dead body. Not reporting the bribe attempt until the day of the game assured Klem of the assignment — Heydler was in no position to make a change. Also curious about the Klem account is that no one appeared to bother, or be in a hurry, to notify Pulliam. And we have to take Klem's word that he spent the eve before the play-off alone.

To complete Klem's magazine account, the Hall of Fame umpire notes that the man who tried to bribe him was barred for life from entering any major league ballpark. He concluded — disingenuously, in that his 1908 affidavit says the money came from Giants players — "I will go to my grave wondering where the money he offered me came from. Certainly not from Tammany Hall, because they didn't care ten dollars worth. And certainly he himself had neither the bank account nor the property to raise any large sum."[6]

Another curious note to Klem's version of the story is that he never mentions the name of Dr. Joseph M. Creamer, the man the National Commission eventually accused and found guilty of the bribe attempt. This is especially interesting in light of the that fact Creamer died in July 1918; concealing the identity of a man dead more than thirty years seems overly solicitous. This would make sense only if Klem were trying to protect someone else more important. Dr. Creamer was the New York Giants team physician at the time of the attempted bribe. It is quite possible that Klem was protecting the name and reputation of another man who had died seventeen years earlier, John McGraw.

McGraw's reputation emerged unscathed following the Creamer episode and other incidents in 1908, even though circumstances involving gamblers in the late season in New York cast legitimate questions in McGraw's direction. But many of these questions were unasked. Was Klem trying to protect McGraw? It is possible, especially in light of Klem's revelation of his close friendship with the Giants manager. Klem told *Collier's:* "McGraw and I developed a strange off-the-field relationship. We frequently dined together during spring training and, in the few years when his team was not in the pennant race, we would dine after a game. I had a rule not to mix socially with any player or manager if his team was in the race."[7] Umpires of today engaging in such behavior would be violating anti-fraternization rules and would be subject to disciplinary action, if not outright dismissal. It must also be noted that during Klem's umpiring career, McGraw's Giants were contenders more often than not.

Klem's reputation for honesty and impartiality is tarnished both by the admission of an off-field friendship with McGraw and by the apparent reluctance to name names in the bribery case. His credibility is not helped any further by his 1951 account differing significantly from his 1908 affidavit in terms of who was offering the money.

As we shall see, reports about Klem's 1908 affidavit indicate that the money came from Giants players. We are free to draw our own conclusions about Klem's role in this mess, but the bottom line is we will never know what really happened, nor the actions and motives of those involved. All we have to work with are their accounts without benefit of cross examination. No one is alive to speak to any other questions.

This brings us to Dr. Creamer. What kind of man was he? Little is known of him beyond what appears in newspaper accounts of the day. Few baseball sources provide much detail. The National Baseball Hall of Fame Library has no biographical file on him. The histories that mention him, and only a handful do, discuss the bribe attempt and his banishment from baseball, and little or nothing else.

It appears that in trying to bribe Klem, Creamer may have been acting out of character and on the orders of others. *Chicago Tribune* reporter Harvey T. Woodruff broke the story in April 1909, describing Creamer as an avid sports physician who had worked with boxers and bicyclists. By all indications he had a prosperous practice.

Creamer's father was a coroner. Creamer took over the medical practice upon the death of his father and enjoyed an "excellent reputation" in sporting circles.[8] Dr. Creamer consistently denied all charges and threatened to sue everyone involved. He told Woodruff that "he intended to bring heavy damage suits against the New York club, the national commission, and Umpires Johnstone and Klem if he was barred out of the Polo Grounds."[9]

The threatened law suit was never filed and Dr. Creamer dropped out of sight after news of the scandal subsided. According to his obituary in the *New York Times* of July 30, 1918, Dr. Creamer "had worked for many years among the poor of the city and was known for the free clinics he maintained at Bellvue, St. Luke's and Polyclinic Hospitals."[10]

Dead at the age of forty-eight, Dr. Creamer has had his impact on baseball history obliterated by the passage of time and the silence of those involved. It will be never known who influenced Dr. Creamer to do what he did, or whether he acted alone or was part of a larger conspiracy. It appears he was not an evil man. His work among the poor may have been atonement, but it may also have been part of his character. That charity work could have led to his early death. His obituary does not list a cause of death, but considering his work at charity clinics, Dr. Creamer could possibly have been an early victim of the influenza epidemic that claimed thousands of lives worldwide in 1918 and 1919. While this brief biography of Dr. Creamer puts us slightly ahead of the story, it provides perspective and an argument that Creamer may indeed have been a patsy.

Returning to the announcement of the probe in late 1908, we face the curious reaction of organized baseball to the situation. Statements that the bribe attempt had come from someone not associated with organized baseball were easily proven untrue. Despite Brush's denials, it was common knowledge among those who covered the Giants that Dr. Creamer was their team physician. In reporting about Giants injuries, reporters cited Creamer often during the season. During the investigation it was revealed that Creamer had been hired by McGraw without Brush's knowledge.

In January 1909, the pages of *Sporting Life* were full of commentary about the league's investigation. The *New York Times* praised the umpires for coming forward and baseball officialdom for going on with the investigation. Despite the apparent gravity of the charges and the composition of the investigating committee, there was a measure of ambivalence about the probe. A *Washington Post* editorial supported the investigation but also paid homage to the position that there were questions that should not be asked. "It is argued that it would have been better for the game had the matter never been made public, and that a suspicion as to the honesty of the sport has been created by ordering the investigation. . . . Had he [National League President Pulliam] kept what knowledge he had to himself there might have been a time in the future when some inkling of the attempt to bribe the umpires would have come out, together with the fact Pulliam had knowledge thereof, in which event there would have been good cause for suspicion."[11]

If the press was ambivalent about and hardly interested in getting to the bottom of the matter, the investigating committee took the cue and moved at its own speed, listening to its leader, John T. Brush. In February, Pulliam finally collapsed under the pressure and took a leave of absence. Heydler, to whom Klem and Johnstone had first related the bribe attempts, was named interim National League president. Seizing the opportunity left open by the transition, Brush issued a preliminary finding. The Brush finding would not be the last word.

Brush consulted attorneys about the attempted bribe and issued a statement that could charitably be called an attempt to "lawyer" his way out of doing anything. Brush wanted to stop the probe because no crime had been committed under New York statutes. The statement reflected the legality but not the morality of the approach to the umpires, "Attempted bribery . . . is a criminal offense only when an effort is made to influence public officials by the use of money. As the umpires were not public officials, but employees of a private corporation, the attempt to bribe them cannot be rated as a crime."[12]

Brush's assertion was a strict interpretation of the statutes of the State of New York. But this reading of the law did not come close to satisfying the Cubs' Murphy, who was outraged and demanded full disclosure. Murphy was still angry over the scalping probe and was likely obeying the time-honored Chicago political and business advice of "don't get mad, get even."

While Murphy's anger may be attributed to sour grapes, he had stature and influence in baseball circles and beyond. His voice would be heard. He owned the best team on the field and had the best political wiring, or clout, in the game. Among Murphy's closest business associates was Charles Phelps Taft, the older brother and political advisor to President Elect William Howard Taft. The relationship with the president elect's brother gave Murphy a great deal of influence among his peers.

The bribery case never went to civil or criminal trial. But Brush's assertion that no laws had been broken was clearly inadequate. Murphy's anger and political connections were apparently noted. In April Brush's committee took the unusual step of banning Dr. Creamer for life from entering major league ballparks. There was no inquiry as to whether Dr. Creamer had acted alone or been acting on orders from others. The committee's finding stated only what action it would take. It offered no other explanation and, further, did not identify Dr. Creamer as the culprit. *Sporting Life*'s commentary shed little light on the matter:

> In this matter the Commission would not hesitate a moment to institute a most rigid prosecution against the offender if they had the power to do so and the corrobative [sic] testimony to sustain the charges made by the umpires. We feel, however, that in the absence of this, the party charged with this offense by the umpires should not go unpunished, and for that reason we will furnish to every major league club owner the name of the person who attempted this offense, with instructions to such club owners to bar him from their respective grounds for all time to come.[13]

The commission hoped the statement would be the last word on the matter. *Sporting Life* offered its support, saying the outcome was the best possible "considering its lack of power and paucity of evidence against the one offender named, and the absolute disconnection of any one, officially or otherwise connected with base ball."[14] *Sporting Life*'s conclusion is curious in that its editors were able to disconnect Dr. Creamer, a Giants employee, from a direct connection to baseball.

The position of both the National Commission and *Sporting Life* reflected a desire to turn attention to the young 1909 season. To both, the umpires' statements were not sufficient grounds for pressing charges or even to conclude that a crime had been committed. Organized baseball had an exit and took it. That exit was the likelihood that no one else would come forward. No one did, and the case closed because no other corroborating evidence surfaced.

From a legal perspective, any conviction would have come down to a question of credibility among the umpires and Dr. Creamer, had such a prosecution been possible using the laws of the day. More disturbing was *Sporting Life*'s assertion, despite evidence to the contrary reported on its own pages, that Creamer had no direct connection with baseball. This position apparently reflected a belief that there were some questions that were better left unasked. The outcome of the investigation could be seen as casting a question upon the umpires' credibility as sole witnesses, but neither Klem nor Johnstone complained. Much to the relief of baseball's leadership, interest in the scandal was waning as the 1909 baseball season began creating its own excitement. However, baseball had to deal with another bombshell before the case was laid to rest.

Two stories by Harvey T. Woodruff of the *Chicago Tribune*, on April 24 and 25, 1909, revealed Dr. Creamer's identity and provided previously unknown information. Woodruff's work made a noise, but the light it shed on the episode was quickly extinguished by lack of interest on the part of the media and official baseball. Nothing can kill a scoop faster than no other media outlet picking up on the story, which was what happened to Woodruff.

Equipped with hindsight and the perspective provided by later investigations of subsequent gambling scandals, we can see that Woodruff's reporting provided fodder for questions that could or should have been asked but were not. Klem's accounts of the incident differ in who was responsible. Remember that Klem's 1951 account says, without naming names, that Dr. Creamer claimed the money to have come from Tammany Hall. Woodruff wrote: "Those who profess to know say that the affidavit of Umpire Klem stated that the man who approached the umpire said he was acting on behalf of three New York players, and these names are understood to have been mentioned in the affidavit, but the investigating committee of the National League could find nothing to substantiate the charges."[15]

That account explains the first approach to Klem. Klem mentions in the *Collier's* article a second approach by Dr. Creamer just before the Cubs-Giants game. According to Woodruff's account, Klem had said in his affidavit that "a man named Dr. Creamer, official physician of the Giants, met Klem under the grand stand at the polo grounds, that the said Creamer, holding a bunch of greenbacks in his right hand, said to Klem: 'Here's $2,500, which is yours if you will give all the close decisions to the Giants and see that they win sure. You know who is behind me and you needn't be afraid of anything. You will have a good job the rest of your life.'" In his affidavit, Woodruff reported, Klem declared that Creamer had mentioned the name of a well-known politician, who, Klem claimed, "does not know Creamer except in a casual way."[16]

Credibility problems abounded for John T. Brush once Woodruff's story hit the streets. His team physician was implicated by an almost unimpeachable witness, who said Giants players had put up the money! It was clear to anyone paying attention that baseball's flagship franchise had a problem. It didn't help that Brush initially denied that Dr. Creamer was a team employee, nor did it look good that the investigation went no further than Creamer.

In fairness to Brush, he was a sick man in 1908 and may not have paid strict attention to detail in the day-to-day operations of the Giants. Thus his denial may not have been as self-serving as it appears. Woodruff's account duly notes Brush's anger over the incident, and his attempt to shift blame for hiring Dr. Creamer to team secretary Fred Knowles, despite evidence that McGraw himself hired the doctor. The fact remains, however, that Brush was the head man of the Giants. He should have known of the hiring, unless he did not want to know so that he could have a measure of deniability.

McGraw's role in this mess is unknowable. It is clear that he hired Creamer as team physician without asking Brush, a curious move but probably one conducted to provide treatment for players and not a bag man for bribes. McGraw does not mention the bribery case in his memoir. He is reported to have been enraged over rumors of a bribe attempt just before the Cubs-Giants game, but little else is recorded about McGraw's thoughts on the matter.[17]

Dr. Creamer went to his grave denying involvement in the affair. Nothing ever came of his threat to sue the Giants, baseball, the umpires, or anyone else involved. He was urged by his friends to come forward with the truth but issued only a brief statement. As noted, Creamer faded from public view after the incident. His statement to Woodruff remains his final say on the matter:

> It is a job to ruin me, he [Dr. Creamer] said. "I never saw Klem or Johnstone to speak to that day or any other day. I did not go outside the grandstand to meet them before the game in question, and I never tried to bribe anybody in my life. I have not decided what I shall do yet, but I have been advised to seek legal redress.
>
> "I acted as the Giants' physician at the request of McGraw and I received payment for my services. Yes, my bill was about $2,800, and it is true that Brush did not want to pay it at first. I earned the money legitimately, and I was on duty every day and gave up much of my valuable time. I have been interested in sports for nearly twenty years and nobody has ever accused me of wrongdoing before. I cannot understand why the umpires have mixed me in this unless it is a conspiracy of some kind."[18]

Creamer's statement is as curious as his subsequent inaction in the legal arena. He spoke volumes when he concluded that the entire matter was a conspiracy of some kind. Why didn't he file suit if his reputation was smeared? Privacy laws being what they then were, he had a good case. Was his subsequent silence purchased? We will never know. It is the stuff of claim and counterclaim, which becomes fertile ground for conspiracy theories but offers little upon which to base a conclusion. Creamer was puzzled as to why the umpires implicated him. A better question to ask is: Why would the umpires cook up such a story if it were not true?

The stench over the case disappeared quickly after Woodruff's stories were published, much to the relief of baseball's establishment. The stakes were high. Had the bribery case been pursued and the umpires' affidavits been substantiated, baseball would have been shaken to its very foundation. The New York Giants franchise was the premier franchise in a business that was beginning to attain respectability and building its image as the national pastime. A blot on the reputation of the Giants would surely impact all other franchises. That is probably why questions as to just what really happened remain unanswered and why a coverup of the incident is plausible.

It is clear baseball dodged a bullet in the 1908 attempted bribery case. It is also clear that something was going on in New York during the waning days of the season. There is no question of the attempt to bribe the umpires. What remains unknown is who was really involved.

The bribery case provides context for suspicions that the late-season Giants-Doves series was not on the level. While a cloud may have hung over the Giants' sweep, there is no definite proof that Boston threw those games. However, evidence that someone tried to fix an earlier series with the Phillies provides room for doubt about the honesty of the Braves series. Word of the Phillies' attempted fix did not emerge until 1920, in the wake of the Black Sox scandal. The account comes from Philadelphia catcher Red Dooin: "All we had to do was name a price. Why, the gamblers opened up a satchel, must have had over $150,000 in it, told our pitchers to help themselves. At the first game at the Polo Grounds, a big man handed me $8,000, told me there was $40,000 more waiting for me. I called big Kitty Bransfield who threw him down the stairs."[19]

Why Dooin or Bransfield, who would later become a major league umpire, did not report the incident provides evidence that players and owners alike had an ambivalent attitude about the gambling and its role in the game. While the amounts of money involved seem exaggerated, Dooin said he did not come forward because the bribe was not taken. This attitude about gambling reigned supreme until the issue was forced in 1920 by the Black Sox.

AFTERWORD: THE YEAR OF THE PITCHER

Despite the potentially sour ending to the 1908 season, we conclude on a positive note. That year remains one of the few in baseball history when pitchers enjoyed almost total domination. In modern baseball, only 1968 comes close to the 1908 season. A major difference between the two years was the reaction of baseball's ruling class.

In 1909, the only major change in the game was the decision to add one more umpire to each league's roster, thus ensuring that a majority of games would be covered by two umpires. The rules change banning the spitball and other doctored pitches would not come until 1920. In 1969, the rules committee wasted no time and reacted swiftly to mound dominance and anemic offense by lowering the height of the pitcher's mound from fifteen to ten inches and shrinking the strike zone. To add insult to injury for the pitching fraternity, in 1969 five teams moved their fences closer to the plate in an attempt to help beleaguered hitters. These reactions helped reestablish the dominance of hitting in the modern game.

In 1908 the American League batting average was .239 (see appendixes I and J for 1908 statistics by league), a mark that would be matched in 1972, the year before the designated hitter rule was installed. In 1968 American League hitters managed a lame .230 mark. During the two previous seasons, junior circuit hitters averaged .240 and .236 respectively. The 1968 American League earned run average was 2.98, the first time it had been under 3.00 since 1918. In 1908 the American League ERA was 2.39, the lowest in American League history. Shutouts recorded in 1908 numbered 132, compared to 154 in 1968. A direct comparison of these figures is not fair because of expansion, but percentage of games gives perspective. In 1908, 21.6 percent of American League games were shutouts, compared to 19 percent sixty years later.

Over in the National League, the hitters also averaged .239 in 1908, likewise the lowest in league history. The .243 mark in 1968 was the lowest league average after 1908. The 1968 National League ERA was 2.99, the first time it had been under three runs since 1919. In 1908 the National League ERA was 2.35, the lowest in major league history.

National League hurlers posted a league record of 185 shutouts in 1968, compared to 163 in 1908. Percentages again show the strength of pitching, as just over one out of four, or 26.5 percent, of games were shutouts in 1908. In 1968 22.8 percent of National League games resulted in shutouts.

We have reviewed the terrific personal performances of 1908, with career-best years by Big Ed Walsh and Christy Mathewson, and 1968 also saw its share of stellar individual achievement. Denny McClain of the Tigers won thirty-one games, becoming the first thirty-game winner since Dizzy Dean in 1934. The Dodgers' Don Drysdale pitched six consecutive shutouts and fifty-eight and two-thirds straight shutout innings, breaking records held by Walter Johnson and Doc White, both of whom were star pitchers in 1908. Finally, Bob Gibson of the Cardinals threw thirteen shutouts and won fifteen consecutive games with an ERA of 1.12. The best ERA of 1908 was Addie Joss's 1.16.

In the June–July 1996 SABR Bulletin, researcher Neil Munro listed fifteen pitchers who, during the twentieth century, allowed fewer than eight base runners per nine innings.[20] Of the fifteen, four pitchers put up the number in 1908 and three in 1968! Of the pitchers on the list, only Greg Maddux (still an active player as of this writing), Dave McNally, and Luis Tiant are not in the Hall of Fame.

There is thus ample proof that the title Year of the Pitcher belongs to both 1908 and 1968, as is illustrated in appendix K. Combine that with the down-to-the-wire pennant races and team and individual achievements, and 1908 was truly a remarkable year — a season to remember for what happened both on and off the diamond.

A. Major League Attendance, 1901–1908

	National	American	Total
1901	1,920,031	1,682,584	3,602,615
1902	1,681,212	2,200,457	3,881,669
1903	2,300,362	2,345,888	4,646,250
1904	2,774,701	3,094,559	5,869,260
1905	2,734,310	3,070,752	5,805,062
1906	2,781,213	2,938,096	5,719,309
1907	2,737,793	3,398,764	6,136,557
1908	3,514,285	3,554,837	7,069,122

Note: Attendance was up 15 percent in 1908, compared to 1907, and 23.6 percent in 1908 compared to 1906.

B. Standings and Attendance Comparison, 1908

American League		National League	
1. Chicago (3)	694,728	New York (2t)	880,700
2. St. Louis (4)	566,793	Chicago (1)	619,807
3. Boston (5)	464,987	Philadelphia (4)	415,171
4. Philadelphia (6)	445,567	Pittsburgh (2t)	366,427
5. Cleveland (2)	414,732	Cincinnati (5)	365,111
6. Detroit (1)	398,058	St. Louis (8)	349,385
7. New York (8)	312,400	Brooklyn (7)	272,900
8. Washington (7)	257,972	Boston (6)	245,284

C. Baseball Dynasties

	Won	Lost	Pct.	No. of World Championships Won
1906–10 Cubs	530	235	.693	2
1942–46 Cardinals	509	263	.659	3
1936–40 Yankees	497	267	.651	4
1910–14 Athletics	488	270	.644	3
1949–53 Yankees	487	281	.634	5
1960–64 Yankees	505	296	.6305	2
1952–56 Dodgers	484	284	.6302	1
1991–96 Braves	482	300	.616	1
1921–25 Giants	461	304	.603	2
1955–59 Yankees	462	308	.600	2

D. American League Umpiring, 1908

UMPIRE SERVICE

	Games	1-Man	2-Man
Hurst	162	9	153
Connolly	158	92	66
Sheridan	156	27	129
O'Loughlin	153	82	71
Evans	151	63	88
Egan	146	28	118
Kerin	8	—	8
Warner	1	—	1

ONE-MAN BY CITY

	Det	Clev	Chi	StL	Bos	Phil	Wash	NY	Total
Connolly	7	8	11	7	13	12	20	14	92
O'Loughlin	11	18	4	6	11	10	10	12	82
Evans	14	8	0	6	10	6	15	3	62
Egan	0	7	0	2	0	3	14	2	28
Sheridan	6	0	2	1	7	2	6	3	27
Hurst	0	0	0	0	3	0	2	4	9
Total	38	41	17	22	44	33	67	38	300

TWO-MAN BY CITY

	Det	Clev	Chi	StL	Bos	Phil	Wash	NY	Total
Hurst/Evans	10	7	9	18	0	0	0	14	58
Sheridan/Egan	19	15	12	0	1	5	0	0	52
Egan/O'Loughlin	2	3	16	4	0	1	0	9	35
Hurst/O'Loughlin	7	0	6	7	8	0	0	0	28
Sheridan/Connolly	0	0	11	8	7	0	0	0	26
Hurst/Sheridan	0	0	0	6	5	13	0	0	24
Sheridan/Evans	1	5	0	0	0	6	0	10	22
Hurst/Connolly	3	0	0	2	0	4	7	6	22
Hurst/Egan	0	0	0	0	9	6	5	0	20
Egan/Connolly	0	3	2	0	0	7	0	0	12
O'Loughlin/Connolly	1	2	0	0	2	0	0	0	5
Egan/Evans	0	0	1	3	0	0	0	0	4
Kerin/Sheridan	0	0	0	4	0	0	0	0	4
Kerin/O'Loughlin	0	0	0	3	0	0	0	0	3
Evans/O'Loughlin	0	0	2	0	0	0	0	0	2
Warner/Hurst	0	0	0	0	0	0	0	1	1
Kerin/Connolly	0	0	1	0	0	0	0	0	1
Total	43	38	59	55	32	48	12	38	319

CONTENDERS — ONE-MAN

	Det/ Clev	Det/ Chi	Det/ StL	Clev/ Chi	Clev/ StL	Chi/ StL	Total
Evans	8	—	3	—	7	2	20
Sheridan	4	8	—	—	1	—	13
O'Loughlin	4	2	2	—	—	—	8
Connolly	—	1	3	—	—	—	4
Egan	—	—	2	—	—	—	2
Total	16	11	10	0	8	2	47

	Det/ Clev	Det/ Chi	Det/ StL	Clev/ Chi	Clev/ StL	Chi/ StL	Total
Egan/O'Loughlin	—	2	—	8	4	6	20
Egan/Sheridan	5	2	2	6	5	—	20
Hurst/O'Loughlin	—	5	5	—	—	4	14
Sheridan/Connolly	—	6	—	—	—	4	10
Hurst/Evans	1	—	—	—	3	3	7
Evans/Sheridan	—	—	—	4	1	—	5
Evans/Egan	—	—	—	1	1	2	4
Hurst/Sheridan	—	—	4	—	—	—	4
Connolly/Hurst	—	2	1	—	—	—	3
Connolly/O'Loughlin	—	—	—	2	—	—	2
O'Loughlin/Evans	—	—	—	2	—	—	2
Total	6	17	12	23	14	19	91
Percentage Two-Man	27%	61%	54.5%	100%	63.6%	90.5%	65.9%

Note: Umpiring data are from the author's research into the 1908 season.

E. National League Umpiring, 1908

UMPIRE SERVICE

	Games	1-Man	2-Man
Emslie	158	72	86
Klem	151	69	83
Rigler	148	69	79
O'Day	138	87	51
Johnstone	134	34	100
Rudderham	115	30	85
Owens	20	6	14
Lanigan	4	4	—

ONE-MAN BY CITY

	Chi	NY	Pgh	Phil	Cin	Bos	Brk	StL	Total
O'Day	19	5	13	3	13	13	11	10	87
Emslie	0	1	11	15	8	12	7	18	72
Klem	8	0	6	15	8	12	12	8	69
Rigler	5	4	10	3	18	14	5	10	69
Johnstone	2	4	1	8	3	6	5	5	34
Rudderham	4	4	0	0	6	8	2	6	30
Owens	0	0	0	0	1	0	5	0	6
Lanigan	0	0	0	0	0	0	4	0	4
Total	38	18	41	44	57	65	51	57	371

TWO-MAN BY CITY

	Chi	NY	Pgh	Phil	Cin	Bos	Brk	StL	Total
Johnstone/Klem	5	15	0	6	7	4	0	8	45
Rudderham/Emslie	5	3	5	0	3	5	10	2	33
Rudderham/Rigler	10	0	4	3	3	0	3	3	26
Johnstone/Rigler	0	10	0	4	0	2	5	0	21
Rudderham/Johnstone	0	0	4	0	0	0	7	5	16
Klem/O'Day	0	12	4	0	0	0	0	0	16
Johnstone/Emslie	4	2	4	5	0	0	0	0	15
Emslie/O'Day	8	4	1	0	0	0	0	0	13
Klem/Emslie	0	4	0	7	0	0	0	0	11
Rigler/O'Day	3	3	4	0	1	0	0	0	11
Emslie/Rigler	0	8	0	0	0	2	0	0	10
Owens/Rigler	0	0	0	3	7	0	0	0	10
Rudderham/Klem	2	0	4	0	0	0	0	3	9
Johnstone/O'Day	4	0	3	0	0	0	0	0	7
Klem/Rigler	0	1	0	0	1	0	0	4	6
Rudderham/O'Day	0	0	0	4	0	0	0	0	4
Owens/Emslie	0	0	0	0	0	0	3	0	3
Owens/Klem	0	0	0	0	0	0	1	0	1
Total	41	62	33	32	22	13	29	25	257

CONTENDERS — ONE MAN

	Chi/NY	Chi/Pgh	Pgh/NY	Total
O'Day	0	8	0	8
Emslie	0	2	0	2
Johnstone	0	0	1	1
Klem	0	0	1	1
Total	0	10	1	12

CONTENDERS — TWO-MAN

	Chi/NY	Chi/Pgh	Pgh/NY	Total
Klem/O'Day	4	0	12	16
O'Day/Emslie	11	0	0	11
O'Day/Rigler	3	1	4	8
Klem/Johnstone	1	5	0	6
Klem/Emslie	0	0	4	4
Johnstone/Emslie	0	4	0	4
O'Day/Johnstone	4	0	0	4
Klem/Rudderham	0	0	2	2
Rigler/Rudderham	0	1	0	1
Total	23	11	22	56
Percentage Two-Man	100%	50%	96%	82.4%

Note: Umpiring data are from the author's research into the 1908 season.

F. American League Ejections, 1908 (51)

Street, Wash 4
Elberfeld, NY Mgr 4
Donovan, Det 3
Jennings, Det Mgr 3
Griffith, NY Mgr 3
Stahl, NY-Bos 3
Bradley, Clev 2
Coughlin, Det 2
Davis, Phil 2
D. Jones, Det 2
F. Jones, Chi Mgr 2
Kleinow, NY 2
McAleer, StL Mgr 1
Altizer, Clev 1
Burchell, Bos 1

Cantillon, Wash Mgr 1
Clymer, Wash 1
Cobb, Det 1
Delahanty, Wash 1
Dougherty, Chi 1
Hughes, Wash 1
Killian, Det 1
McGuire, Bos Mgr 2
McGuire, Wash 1
Moriarty, NY 1
Mullin, Det 1
Powers, Phil 1
Unglaub, Bos 1
Warner, Wash 1
Winter, Bos 1

EJECTIONS BY UMPIRES

O'Loughlin 16
Evans 6
Connolly 5
Sheridan 4
Egan 3
Hurst 3

Evans / Hurst 8
Sheridan / Egan 8
Hurst / Connolly 2
Egan / Connolly 1
O'Loughlin / Egan 1

EJECTIONS BY TEAM

Detroit Tigers 13
New York Highlanders 12
Washington Senators 10
Boston Red Sox 6

Chicago White Sox 3
Cleveland Naps 3
Philadelphia Athletics 3
St. Louis Browns 1

Note: Ejection data are from SABR ejection files and author's research.

G. National League Ejections, 1908 (48)

McGraw, NY. 7
Donlin, NY 6
Kelley, Bos Mgr 5
Dooin, Phil 4
Evers, Chi 3
Ganzel, Cin Mgr 3
Doyle, NY 3
Chance, Chi Mgr 2
Gleason, Phil Coach 2
McGann, Bos 2
Magee, Phil. 2
Dahlen, Bos 2
Abbaticchio, Pgh 1
Bergen, Brk. 1
Bowerman, Bos 1
Bransfield, Phil. 1
Bresnahan, NY 1

Browne, Bos 1
Charles, StL 1
Clarke, Pgh Mgr 1
Doolan, Phil 1
Gilbert, StL 1
Grant, Phil 1
Hofman, Chi. 1
Huggins, Cin. 1
Karger, StL 1
Knabe, Phil 1
Lewis, Brk 1
Murray, Phil 1
Raymond, StL. 1
Snodgrass, NY. 1
Swacina, Pgh. 1
Taylor, NY 1
Tenney, NY 1

EJECTIONS BY UMPIRE

O'Day 11
Johnstone 10
Rigler. 10
Rudderham 10
Emslie 7
Klem 7

Rudderham/Emslie 2
Rigler/Rudderham 2
Klem/Johnstone 2
O'Day/Rigler 2
Emslie/Klem 1
Emslie/Rigler. 1
Rigler/Klem. 1

EJECTIONS BY TEAM

New York Giants. 20
Philadelphia Phillies 13
Boston Doves 11
Chicago Cubs 6

Cincinnati Reds 4
St. Louis Cardinals 4
Pittsburgh Pirates. 3
Brooklyn Superbas. 2

Note: Ejection data are from SABR ejection files and author's research.

H. Comparing Kling and Bresnahan, 1902–10

KLING AND BRESNAHAN AS DEFENSIVE CATCHERS

		PO	Assists	Errors	DP	Fielding Pct.
1902	Bresnahan	(played as utility player, 38 games catching)				
	Kling	471	158	17	16	.974
1903	Bresnahan	(played mainly in outfield, 11 games catching)				
	Kling	565	189	24	13	.969
1904	Bresnahan	(played mainly in outfield, 0 games catching)				
	Kling	499	135	17	6	.974
1905	Bresnahan	492	114	19	15	.970
	Kling	538	136	24	12	.966
1906	Bresnahan	407	125	14	6	.974
	Kling	502	126	12	7	.982
1907	Bresnahan	483	94	8	11	.986
	Kling	499	109	8	11	.987
1908	Bresnahan	657	140	12	12	.985
	Kling	596	149	16	11	.979
1909	Bresnahan	211	121	22	11	.960
	Kling	(did not play)				
1910	Bresnahan	295	100	16	11	.961
	Kling	407	118	11	10	.979

		BA	RBI	HR
1902	Bresnahan	.292	22	1
	Kling	.286	57	0
1903	Bresnahan	.350	55	4
	Kling	.297	68	3
1904	Bresnahan	.284	33	5
	Kling	.243	46	2
1905	Bresnahan	.302	46	0
	Kling	.218	52	1
1906	Bresnahan	.281	43	0
	Kling	.312	46	2
1907	Bresnahan	.253	38	4
	Kling	.284	43	1
1908	Bresnahan	.283	54	1
	Kling	.276	59	4
1909	Bresnahan	.244	23	0
	Kling	(did not play)		
1910	Bresnahan	.278	27	0
	Kling	.269	32	2

BRESNAHAN AND KLING CAREER COMPARISON

	BA	Hits	RBI	HR	Slugging
Bresnahan	.280	1253	530	26	.379
Kling	.271	1151	513	61	.357

I. American League Team Record, 1908

	W	L	GB	Pct.	BA	Runs	ERA	Fielding
Detroit	90	63	—	.588	.264	645	2.40	.953
Cleveland	90	64	.5	.584	.239	570	2.02	.962
Chicago	88	64	1.5	.579	.224	535	2.22	.966
St. Louis	83	69	6.5	.547	.245	543	2.15	.964
Boston	75	79	15.5	.487	.246	563	2.27	.955
Philadelphia	68	85	22	.444	.225	487	2.57	.957
Washington	67	85	22.5	.441	.235	479	2.34	.947
New York	51	103	39.5	.331	.236	458	3.16	.947
League Average					.239	535	2.39	.958

	Det	Clev	Chi	StL	Bos	Phi	Wash	NY	Wins
Detroit	—	9	13	12	11	14	16	15	90
Cleveland	13	—	14	11	12	16	8	16	90
Chicago	9	8	—	11	16	13	15	16	88
St. Louis	10	11	10	—	7	13	15	17	83
Boston	11	10	6	15	—	9	11	12	75
Philadelphia	8	6	9	8	12	—	11	14	68
Washington	5	14	6	7	11	11	—	13	67
New York	7	6	6	5	10	8	9	—	51
Losses	63	64	64	69	79	84	85	103	—

AMERICAN LEAGUE BATTING LEADERS

Average
Cobb, Det	.324
Crawford, Det	.311
Gessler, Bos	.308
Hemphill, NY	.297
McIntyre, Det	.295

Runs Batted In
Cobb, Det	101
Crawford, Det	80
Ferris, StL	74
Lajoie, Clev	74
Rossman, Det	70

Stolen Bases
Dougherty, Chi	47
Hemphill, NY	42
Schaefer, Det	40
Cobb, Det	39
J. Clarke, Clev	37

Home Runs
Crawford, Det	7
Hinchman, Clev	6
Davis, Phil	5
Niles, Bos-NY	5
Stone, StL	5

Hits
Cobb, Det	188
Crawford, Det	184
Lajoie, Clev	168
McIntyre, Det	168

Runs
McIntyre, Det	105
Crawford, Det	102
Schaefer, Det	96

Winning Percentage

Donovan, Det	.731
Walsh, Chi	.727
Joss, Clev	.667
Summers, Det	.667
Young, Bos	.656

Earned Run Average

Joss, Clev	1.16
Young, Bos	1.26
Walsh, Chi	1.42
Johnson, Wash	1.64
Summers, Det	1.64

Wins

Walsh, Chi	40
Joss, Clev	24
Summers, Det	24
Young, Bos	21
Waddell, StL	19

Shutouts

Walsh, Chi	12
Joss, Clev	9
Powell, StL	6
Vickers, Phil	6
Johnson, Wash	6

Strikeouts

Walsh, Chi	269
Waddell, StL	232
Hughes, Wash	165
Dygert, Phil	164
Johnson, Wash	160

Innings Pitched

Walsh, Chi	464
Joss, Clev	325
Howell, StL	324

J. National League Team Record, 1908

	W	L	GB	Pct.	BA	Runs	ERA	Fielding
Chicago	99	55	—	.643	.249	625	2.14	.969
New York	98	56	1	.636	.267	652	2.14	.962
Pittsburgh	98	56	1	.636	.247	585	2.12	.964
Philadelphia	83	71	16	.539	.244	503	2.10	.963
Cincinnati	73	81	26	.474	.227	488	2.37	.959
Boston	63	91	36	.409	.239	537	2.79	.962
Brooklyn	53	101	46	.344	.213	375	2.47	.961
St. Louis	49	105	50	.318	.223	372	2.64	.946
League Average					.239	517	2.35	.961

	Chi	NY	Pgh	Phil	Cin	Bos	Brk	StL	Wins
Chicago	—	11	10	9	16	16	18	19	99
New York	11	—	11	16	14	16	16	14	98
Pittsburgh	12	11	—	13	14	15	13	20	98
Philadelphia	13	6	9	—	12	12	17	14	83
Cincinnati	6	8	8	10	—	14	16	11	73
Boston	6	6	7	10	8	—	12	14	63
Brooklyn	4	6	9	5	6	10	—	13	101
St. Louis	3	8	2	8	11	8	9	—	105
Losses	55	56	56	71	81	91	101	105	—

NATIONAL LEAGUE BATTING LEADERS

Average

Wagner, Pgh	.354
Donlin, NY	.334
Doyle, NY	.308
Bransfield, Phil	.304
Evers, Chi	.300

Home Runs

Jordan, Brk	12
Wagner, Pgh	10
Murray, StL	7
Tinker, Chi	6
Donlin, NY	6

Runs Batted In

Wagner, Pgh	109
Donlin, NY	106
Seymour, NY	92
Bransfield, Phil	71
Tinker, Chi	68

Hits

Wagner, Pgh	201
Donlin, NY	198
Lobert, Cin	167
Murray, StL	167

Stolen Bases

Wagner, Pgh	53
Murray, StL	48
Lobert, Cin	47
Magee, Phil	40
Evers, Chi	36

Runs

Tenney, NY	101
Wagner, Pgh	100
Leach, Pgh	93
Clarke, Pgh	83
Evers, Chi	83

Winning Percentage

Reulbach, Chi	.774
Mathewson, NY	.771
Brown, Chi	.763
Maddox, Pgh	.742
Willis, Pgh	.686

Wins

Mathewson, NY	37
Brown, Chi	29
Reulbach, Chi	24
Maddox, Pgh	23
McQuillan, Phil	23
Willis, Pgh	23
Wiltse, NY	23

Strikeouts

Mathewson, NY	259
Rucker, Bkn	199
Overall, Chi	167
Raymond, StL	145
Reulbach, Chi	133

Earned Run Average

Mathewson, NY	1.43
Brown, Chi	1.47
McQuillan, Phil	1.53
Camnitz, Pgh	1.56
Coakley, Cin-Chi	1.78

Shutouts

Mathewson, NY	12
Brown, Chi	9
Camnitz, Pgh	7
McQuillan, Phil	7
Reulbach, Chi	7
Wiltse, NY	7

Innings Pitched

Mathewson, NY	391
McQuillan, Phil	360
Rucker, Brk	333
Wilhelm, Brk	332
Wiltse, NY	330
Raymond, StL	324
Willis, Pgh	305

K. Pitchers Allowing Fewer than Eight Runners per Nine Innings

Pitcher	Year	Team	Runners/9 In
Walter Johnson	1913	Wash (AL)	7.257
Addie Joss	1908	Clev (AL)	7.311
Christy Mathewson	1909	NY (NL)	7.454
Greg Maddux	1995	Atl (NL)	7.482
Ed Walsh	1910	Chi (AL)	7.476
Christy Mathewson	1908	NY (NL)	7.604
Mordecai Brown	1908	Chi (NL)	7.723
Pete Alexander	1913	Phil (NL)	7.821
Sandy Koufax	1965	LA (NL)	7.831
Juan Marichal	1966	SF (NL)	7.878
Bob Gibson	1968	StL (NL)	7.889
Dave McNally	1968	Balt (AL)	7.912
Ed Walsh	1908	Chi (AL)	7.914
Sandy Koufax	1963	LA (NL)	7.958
Luis Tiant	1968	Clev (AL)	7.979

Source: Neil Munro, "20th Century Pitchers with Fewer than Eight Baserunners per Nine Innings Pitched," SABR Bulletin 26, no.6 (June–July 1996), 11.

Notes

Introduction

1. *Spalding's Official Base Ball Guide,* 1909 (New York: American Sports, 1909), 81.
2. *Reach Official American League Guide,* 1909 (Philadelphia: A. J. Reach, 1909), 7.
3. "Purchase Grounds," *Sporting Life,* 4 July 1908, 11.
4. "National League News," *Sporting Life,* 8 August 1908, 16.
5. *Spalding's Guide,* 1909, 344–45.
6. Marc Okkonen, *Baseball Memories 1900–1909* (New York: Sterling, 1992), 69.
7. "Freak or Fixture," *Sporting Life,* 13 June 1908, 4.
8. G. Edward White, *Creating the National Pastime: Baseball Transforms Itself 1903–1953* (Princeton NJ: Princeton University Press, 1996), 161–63.
9. Alex Chadwick, *Illustrated History of Baseball* (Edison NJ: Chartwell Books, 1995), 32–33. Song words in Geoffrey C. Ward and Ken Burns, *Baseball: An Illustrated History* (New York: Alfred A. Knopf, 1994), 96–97. Mike Shatzkin, ed., *The Ballplayers: Baseball's Ultimate Biographical Reference* (New York: William Morrow, 1990), 1067.
10. Chadwick, *Illustrated History of Baseball,* 33.

1. Baseball Turned Upside Down

1. Charles C. Alexander, *John McGraw* (New York: Viking, 1988; reprint, Lincoln: University of Nebraska Press, 1995), 121. Page citation from reprint edition.
2. John J. Evers and Hugh Fullerton, *Touching Second: The Science of Baseball* (Chicago: Reilly and Britton, 1910), 160.
3. Evers and Fullerton, *Touching Second,* 16–17.
4. Okkonen, *Baseball Memories,* 224.
5. David Bauer, ed., *Baseball's 20 Greatest Teams of All Time* (New York: Time Inc. Magazine Company, 1991), 42.

2. The Game in 1908

1. Stephen A. Reiss, *Touching Base: Professional Baseball and American Culture in the Progressive Era* (Westport CT: Greenwood Press, 1980), 33.

2. "New Scale of Prices Is Set for Games at West Side Park," *Chicago Tribune*, 14 March 1908, 10.

3. Reiss, *Touching Base*, 62.

4. "The American's War," *Sporting Life*, 15 August 1908, 1.

5. "Ladies Day for West Side," *Chicago Tribune*, 28 March 1908, 10.

6. G. H. Fleming, *The Unforgettable Season* (New York: Holt, Rinehart and Winston, 1981), 70.

7. Grantland Rice, "A Timely Warning," *Sporting Life*, 24 April 1909, 4.

8. HEK (byline), "Some Offside Plays," *Chicago Tribune*, 5 January 1908.

9. "Rooters Clubs Hit by Murphy," *Chicago Tribune*, 2 March 1908, 12.

10. "Firm Stand by Johnson," *Chicago Tribune*, 12 March 1908, 8; "Johnson's Jots," *Sporting Life*, 21 March 1908, 8.

11. Francis C. Richter, "Current Comment," *Sporting Life*, 4 April 1908, 4.

12. "Cowardly Attack," *Sporting Life*, 10 October 1908, 11.

13. I. E. Sanborn, "Hofman Signs Contract," *Chicago Tribune*, 1 March 1908, sec. 3, 2.

14. Francis C. Richter, "The Proper Solution," *Sporting Life*, 15 February 1908, 4.

15. Lawrence S. Ritter, *Glory of Their Times* (New York: William Morrow, 1984), 99.

16. Fleming, *Unforgettable Season*, 36.

17. Benjamin G. Rader, *Baseball: A History of America's Game* (Urbana: University of Illinois Press, 1992), 89.

18. Okkonen, *Baseball Memories*, 29–78.

19. Francis C. Richter, "A Current Comment," *Sporting Life*, 25 July 1908, 4.

20. Paul Dickson, *Baseball's Greatest Quotations* (New York: Harper Collins, 1991), 44.

21. "The Referee," *Chicago Tribune*, 12 April 1908, sec. 3, 1.

22. "That New Rule," *Sporting Life*, 18 April 1908, 11.

23. Charles C. Alexander, *Our Game* (New York: Henry Holt, 1991), 87.

24. Evers and Fullerton, *Touching Second*, 75.

25. *World's Championship 1905: The Great World Series Program Collection* (Santa Clara CA: Robert D. Opie, 1983), 8.

26. William J. Slocum and Bill Klem, "I Never Missed One in My Heart," *Collier's*, 3 March 1951, 60.

27. Slocum and Klem, "Never Missed," 30.

28. Slocum and Klem, "Jousting with McGraw," *Collier's*, 7 April 1951, 30.

29. Quoted in Evers and Fullerton, *Touching Second*, 188.

30. I. E. Sanborn, "Fans Would Improve Game," *Chicago Tribune*, 5 January 1908, sec. 3, 3.

31. Fleming, *Unforgettable Season*, 74–75.

32. James H. Kahn, *The Umpire Story* (New York: Putnam, 1953), 233.

33. Interview with John Kovach, former curator of the New York Central Museum in Elkhart.

34. Fleming, *Unforgettable Season*, 29–30.

35. "Hedges Hot," *Sporting Life*, 15 August 1908, 11.

36. Shatzkin, ed., *The Ballplayers*, 286.

37. "Ready to Play," *Sporting Life*, 7 March 1908, 4.

38. Charles H. Zuber, "Tie Impossible," *Sporting Life*, 12 October 1907, 7.

39. "Concerning Postponement," *Sporting Life*, August 15, 1908, 9.

40. "Postponed Games," *Sporting Life*, 18 July 1908, 4.

3. The Teams of 1908

1. Evers and Fullerton, *Touching Second*, 45.

2. Ty Cobb with Al Stump, *My Life in Baseball* (New York: Doubleday, 1961; reprint, Lincoln: University of Nebraska Press, 1993), 192 (reprint ed.).

3. Lyle Spatz, "SABR Picks 1900–1948 Rookies of the Year," *Baseball Research Journal* no. 15 (1986): 2–4.

4. Lee Allen, *Cooperstown Corner: Columns from the Sporting News* (Cleveland: SABR, undated), 25–27.

5. Shatzkin, ed., *The Ballplayers*, 233.

6. Scott Longert, *Addie Joss: King of the Pitchers* (Cleveland: SABR, 1998), 18.

7. Scott Longert, "Bill Bradley," *National Pastime* no. 16 (1996): 128.

8. *USA Today*, 9 November 1996, Sports, 1.

9. Shatzkin, ed., *The Ballplayers*, 540.

10. Quoted in Ritter, *Glory*, 56.

11. Robert L. Tiemann and Mark Rucker, eds., *Nineteenth Century Stars* (Kansas City MO: SABR, 1989), 36.

12. Shatzkin, ed., *The Ballplayers*, 1058.

13. Shatzkin, ed., *The Ballplayers*, 974.

14. Harvey Frommer, *Shoeless Joe and Ragtime Baseball* (Dallas: Taylor Publishing, 1992), 26.

15. Henry W. Thomas, *Walter Johnson: Baseball's Big Train*, (Washington DC: Phenom Press, 1995; reprint, Lincoln: University of Nebraska Press, 1998), 10 (reprint ed.).

16. "One Sore Spot," *Sporting Life*, 17 October 1908, 4.

17. J. Ed Grillo, "Cantillon's Conduct," *Sporting Life*, 7 November 1908, 2.

18. Thomas, *Walter Johnson*, 67.

19. *Reach Guide*, 1909, 35.

20. Paul J. Zingg and Mark D. Madieros, *Runs, Hits and an Era: The Pacific Coast League, 1903–1958* (Urbana: University of Illinois Press, 1994), 48.

21. "Eastern catcher," in Evers and Fullerton, *Touching Second*, 97.

22. Arthur R. Ahrens, "Tinker vs. Matty: A Study in Rivalry," *Baseball Research Journal* 1, no. 3 (1998): 129.

23. John P. Carmichael, ed., *My Greatest Day in Baseball* (New York: A. S. Barnes, 1945; reprint, Lincoln: University of Nebraska Press, 1996), 135 (reprint ed.).

24. William J. Slocum and Bill Klem, "Diamond Rhubarbs," *Collier's*, 14 April 1951, 30.

25. Evers and Fullerton, *Touching Second*, 64.

26. Noel Hynd, *The Giants of the Polo Grounds* (Dallas: Taylor Publishing, 1995), 194.

27. *Reach Guide*, 1909, 89.

28. Quoted in Shatzkin, ed., *The Ballplayers*, 110.

29. David S. Neff and Richard M. Cohen, eds., *The Sports Encyclopedia: Baseball*, 16th edition (New York: St. Martin's Griffon, 1996), 582.

30. Spatz, "SABR Picks Rookies," 2–4.

31. Ritter, *Glory*, 109

32. Ritter, *Glory*, 118.

33. J. Kent Steele, "A Tragic Link," *National Pastime* no. 17 (1997): 118.

34. Shatzkin, ed., *The Ballplayers*, 943.

4. The Men in Blue

1. *Spalding's Guide*, 1909, 351.

2. Okkonen, *Baseball Memories*, 18.

3. Slocum and Klem, "Jousting with McGraw," 30.

4. "O'Day Differs," *Sporting Life*, 24 October 1908, 12.

5. "Current Comment," *Sporting Life*, 6 June 1908, 4.

6. "New Rule Point," *Sporting Life*, 9 May 1908, 11.

7. "President Johnson Overrules O'Loughlin," *Sporting Life*, 20 June 1908, 1.

8. "Harry Pulliam," *Sporting Life*, 4 April 1908, 6.

9. Billy Evans, *Umpiring from the Inside* (n.p., 1947), 11.

10. Shatzkin, ed., *The Ballplayers*, 316.

11. Evans, *Umpiring*, 13.

12. Shatzkin, ed., *The Ballplayers*, 825.

13. Larry Gerlach, "Umpires," in *Total Baseball*, ed. John Thorn and Pete Palmer (New York: Warner Books, 1989), 466.

14. Evans, *Umpiring*, 77.

15. Joe Dittmar, "Tim Hurst, Umpire," *National Pastime* no. 17 (1997): 99.

16. Shatzkin, ed., *The Ballplayers*, 506–7.

17. Evans, *Umpiring*, 22.

18. William Patten and J. Walker McSpadden, *The Book of Baseball: The National Game from the Earliest Days to the Present Season* (New York: P. F. Collins & Son, 1911), 115.

19. *Sporting Life*, 10 October 1908, 11.

20. Shatzkin, ed., *The Ballplayers*, 576.

21. William J. Slocum and Bill Klem, "My Last Big League Game," *Collier's*, 21 April 1951, 74.

22. Henry O'Day Biographical File, National Baseball Hall of Fame Library.

23. O'Day Biographical File.

24. O'Day Biographical File.

25. Shatzkin, ed., *The Ballplayers*, 311.

26. Shatzkin, ed., *The Ballplayers*, 538.

27. Ronald A. Mayer, *Perfect!* (Jefferson NC: McFarland, 1991), 74.

5. April

1. "Bad Language," *Sporting Life*, 25 April 1908, 9.

2. "National League News," *Sporting Life*, 2 May 1908, 9.

3. "American League News," *Sporting Life*, 2 May 1908, 11.

4. Evers and Fullerton, *Touching Second*, 211–12.

5. "Cubs Nosed Out 3–2 by Cardinals," *Chicago Tribune*, 19 April 1908, sec. 3, 1.

6. "National League News," *Sporting Life*, 2 May 1908, 9.

7. Dennis DeValeria and Jeanne Burke DeValeria, *Honus Wagner: A Biography* (New York: Henry Holt, 1995), 178.

8. "Robbed of Game by Crowd," *Chicago Tribune*, 23 April 1908, 8.

9. Francis C. Richter, "Current Comment," *Sporting Life*, 25 April 1908, 4.

10. *Sports Encyclopedia North America*, vol. 5, ed. John D. Windhausen, 1993, s.v. Baseball Writers Association of America, 89–90.

11. "Johnson's Joy," *Sporting Life*, 24 October 1908, 2.

12. "Writers Association," *Sporting Life*, 5 August 1908, 2.

13. *Sports Encyclopedia*, 90.

14. Harold Seymour, *Baseball: The Early Years* (New York: Oxford University tPress, 1960), 351.

6. May

1. Grantland Rice, "Get in the Game," *Sporting Life*, 2 May 1908, 4.

2. "An Innovation," *Sporting Life*, 2 May 1908, 2.

3. "Jennings Optimistic," *Sporting Life*, 2 May 1908, 2.

4. Francis C. Richter, "Quaker Quips," *Sporting Life*, 30 May 1908, 3.

5. "American League Notes," *Sporting Life*, 23 May 1908, 11.

6. " 'Ware the Weed,' " *Sporting Life*, 16 May 1908, 4.

7. "National League News," *Sporting Life*, 16 May 1908, 9.

8. "McGraw Predicts Downfall of the Cubs," *Sporting Life*, 6 June 1908, 1.

9. "McGraw Predicts," 1.

10. "Ebbet's Eyes," *Sporting Life*, 30 May 1908, 6.

11. "Symposium upon the 'Spit Ball,' "*Spalding's Guide*, 1909, 33–51.

12. "Symposium," 33.

13. "Symposium," 35.

14. Fleming, *Unforgettable Season*, 154.

15. "Fading Away," *Sporting Life*, 19 September 1908, 2.

16. "A Pitcher's View," *Sporting Life*, 5 September 1908, 11.

17. Henry O'Day, "A Big League Umpire's View," *Baseball Magazine*, June 1908, 32.

18. Evers and Fullerton, *Touching Second*, 113.

19. "Mack's Dictum," *Sporting Life*, 18 July 1908, 11.

7. June

1. "McAleer's Men," *Sporting Life*, 18 July 1908, 11.

2. "Smith Huffed," *Sporting Life*, 27 June 1908, 1.

3. Charles C. Alexander, *Ty Cobb* (New York: Oxford University Press, 1984), 68.

4. "American League Notes," *Sporting Life*, 20 June 1908, 11; Alexander, *Ty Cobb*, 68.

5. "Press Pointers," *Sporting Life*, 4 July 1908, 4.

6. "Press Pointers," 4.

7. "Gambling and Baseball," *Sporting Life*, 11 July 1908, 4.

8. "Wagner's Record," *Sporting Life*, 4 July 1908, 5.

9. "Chaotic 'Cubs,' " *Sporting Life*, 1 August 1908, 7.

8. July

1. "American League Notes," *Sporting Life*, 25 July 1908, 7.

2. "American League Notes," *Sporting Life*, 25 July 1908, 7.

3. "2 Umpires," *Sporting Life*, 18 July 1908, 1.

4. "Merkle Blood Poisoning," *Sporting Life*, 18 July 1908, 1.

5. "Protest Wins," *Sporting Life*, 18 July 1908, 6.

6. Fleming, *Unforgettable Season*, 143.

7. W. A. Phelon, "Chicago Gleanings," *Sporting Life*, 1 August 1908, 8.

8. Fleming, *Unforgettable Season*, 114.

9. "National League News," *Sporting Life*, 18 July 1908, 9.

10. Bill James, *Whatever Happened to the Hall of Fame?* (New York: Fireside, 1995), 178.

11. Bill James, *The Bill James Historical Baseball Abstract* (New York: Villard Books, 1988), 354.

9. August

1. "Manager McGraw Pays His Respects to Detroit," *Sporting Life*, 1 August 1908, 1.

2. "Giants-Tigers Will Be Contestants," *Sporting Life*, 22 August 1908, 1.

3. "American League Notes," *Sporting Life*, 29 August 1908, 11.

4. "American League Notes," *Sporting Life*, 15 August 1908, 10.

5. "Washington Players," *Sporting Life*, 15 August 1908, 19.

6. "Young Honored," *Sporting Life*, 22 August 1908, 7.

7. "A Possible Upheaval," *Sporting Life*, 29 August 1908, 1.

8. White, *Creating the National Pastime*, 161–62.

9. "National League News," *Sporting Life*, 29 August 1908, 9.

10. "National League News," *Sporting Life*, 15 August 1908, 9.

11. *Spalding's Guide*, 1908 (New York: American Sports, 1908), 321.

12. *1999 Official Baseball Rules* (Wichita KS: National Baseball Congress, 1999), 16.

13. DeValeria and DeValeria, *Honus Wagner*, 188.

14. James, *Abstract*, 188.

15. "A Vain Protest," *Sporting Life*, 12 September 1908, 4.

16. Lowell Reidenbaugh, *Baseball's 25 Greatest Pennant Races* (St. Louis: Sporting News, 1986), 22.

17. David Nemec, *The Rules of Baseball* (New York: Lyons and Burford, 1994), 133.

18. Fleming, *Unforgettable Season*, 209.

19. Reidenbaugh, *Pennant Races*, 22.

20. *1999 Official Baseball Rules*, 43.

10. September

1. "Cobb in Disfavor," *Sporting Life*, 5 September 1908, 1.

2. "Chase Chase Chase," *Sporting Life*, 12 September 1908, 7.

3. Thomas, *Walter Johnson*, 56–59.

4. "American League News," *Sporting Life*, 19 September 1908, 11.

5. "American League News," *Sporting Life*, 12 September 1908, 11.

6. Charles H. Zuber, "Races Are Not Fixed!" *Sporting Life*, 19 September 1908, 1.

7. "Cowardly Attack," *Sporting Life*, 12 September 1908, 11.

8. "A Regrettable Incident," *Sporting Life*, 3 October 1908, 4.

9. Ronald A. Mayer, *Christy Mathewson: A Game by Game Profile of a Legendary Pitcher* (Jefferson NC: McFarland, 1993), 166.

10. Charles Dryden, "Pfeister's Case," *Sporting Life*, 10 October 1908, 9.

11. Charles A. Alexander, *Rogers Hornsby: A Biography* (New York: Henry Holt, 1995), 113.

12. Evers and Fullerton, *Touching Second*, 116.

13. Lowell Reidenbaugh, *Baseball's 50 Greatest Games* (St. Louis: Sporting News, 1986), 48.

14. Nemec, *Rules of Baseball*, 132–33.

15. Donald Dewey and Nicholas Acocella, *The Biographical History of Baseball* (New York: Carroll and Graf, 1995), 366–67.

16. Slocum and Klem, "Never Missed," 59–60.

17. Slocum and Klem, "Never Missed," 59.

18. Slocum and Klem, "Jousting with McGraw," 52.

19. Slocum and Klem, "Jousting with McGraw," 52.

20. Slocum and Klem, "Jousting with McGraw," 52.

21. Slocum and Klem, "Jousting with McGraw," 53.

22. John McGraw, *My Thirty Years in Baseball* (New York: Boni and Liveright, 1923; reprint, Lincoln: University of Nebraska Press, 1995), 182 (reprint ed.).

23. Harold Seymour, *Baseball: The Golden Age* (New York: Oxford University Press, 1971), 150.

24. Fleming, *Unforgettable Season*, 223.

25. Christy Mathewson, *Pitching in a Pinch* (New York: Putnam, 1912; reprint, Lincoln: University of Nebraska Press, 1994), 175 (reprint ed.).

26. A. R. Cratty, "In Pittsburgh," *Sporting Life*, 17 October 1908, 10.

11. October

1. Longert, *Joss*, 101.

2. Mayer, *Perfect!*, 56.

3. Carmichael, ed., *Greatest Day*, 79.

4. Franklin Lewis, *The Cleveland Indians* (New York: Putnam, 1949), 60.

5. J. M. Murphy, "Napoleon Lajoie Modern Baseball's First Superstar," *National Pastime*, Spring 1988, 30.

6. Longert, *Joss*, 103.

7. Richard E. Derby Jr., "The Race," unpublished. Copy in author's possession.

8. Data derived from author's research of umpiring during the 1908 season.

9. Fleming, *Unforgettable Season*, 276.

10. Fleming, *Unforgettable Season*, 284.

11. "Fans at Polo Grounds," *New York Times*, 5 October 1908, 8.

12. Charles Dryden, "Pirates Fighting — See Glories Go," *Chicago Tribune*, 5 October 1908, 2.

13. DeValeria and DeValeria, *Honus Wagner*, 195.

14. Shatzkin, *The Ballplayers*, 3.

15. Dryden, "Pirates Fighting," 2.

16. Dryden, "Pirates Fighting," 2.

17. Alexander, *McGraw*, 135.

18. Carmichael, ed., *Greatest Day*, 175.

19. Carmichael, ed., *Greatest Day*, 174.

20. Evers and Fullerton, *Touching Second*, 192–93.

21. Carmichael, ed., *Greatest Day*, 178.

22. Carmichael, ed., *Greatest Day*, 178–79.

23. W. Ross Tenney, "The Cubs' Pennant Ride," *Sporting Life*, 24 October 1908, 9.

12. Scandals of 1908

1. Reiss, *Touching Base*, 35.

2. Reiss, *Touching Base*, 55–56.

3. "The Bribery Charge," *Sporting Life*, 19 December 1908, 4.

4. Slocum and Klem, "Jousting with McGraw," 52.

5. Slocum and Klem, "Jousting with McGraw," 52.

6. Slocum and Klem, "Jousting with McGraw," 52.

7. Slocum and Klem, "Jousting with McGraw," 52.

8. Harvey T. Woodruff, "Bar Dr. Creamer from All Ball Parks," *Chicago Tribune*, 24 April 1909, 8.

9. Woodruff, "Bar Dr. Creamer," 8.

10. Obituary, *New York Times*, 30 July 1918.

11. "The Bribery Scandal," *Sporting Life*, 9 January 1909, 6.

12. "The Bribery Case Likely to be Smothered," *Sporting Life*, 13 February 1909.

13. "Court Decrees," *Sporting Life*, 24 April 1909, 7.

14. "The Bribery Case," 4.

15. Woodruff, "Bar Dr. Creamer," 8.

16. Woodruff, "Bar Dr. Creamer," 8.

17. Ray Robinson, *Matty: An American Hero* (New York: Oxford University Press, 1993), 105–6.

18. Harvey T. Woodruff, "East Hears of Dr. Creamer," *Chicago Tribune*, 25 April 1909, pt. 3, 1–2.

19. Eliot Asinof, *Eight Men Out: The Black Sox and the 1919 World Series* (New York: Holt, Rinehart and Winston, 1963), 234.

20. Neil Munro, "20th Century Pitchers with Fewer than Eight Baserunners per Nine Innings Pitched," SABR Bulletin 26, no.6 (June–July 1996), 11.

Bibliographic Essay

Historic research leaves the author dependent upon the works of others to a large extent. Assessing sources and confirming the information they conveyed was a constant process in preparing this book. Here is an evaluation of some of the sources consulted for *More than Merkle*.

Any study of 1908 should include detailed reading of G. H. Fleming's *Unforgettable Season* (New York: Holt, Rinehart and Winston, 1981). It inspired me to write this book. Fleming's work remains an important contribution to the body of baseball history, and it is an excellent study of sports journalism of its day.

William J. Slocum's 1951 interviews with Bill Klem in *Collier's Magazine* are also invaluable. Klem's career spanned several decades, and this series of interviews provides much insight into umpires and umpiring.

Two books also provide detail on the Dead Ball Era. Johnny Evers's *Touching Second* (with Hugh Fullerton; Chicago: Reilly and Britton Company, 1910) is as good a baseball book as any written in the twentieth century. The eyewitness insights are illuminating but require scrutiny. The title did not refer to Fred Merkle, though some have believed it did and have therefore dismissed the book. However, Evers discusses this incident of 1908 only briefly. His analysis of the Dead Ball game deserves attention. Evers was an excellent player with an outstanding mind for the game. The other work is Billy Evans's *Umpiring from the Inside* (n.p., 1947). It is as good an umpire's manual as any I have seen. A pioneer umpire, Evans pays homage to his colleagues and provides a valuable source for major league umpiring.

Memoirs by figures of the time were helpful, but as is the case with all memoirs, they must be used with caution. Historians know that memoirs are useful tools, but often they reveal as much in what they don't say as in what they do include. The ghostwritten memoirs of John McGraw (*My Thirty Years in Baseball* [New York: Boni and Liveright, 1923; reprint, Lincoln: University of Nebraska Press, 1995]) and Christy Mathewson (*Pitching in a Pinch* [New York: Putnam, 1912; reprint, Lincoln: University of Nebraska Press, 1994]) are above average for the genre but, as in the case of *Touching Second*, require verification from independent sources.

Sporting Life, a weekly newspaper that covered baseball during the Dead Ball Era, receives little respect from some researchers. Because it also covered billiards and skeet, some believe it neglected baseball. It did not. It was a worthy competitor of the *Sporting News*. *Sporting Life* contains a mother lode of information for researchers. Part of the reason for its neglect is that *Sporting Life* ceased publication before the Lively Ball Era, while *Sporting News* continued.

Contemporary newspaper accounts remain important sources, although some of the papers that covered the Dead Ball Era are long gone. Sportswriting of the era remains a vital part of any study of early-twentieth-century American culture. In working with newspapers of the day, a researcher gains the understanding that contemporary journalism, for better or worse, is a first rough draft of history.

Publications of the Society for American Baseball Research (SABR) are invaluable to any researcher wishing to dot the *i*'s and cross the *t*'s; it often added sinew and muscle to this work.

Recent biographies of Dead Ball Era heroes made significant contributions to this work. The long-awaited biographies of Honus Wagner by Dennis and Jean Burke DeValeria (New York: Henry Holt, 1995) and Arthur Hittner (Jefferson NC: McFarland and Co., 1996) filled in blanks. Charles Alexander's works on John McGraw (New York: Viking, 1988; reprint, Lincoln: University of Nebraska Press, 1995), Ty Cobb (New York: Oxford University Press, 1984), and Rogers Hornsby (New York: Henry Holt, 1995) provided vital perspective. Biographies of Walter Johnson by Henry Thomas (Washington DC: Phenom Press, 1995; reprint, Lincoln: University of Nebraska Press, 1998) and by Jack Kavanaugh (South Bend IN: Diamond Communications, 1995) are excellent, but Thomas earns a special nod for such a finely written and illustrated book about his grandfather. *Shoeless Joe and Ragtime Baseball* by Harvey Frommer (Dallas: Taylor Publishing, 1992) should not be overlooked by anyone interested in one of baseball's tragic heroes and in early-twentieth-century baseball. One work of fiction deserves mention: Eric Rolfe Greenberg's *The Celebrant* (Lincoln: University of Nebraska Press, 1983). This novel about Christy Mathewson captures the ambiance of the era.

Ronald Mayer's game-by-game analysis of Christy Mathewson's career (Jefferson NC: McFarland, 1993) is a wonderful source, and his account of Addie Joss's 1908 gem in *Perfect!* (Jefferson NC: McFarland, 1991) provides excellent information on how the game was played. The environment of Dead Ball Era baseball is well handled in Philip Lowry's study of ballparks, *Green Cathedrals* (Reading MA: Addison Wesley Publishing Co., 1992) and Marc Okkonen's *Baseball Memories: 1900–1909* (New York: Sterling, 1992). Okkonen's work provides details about uniforms, ballparks, and newspaper coverage and other valuable information for the Dead Ball Era.

Providing insights, opinion, and fact about many of the figures of 1908 were general references such as the *Baseball Encyclopedia*; *The Bill James Historical Baseball Abstract* (New York: Villard Books, 1988); *The Sports Encyclopedia: Baseball*, 16th edition, edited by David S. Neff and Richard M. Cohen (New York: St. Martin's Griffon, 1996); *The Ballplayers*, edited by Mike Shatzkin (New York: William Morrow, 1990); *Total Baseball*, edited by John Thorn and Pete Palmer (New York: Warner Books, 1989); Donald Dewey and Nicholas

Acocella's *The Biographical History of Baseball* (New York: Carroll and Graf, 1995) and *The Ball Clubs* (New York: Harper Perennial, 1996); and Daniel Okrent and Harris Lewine's *The Ultimate Baseball Book* (Boston: Houghton Mifflin, 1991).

There are other good studies of baseball during the Dead Ball Era. Daniel Ginsberg's *The Fix Is In: A History of Baseball Gambling and Game Fixing Scandals* (Jefferson NC: McFarland, 1995) gives a wonderful view of baseball and its relationship with gambling. Stephen Reiss provides considerable social insight in his *Touching Base: Professional Baseball and American Culture in the Progressive Era* (Westport CT: Greenwood Press, 1980). Robert Burk's *Never Just a Game: Players, Owners and American Baseball to 1920* (Chapel Hill: University of North Carolina Press) rounds out this trilogy of works about baseball off the diamond.

Finally, we must salute Lawrence Ritter's seminal works of oral history. *The Glory of Their Times* (New York: William Morrow, 1984) is a classic and stands as an example of what we lose if we do not talk to and with our elders. The companion pictorial volume, *The Image of Their Greatness* (New York: Crown, 1992), done by Ritter with Donald Honig, puts faces to the names. Ritter was not the first to assemble oral history. John P. Carmichael's *My Greatest Day in Baseball* (New York: A. S. Barnes, 1945; reprint, Lincoln: University of Nebraska Press, 1996) supplies valuable accounts from players who died before Ritter could interview them and makes a strong contribution to the study of early baseball.

Index

Polo Grounds, 67; July attendance, 144–45

Powell, Jack, 50, 128, *236*

Powers, C. B., on spitballs, 123

Powers, Michael "Doc," 55; ejection of, *231*

Pulliam, Harry C.: and committee to probe attempted bribes, 213, 217–18; and Cub-Pirate double-header protest, 142; on gambling, 155; meets with baseball writers, 114; and Merkle hearing, 192; on rain delays, 33; ruling on Gill play, 162; ruling on Merkle game, 173; suicide of, xxiv, 178–79; support of umpires, 91–92

Raymond, Arthur "Bugs," 84, *238*; ejection of, *232*; rumored trade to Cubs, 133, 135

Reese, John D. "Bonesetter," 175, 200; treats Pfiester, 175

Reiss, Stephen A.: on World Series attendance, 212; on gambling, 12–13; on ticket scalping, 212

reserve clause, 36

Reulbach, "Big Ed," 3, 7–8, 109, 135, 143, 146, 156, 191, 199–200, *238*; doubleheader vs. Brooklyn, xxiv, 174; season performance of, 66; in World Series, 203

Rhoades, Bob "Dusty," 43; no-hitter, 166

Rice, Grantland, 14–15, 115–16

Richie, Lew, 75

Richter, Francis: on bottle ban, 18; and Gill play, 161; on improving offense, 22; and Merkle game, 173; on rooting clubs, 16. See also *Sporting Life*

Rigler, Cy, 100; and Cub-Pirate controversy, 195; ejections by, *232*;

games worked by, *229–30*; and hand signals, 100; use of hotel registers, 94; and Wiltse no-hitter, 144

Ritchey, Claude, 81

Ritter, Lew, 83

Robison, Matthew Stanley, 84

Rohe, George, 7

rooters clubs, 15–17

Rossman, Claude, 40, 168, 185, 235; injured, 130; about Jennings' leadership, 150; in World Series, 204–5

rowdyism, 13, 105. *See also* Johnson, Ban; Pulliam, Harry C.; rooters clubs

Rucker, Nap, 81, *238*; no-hitter, 176–77

Rudderham, John E., 100; and controversial call vs. Pirates, 111; ejections by, *232*; fired by Pulliam, 178–79; games worked by, *228–30*

Rule 4.09 (a), 160

Rule 9.05 (a), 162

Rule 59, 160

rule changes: in American League on playing all games, 31–32; in shape of home plate, 19; in foul strikes, 20–21; affecting season, 31–34; in National League on playing all games, 32; in pitcher's mound height, 122; on rain delays and postponements, 33–34

The Rules of Baseball (Nemec), on Gill play, 161, 178

Rupp, Joseph: Inquisitive Fan letter, 137–38

Ruppert, Jacob, 62

Ruth, Babe, 101

Ryan, Jack, 189

Ryan, Nolan, xxiv, 128

games worked by, 226; as substitute umpire, 96

Washington Nationals (Senators), 56–59, 234–35; attendance, 225; and investigation of Cantillon, 59; Johnson returns to, 127; mastery over Cleveland, 45, 59, 152. *See also* Johnson, Walter "Big Train"; Street, Charles "Gabby"

Washington Park, 82

Washington Post, on bribery probe, 217–18

weather problems, 116

Weiss, George, 31

Wermer, Jake, 79

West Side Grounds, 62; ban on profanity at, 105

Whatever Happened to the Hall of Fame? (James), on Tinker, Evers, and Chance, 147

White, Guy "Doc," 5, 46–47, 107, 186, 188–90, 224

White Sox Rooters' Association, 16–17. *See also* Cantwell, Robert E.

Wilhelm, Irvin "Kaiser," 83, *238*

Willett, Ed, 41; in July, 139

Williams, Jimmy "Buttons," 49, 51, 106, 188–89

Willis, Vic, 74, 131, 145, 176, 194, *238*; and Gill play, 159–60; in Hall of Fame, 71

Wilson, Owen "Chief," 73, 196; and Gill play, 159

Wilson, Parke A., 183

Wilson, W. L., 183

Wilson, William C., 183

Wiltse, George "Hooks," 68–69, 121, 157, 171, 173, 198, *238*; no-hitter, 144

Winter, George, 52–53; ejection of, *231*

women, 13–15

Wood, Joseph "Smokey Joe," 52; debuts, 169; signs with Red Sox, 142

Woodruff, Harvey T., Dr. Creamer story, 216, 220–22

Wrigley Field, xxi

Yeager, "Little Joe," 135

Young, Denton True "Cy," 119, 166, *236*; and cigarette smoking, 119–20; and Cy Young Day, 154; in Hall of Fame, 52; no-hitter, xxiv, 128; season performance of, 52

Young, Irving "Young Cy," 81, 145

Zimmerman, Henry "Heinie," 63–64, 135, 143; fights Sheckard and Chance, 132–33; injured, 132; rumored trade of, 133

Zuber, C. H.: quotes Comiskey on honest pennant races, 168; on spitballs, 124